DR IAIN WEST'S
CASEBOOK

DR IAIN WEST'S CASEBOOK

Chester Stern

LITTLE, BROWN AND COMPANY

A *Little, Brown* Book

First published in Great Britain in 1996
by Little, Brown and Company

A CIP catalogue record for this book
is available from the British Library.

ISBN 0 316 87788 3

Set in Plantin by M Rules
Printed and bound in Great Britain by
Clays Ltd, St Ives plc

Little, Brown and Company (UK)
Brettenham House
Lancaster Place
London WC2E 7EN

It is not the author's wish to cause distress to any of the families of the victims mentioned in this book. The details of suffering are by their nature harrowing but are factual information and almost all are a matter of public record.

CONTENTS

INTRODUCTION   *1*

CHAPTER 1 **ROBERT MAXWELL:**
           The mysterious death of a tycoon at sea   *7*

CHAPTER 2 **INTERNATIONAL TERRORISM**

WPC Yvonne Fletcher   *37*
The Brighton bomb   *49*
Mostaghimy Tehrani Gholam Hossein   *56*
Kenneth Howorth   *61*
The Hyde Park bombing   *65*
A crime against Christmas – the Harrods bombing   *70*
Ali El Giahour   *75*
Abdullah Rahim Sharif Ali   *81*

CHAPTER 3 **ESPIONAGE AND INTRIGUE**

Robert Ouko   *87*
Ludmilla Klimova   *105*
Dr Cyrus Hashemi   *110*

CHAPTER 4 **WAR CRIMES:**
           Saddam's Chemical Warfare Atrocities   *119*

CHAPTER 5 **DISASTERS**

Hillsborough   *141*

The King's Cross fire 153
The Clapham rail crash 163

CHAPTER 6 **'OLD BONES'**

Pete Marsh 177
The body in Chichester harbour 188
The Abingdon skull 190

CHAPTER 7 **MURDER – DOMESTIC**

Dr John Baksh 195
Andrew Alder 206
Barbara Gaul 213

CHAPTER 8 **MURDER**

Vishal Mehrota 222
The Babes in the Wood 228
Rachel McLean 240
The American and the rent boys 246

CHAPTER 9 **SERIAL KILLERS**

Michael Lupo 249
Colin Ireland 257

CHAPTER 10 **SUICIDES**

Graham Backhouse 271
Vicky de Lambray 275
John McCarthy 278

CHAPTER 11 **FOREIGN INQUIRIES**

The Zimbabwean hostages 284
The body in the Maltese Crusaders' well 292
Victor Bruce 297
Mrs Arah Hector 301

CHAPTER 12 **GANGLAND KILLINGS**

John Fordham 307
The Surrey torso murder 317

Graeme Woodhatch   330
Murder at the 39 Club   339

CHAPTER 13 DEATHS 'IN CUSTODY'

Lee Clegg   352
Joy Gardner   358
Kevin Gately   363
Colin Roach   372
John Mikkleson   382
Kenny Baker   387
Orville Blackwood   392

CHAPTER 14 CHILD ABUSE

Jasmine Beckford   397
Tyra Henry   401

INTRODUCTION

Death is a way of life for Iain West and his passport to a fascinating but rarely glamorous jet-setting lifestyle, for Dr West is one of Britain's foremost pathologists. He is a special kind of detective. His job is to carry out the physical examination of victims of fatal crimes, or accidents, or of the bodies of people who have died in mysterious circumstances. A dead body can produce a host of clues imperceptible to the untrained eye: a fresh blemish on the skin, details of the victim's last meal, tell-tale signs emerging from the microscope.

Inevitably Iain West has been involved in unravelling some of the most sensational headline-grabbing cases and is frequently plunged into controversy as his findings throw new light on contentious legal disputes. The famous pathologists of the past – men like Sir Bernard Spilsbury, Professor Francis Camps and Professor Keith Simpson – all became stars of their grisly profession. Each in his own way established a worldwide reputation for the skill of his detective work and his learned presence in the witness box. But all that came before the days of global communication and international crime

With the growth in terrorism, the surge in international organised crime and the explosion of satellite television, Iain West's fame has spread along with the demand for his unique expertise. He is regularly commissioned by foreign governments and other international bodies. Often accompanied by his beautiful blonde Yugoslav wife Vesna – also a pathologist – he travels the world, his macabre skills and tools of the trade with him, probing death in many bizarre forms. Meanwhile, in London, as head of the department of Forensic Medicine at Guy's Hospital, he has his hands more than full with Home Office cases and inquiries led by Scotland Yard and other British police forces.

There was no medical tradition in the West family. Iain's father was an RAF officer, and his young son born in Glasgow at the end of the war led the nomadic existence common to most service children. He grew up travelling around the country wherever his father was posted, moving from school to school and completing a patchwork education. Finally he found himself at medical school in Edinburgh.

'I don't know what drew me to medicine,' he said. 'I was interested in the biological side of science.'

Graduating from Edinburgh University in 1967, he moved south and finished clinical medicine in Kent before beginning his training as a pathologist in 1970. His early work as a junior pathologist, carried out in the drab and humdrum surroundings of Kent and south London, eventually led to a post in the pathology department at Lewisham Hospital.

'I'd had an interest in pathology but I wasn't determined to become a pathologist by any means. I had jobs in medicine – orthopaedics, casualty – at a hospital at Ashford in Kent,' he said. 'Then I developed an interest in the clinical aspect of pathology while working in the rhesus babies unit and treating haemophiliacs at Lewisham Hospital.'

INTRODUCTION

A teaching post at Cambridge University followed in 1971 with an attachment to the world famous Addenbrookes Hospital, where he worked under another legendary pathologist, Austen Gresham. 'At that stage I thought that my career lay in haematology,' said Dr West. 'I was also interested in the medico-legal aspects of haematology – paternity testing, and so on.'

In 1974 it was back to join Professor Hugh Johnson at St Thomas's, one of London's five big teaching hospitals, where a consultancy followed in 1978. 'For some reason I decided that I'd like to try forensic medicine for a year – I'd done quite a few postmortems and some histopathology – so I joined Hugh Johnson at St Thomas's in 1974. It's been a long year,' he quipped. He moved to Guy's in 1984 at the tail end of the careers of the two most influential pathologists in the history of that great institution, Professor Keith Mant and Professor Keith Simpson, from whom, he acknowledges, he learned a great deal.

Iain West is very conscious that he is treading in the footsteps of the great men in the field and acutely aware of the invaluable lessons he has learned from those he has come into contact with. 'I am very grateful to Hugh Johnson – a very fine pathologist who taught me an awful lot,' he said. 'I am also very grateful to Austen Gresham at Cambridge, who taught me how to do a postmortem properly. Another excellent pathologist. I also appreciated the advice I was given over the years by people like Keith Mant and Keith Simpson. I knew Simpson after he had retired from the university very much towards the end of his career. Certainly in the earlier years that I knew him he had an acute mind. He was regarded as a bit of an aloof figure – somebody who would be difficult to get on with. But I always found him willing to help and give advice.'

So what is it that sets these big-name pathologists apart from the rest? Is it their style in the witness box or is it their academic brilliance? 'Everyone adopts their own way of giving evidence – their own style in the witness box,' said Iain West. 'They either enjoy court or they don't. If you don't, you should not be in this game. As for the way of working, I've got Simpson's notes from his early days; in those days the note-taking was meticulous, the work was of a very high standard. I was able to observe his work at first hand only towards the end of his career, but even then it was clear that he was a forensic pathologist who had had a proper training in pathology. And that wasn't the case with some. He and Donald Teare had a very sound training in pathology before they became forensic pathologists. I had a lot of time for them both.'

What then is the difference between the modern pathologist and those great men of a bygone era like Sir Bernard Spilsbury who was such a star in his day? 'We do many more cases,' said Dr West. 'They seemed to deal with more cases of poisoning than we do. But a modern pathologist now would expect to carry out the number of homicide cases that Spilsbury did in the whole of his career in a period of perhaps ten years. We also have the benefits of the dramatic developments in the fields of forensic science and medicine. The forensic scientist makes a major contribution to most homicide cases nowadays – a relatively rare state of affairs sixty or seventy years ago.'

Watching Dr West, you are struck by the painstaking work of threading together elusive clues. His large office in a small block at Guy's in south London is a laboratory of death incongruously situated in an institution for saving lives. It is as much a home as a workplace for this remarkable immaculately dressed Scot.

INTRODUCTION

This book takes us inside the fascinating world of Iain West – a personal casebook of his most interesting cases over the past twenty years. Using his case notes, photographs, charts and scientific data, alongside his vivid recollections, I have been able to piece together the investigations.

CHAPTER 1

ROBERT MAXWELL:
The mysterious death of a tycoon at sea

The first sign that anything was amiss in the larger-than-life world of Robert Maxwell came just after noon on Tuesday 5 November 1991 when three people anxiously entered the harbourmaster's office at Los Cristianos on the south-west coast of Tenerife in the Canary Islands. It was a meeting the outcome of which was to have massive repercussions around the world – from the money markets of Wall Street and Tokyo to the boardrooms of London and the secret spy headquarters of Moscow and Tel Aviv.

Leading the worried delegation was Gus Rankin, captain of Robert Maxwell's 450-ton motor yacht *Lady Ghislaine*. With him were a senior member of the crew and a Spanish interpreter. The two seamen had come ashore in a small motor launch from the yacht, which had dropped anchor in the bay some three hours earlier. Breathlessly they told their story.

A business telephone call from New York had been received on board for Mr Maxwell at 11 am and had been put through to his stateroom, but there was no reply. The sixty-eight-year-old media tycoon had last been heard of in the cabin from which he had telephoned the bridge at 4.55 that morning to ask for the air conditioning to be turned down. Alerted to a problem, Mr Rankin went to his boss's cabin ten minutes later. Significantly, he found the staterooms, including the study and the bathroom, locked from the outside. When he could not find the publisher, he ordered the ship to be thoroughly searched from stem to stern. After four fruitless searches by the eleven-strong crew he decided to raise the alarm.

Robert Maxwell was reported missing at sea.

By 2 pm the Tenerife authorities had launched a massive air and sea search involving three helicopters and a fixed wing aircraft. During the previous night *Lady Ghislaine* had been cruising towards Tenerife from the neighbouring island of Grand Canary and had covered sixty miles between the time Maxwell was last known to be on board and the time she anchored off Los Cristianos. At 5.46 pm Robert Maxwell's naked body was spotted by a Fokker aircraft floating 20 miles south-west of Maspalomas, the southern tip of Grand Canary. It was winched on to a helicopter and taken to Gando airport, Las Palmas.

The grim discovery sparked off a chain reaction in Maxwell's business empire, which led to the uncovering of crime and corruption on a massive scale perpetrated secretly by the crooked businessman over many years, ultimately ending with the criminal trial of his two sons. But, more intriguingly, his death gave birth to a series of wild and bizarre theories about how and why he died – or if he was dead at all.

Madeleine Hult, a blonde Swedish-born former stewardess on the yacht, came forward to say that she had overheard Maxwell, a few months earlier, discussing plans to fake his own death and slip away to South America to escape his mounting financial problems. Her story led to speculation that the body found floating in the sea was that of a double.

Preposterous though the suggestion might have sounded, the local Spanish police nonetheless took the precaution of running tests on Maxwell's fingerprints rather than relying on the family's identification of the body. It is not known quite how hard they tried and they did not have the sophisticated equipment available to detectives in London, but, curiously, they were unable to confirm identity of the corpse by means of dental records or fingerprints. Their reports consistently refer to the body as being of athletic build – a description not normally attached to Robert Maxwell in his later years.

The Maxwell family very quickly ordered an investigation into the backgrounds of *Lady Ghislaine*'s crew in case one of them had been planted on board to murder him and make it look like an accident. The yacht was impounded and forced to remain berthed at a fishing port outside the Tenerife capital of Santa Cruz.

As with most suspicious deaths, the real truth ought to have been easy enough to fathom through the detective skills of the pathologists, but in the case of Robert Maxwell the process was clouded by inexperience, indecision and outside interference. *Lady Ghislaine* was allowed to put to sea the day after the tragedy, for instance, and a succession of visitors probably destroyed vital evidence. Investigators broke basic rules by smoking on board and not wearing gloves. Also, the clumsy use of embalming fluid and other preservatives in the mortuary rendered a more sophisticated forensic investigation almost impossible at a later stage.

Within hours of his body being recovered, Spanish doctors declared that Maxwell had died of a heart attack. A preliminary examination before the formal autopsy showed no signs of violence, they said. 'All the signs are that it was a case of natural death and it seems probable that it was some kind of cardiac or cardiovascular attack,' said a spokesman at the Las

Palmas Institute of Forensic Medicine. This caused Maxwell's New York lawyer Samuel Pisar to assert publicly that his client had never experienced any heart trouble although he was overweight and suffered from lingering colds because part of a lung had been removed more than thirty years earlier. Two days later the Spanish authorities seemed to have satisfied themselves that the 6 feet 2 inches 20-stone billionaire had died from a heart attack before he fell into the Atlantic. But his family were convinced that he was alive when he hit the water and had suffered a fatal heart attack in the desperate struggle to survive. This point was, of course, crucial to any future insurance claim, since it would mean that his death was an accident and had not occurred from natural causes.

The local judge investigating the death, Miss Isabel Oliva, moved to scotch rumours that the case had been peremptorily closed, announcing that she had authorised samples from Mr Maxwell's body to be sent to Madrid for analysis and toxicology tests, including scrapings from beneath his fingernails to establish whether he might have been involved in a struggle. Scientists at the Madrid National Toxicology Institute were specifically asked to examine the dead man's organs to check for traces of substances known to attack the central nervous system, amid fears that he might have been killed by a poison that produces the symptoms of a heart attack.

The Maxwell family's lawyer in the Canaries, Julio Hernandez Claverie, gave public voice to the suspicion that was on everyone's lips: 'Mr Maxwell was a man who had many enemies, powerful enemies. There has to be a possibility that he was murdered.'

Maxwell's daughter Christine then claimed that her father had been murdered by the injection of an air bubble into his bloodstream to induce an embolism. He had just had a medical and his heart was in good shape, she said. Her theory was initially discounted because such a method would have left a mark from the injection needle, and it was widely assumed that no such mark had been found. But later it emerged that the pathologists who carried out the first postmortem found a minute perforation of the skin below one ear which they could not readily explain.

Ten days before his death Maxwell had been named in a book as an agent of the Israeli secret service Mossad. Now conspiracy theorists began claiming he had been silenced by Mossad to prevent his leaking details of their most clandestine operations over the years. Many pooh-poohed this idea, but it was curious that the crime correspondent of the *Jerusalem Post* was tipped off, in Jerusalem, about Maxwell's death a full forty-five minutes before it was officially declared to the world in London.

The mystery deepened when witnesses came forward to report that an unidentified yacht had been spotted shadowing the *Lady Ghislaine* the day before the tragedy. The vessel was seen in company with the dead publisher's yacht at Punta de Abona, a picturesque bay in southern Tenerife where Maxwell had spent several hours on the Monday before his death. Two fishermen observing from a headland said both ships were anchored close together and a swimmer was seen near the unidentified yacht at one point. The vessel bore no name, national flag or other identifying marks, and followed the *Lady Ghislaine* when she set sail in the direction of Santa Cruz. Later reports indicated that yachts similar to Mr Maxwell's were seen close to the *Lady Ghislaine* on at least three occasions before and after his disappearance. Indeed, intriguingly, the last order reportedly given by Captain Rankin to his first officer Grahame Shorrocks before he turned in at midnight on the night of the tragedy was, 'Call me if any craft shows up on the radar within five miles.'

As speculation grew wilder, attention was paid to discrepancies in the crew manifest of *Lady Ghislaine,* lodged with the Spanish port authorities, which put the number of crew as high as thirteen during the last voyage, while the captain insisted there had been only eleven plus Mr Maxwell. The maritime authorities also investigated suggestions that the vessel had deviated several times from her declared route during the last fateful sailing.

Several experts on the layout and workings of the *Lady Ghislaine* declared themselves baffled as to how Mr Maxwell could have fallen into the water. All her decks were surrounded by large banisters, like an ocean liner, making it impossible to topple overboard accidentally. The only other possibility was that Mr Maxwell had fallen into the sea over the wire at the side of the vessel. But the motor launches were kept there and the distance between them and the wire was less than twelve inches – far too small a gap for Maxwell to have squeezed his bulky frame through. Even had that occurred, marine engineers said the design of the ship meant that his body would have been sucked underneath and chopped up by the propeller blades

The suggestions of foul play persisted, and soon a new mystery about the time of death began to emerge. A confidential police report laid great stress on the fact that the body showed only slight signs of rigor mortis and the skin displayed none of the puckering consistent with long immersion in water. If the body had been in the sea all day, why were there no signs of sunburn? Algae trapped between his fingers and toes were analysed to see whether they could have come from an area outside the point where he had supposedly fallen into the sea. The crew of a search and rescue aircraft which, earlier in the day, had repeatedly passed over the area where the body was subsequently found had seen nothing and were astonished at the later discovery.

Quite early on, the idea of suicide was mooted and as new scandalous revelations emerged daily over Maxwell's business dealings, even the most sceptical were forced to consider it. Most of the £426m that disappeared from his company pension funds went missing in September and October of that year. Most of the £100m he took from the Mirror Group accounts had disappeared just days before his final voyage. Six days before his death he had agreed to repay, within six days, a £55m loan from the Swiss Bank Corporation but, as he sailed, he sent several messages to the bank asking to delay the payment. The bank refused, and threatened to call in receivers to one of his companies.

Everyone who knew Robert Maxwell, however, agreed that suicide was unlikely. It was alien to his character. He was a born fighter who had been through financial crises before. It is also the experience of doctors that people intending suicide by drowning seldom do so naked. The axiom is that if someone is found in water unclothed or wearing a swimming costume, the death was probably accidental. Suicides sometimes remove their jacket and coat, which are usually then carefully folded up and left on the beach or deck, but in general they are neatly dressed. Pathologists are also extremely cautious in assuming accidental death in cases where a body has been immersed in water and there is no actual evidence of drowning, particularly if there is any evidence of other injury.

Iain West's great predecessor, the late Professor Keith Simpson, once wrote: 'Suspicious injuries, or no injuries at all, require the same commonsense interpretation. There must be some significant ominous finding before real suspicions should be aroused.'

Examination of the hands and nails is vitally important when looking at a body found in water. The pathologist makes a search under the nails, not just for evidence of skin which might have been scratched from an assailant, but also because the dead person when falling might have made a grab for anything nearby. Fragments of fibre from rope, wood splinters, paint from the rails, polish from the deck might have lodged beneath the nails, which could also give a clue by being torn or scratched.

On the assumption that Maxwell went over the side relatively soon after his last communication with the crew, he would have been in the sea for more than twelve hours by the time his body was recovered. Rigor mortis comes on more quickly in bodies immersed in water than in those exposed to the air, and although the actual timing depends on the temperature of the sea, it is usually fully established by five to seven hours. Since rigor mortis was apparently not fully established when his body was recovered, did he remain alive by swimming for several hours, or was his lifeless body dumped shortly before it was found?

The Spanish pathologists also looked for clues in the dead man's stomach contents to determine the degree of digestion which his last meal had undergone before he died. Were the clams he ate for his last meal sound, or could he have been sick leaning over the rails when he lost consciousness?

The classic signs of death by drowning include water in the lungs and stomach. In the case of salt water, the chloride content in the blood increases on the left-hand side of the heart. In fact, so soon after drowning, the body should not have surfaced because it would have sunk due to the excessive amounts of water swallowed. There was very little water in Maxwell's lungs, but that does not necessarily mean that he was not alive when he went overboard. The sudden shock of hitting the cold water could have stopped his heart instantly, but would not explain the other signs suggesting that the body had not been immersed for many hours.

Another problem was to time the moment when his forehead was bruised. If he had died in his cabin, and the bruise occurred because his head hit the side of the ship as he was pushed overboard, the bruise would be identical to one suffered if he was hit on the head seconds before death.

Within days, suspicions arose that the postmortem examination had been hopelessly botched and an opportunity to glean vital evidence missed. The local pathologist Dr Carlos Lopez Lamela admitted that the equipment and facilities available to him were desperately inadequate for the task, hence his complete failure to establish the cause and precise timing of death. 'We are not the world's best,' he said. 'I think we carried out the initial autopsy correctly and professionally, but we are open to criticism. I must admit one can be mistaken.'

He was perplexed by the conflict of evidence over how long the body had been in the sea and hampered because the military authorities who recovered the body had made no report at the scene. Poor Dr Lamela had twice begged the Maxwell family to permit British forensic experts to be involved in his investigation, but twice he was refused. Nothing was to be allowed which would delay the body being released for the funeral in Israel before the end of the week, in accordance with Jewish tradition.

Meanwhile the growing international scepticism over the competence of the Spanish pathologists was thrown into sharp focus by the publication of an amusing anecdote about one of Iain West's illustrious predecessors, and the story came from a most unlikely source. The former MI6 spy and inveterate newspaper correspondent James Rusbridger, recalling a

British wartime counter-espionage operation, wrote to the *Daily Telegraph*:

> The problems of determining how Robert Maxwell died are reminiscent of the time, in April 1943, when Naval Intelligence was preparing to float ashore on the Spanish coast the body of a 45-year-old Welsh barman, Emlyn Howells. It was dressed as a major in the Royal Marines, and clutched a briefcase full of bogus Allied invasion plans.
>
> Howells had died of bronchial pneumonia in January and the authorities contacted the eminent pathologist, Sir Bernard Spilsbury, for his opinion as to whether a postmortem would show the absence of sea water in the lungs. Sir Bernard replied: 'You have nothing to fear from a Spanish postmortem; to detect this man had not drowned at sea would need a pathologist of my experience – and there aren't any in Spain.'

Gradually it emerged, however, that Dr Lamela and his two colleagues had not found evidence of a heart attack and, contrary to the earlier announcements, had not concluded that Maxwell died of natural causes before falling in to the sea. They did admit to finding blockages of up to 95 per cent in some of Maxwell's coronary arteries, which was puzzling to many observers since the family always insisted that his heart was in excellent condition. But documents the family supplied underpinned the finding, claimed Dr Lamela, that it was Mr Maxwell's heart condition that was the primary cause of death.

Mr Maxwell's reported behaviour just before his death was compatible with that of a man heading for a fatal coronary disorder. He was evidently feeling hot and cold and suffering from nausea. A man in this condition, reasoned Dr Lamela, might need only a slight movement of the boat to pitch overboard, especially if he was vomiting over the side at the time. Traces of vomit were found in the dead man's respiratory tract and lungs, and traces of a drug only found in seasickness pills carried on board the ship were also discovered in the body.

One objection to this theory is the coincidence that the publisher's vulnerable heart happened to give out on the very day he was due to pay back a debt whose return would trigger the collapse of his empire. But suicide still looked unlikely. People who want to end their lives by jumping into the sea give themselves up willingly to the waves with much clearer evidence of drowning. In these circumstances a body usually takes two to three days to resurface. He would also have been expected to have been found face down in the foetal position, yet when found he was face up with his arms and legs splayed out. There was also no damage from the yacht's propellors.

When the final Spanish ruling came, it said that Maxwell probably suffered a heart attack and fell overboard accidentally from his £15m yacht. It was a ruling which was to open up a wrangle between insurers and the Maxwell companies. A personal accident insurance policy on him was worth £20m, but a verdict of anything other than accident or homicide meant that the insurers would not have to pay out.

Insurers have the right to make up their own minds whether a death was accidental, and those firms or individuals likely to benefit from it can then challenge their view in the courts if necessary. With this in mind, the insurers underwriting the massive policy commissioned Iain West to investigate. The decision to bring him in was taken late. Almost too late.

'The loss adjusters approached me and asked me to fly to the Canary Islands to carry out an examination on their behalf,' Dr West recalled. 'So I went over to the Maxwell Communication people and met Ian Maxwell and his staff; it rapidly became apparent that it was going to be impossible to carry out a postmortem in Tenerife – it would have to be done in Israel. The reason was the shortness of time. Jewish religion required that the burial take place before the end of the week, and a huge State funeral was planned for the following Sunday in Jerusalem, where Mr Maxwell was to be buried on the Mount of Olives.

'I was told that we would not be allowed to do the post-mortem personally – it would be carried out by the Israelis,' said Dr West. 'I knew the Israeli pathologist involved. I'd met him some years before – a pleasant enough chap who seemed very competent. I decided, however, that it would be better to have two pathologists from our side as well.'

He chose his wife, Dr Vesna Djurovic, to accompany him, and a letter sent from Continental Insurance International on 7 November 1991 confirms that 'as personal accident insurers of the above (Robert Maxwell) we wish to retain you and Dr Djurovic to examine the body of the deceased as a matter of urgency in order to provide an independent opinion of the cause of death. We should be grateful if you could also consider the likelihood of there being any previous history of heart disease or other physical defect or infirmity.' The letter adds, 'Your assistance at such short notice is much appreciated.' With all the international hullabaloo triggered off by Maxwell's death, it was difficult to imagine that just two days had passed since his body had been pulled from the Atlantic.

'The next problem was that all the flights to Israel were fully booked and we couldn't get any seats,' said Iain West. 'We thought we might have to charter an aircraft, but we managed to get a couple of seats on the Maxwell plane that was going out to the funeral. We went from Farnborough on a small jet, landed at a military airfield just outside Jerusalem, and were taken straight to Tel Aviv for the postmortem.'

It was late in the evening of Saturday 9 November. Maxwell had been dead just four days and his funeral was less than twelve hours away. There was no time to be lost. This was to be a momentous autopsy with important international implications, both politically and economically, so Dr West began his report by formally recording the names of all those present:

> At 10.15 pm on Saturday 9th November 1991 at the Institute of Forensic Medicine, Tel Aviv, I performed a second postmortem examination on the body of Robert Maxwell, aged 68 years.
>
> Also taking part in the examination were: Dr Jehude Hiss and Dr Birtolon Levy, forensic pathologists from the Institute in Tel Aviv, Professor Baruch Arensburg, professor of anatomy and forensic pathology from the Institute in Tel Aviv, Dr Vesna Djurovic, forensic pathologist from the department of forensic medicine at Guy's Hospital. Also present at the postmortem examination was Dr Esther Daniels-Phillips, forensic pathologist from the Institute in Tel Aviv. The mortuary technician was Mr Eliezek Lipstein. The photographs, X-rays and video recording were carried out by Mr Naim Batsri. Also present was Miss Edna Barez, secretary to Dr Hiss.

'Although I was strictly speaking not the person doing the postmortem,' said Dr West, 'they were quite happy to let me help run things, and effectively the tasks were shared out. An effort was made to ensure that everybody saw it all.'

Maxwell's body was stretched out on the mortuary table encased in a wrapping of coarse muslin with the inscription 'Maxwell R' scrawled with a magic marker on the material. The head was exposed, but the whole clumsy package was held together by ropes tied around the ankles, thighs and chest.

'It was physically an extremely unpleasant autopsy,' remembered Dr West. 'The embalming fluid that they had placed in the body was almost neat formalin and it was quite difficult to breathe in that atmosphere. One could only work for a few minutes at a time on the interior of the body simply because one's eyes, nose and respiratory tract became affected quite quickly.

'There were a lot of organs and tissues missing. Most of the heart had been taken. Quite a number of organs couldn't be found. And there were also some red herrings, like a collection of blood within the skull. We looked at that and said, "They couldn't have missed an extradural of that size, surely," and then quickly realised that this was a product of the fixation by the embalming fluid.

'Normally, when the skull is opened following a post-mortem, the blood drains. Obviously that had not happened here. The Spanish had not drained its interior fully but had just placed embalming fluid in there so, as a result, the blood which was present inside the skull vault had hardened. Because of gravity it had hardened in a layer which made it look like a haemorrhage at the back of the skull.'

Most of the postmortem was straightforward. The body was covered with bruises and abrasions – every one of which was measured and tabulated – but most of these could be attributed to damage inflicted while the body was in the sea, during the operation to recover it, or during the first postmortem.

But Dr West and the other pathologists involved did make several crucial and highly significant discoveries which the

Spanish had missed. The clues are in the postmortem report as it refers to the examination of the muscles in Mr Maxwell's back:

> Dissection of the skin of the back showed an extensive 5 by 2 inches haemorrhage along the line of the left infraspinatous muscle. *Some of the muscle fibres were torn and the haemorrhage involved most of the muscle.* There was a 5 by ½ inch extensive haemorrhage into the paraspinal muscle on the left side extending from the twelfth thoracic vertebrae to the level of the fourth and fifth lumbar vertebrae. There was a small area of haemorrhage inside the right psoas muscle.

'Those were the most significant findings,' said Dr West. 'The muscle on the back of the left shoulder was quite badly torn and the muscle on the lower left side of the spine had a bruising over its surface. There was a tear on the right side of the psoas muscle which lies to the side of the spine within the abdomen.'

Now, at least, there was some evidence from which to develop a theory. Did Mr Maxwell fall into the sea because he was hanging on to the side of *Lady Ghislaine* when his excessive weight ripped the muscles in his back, causing him excruciating pain and forcing him to let go? If so, was he hanging there because he had been pushed, had fallen, or had jumped and changed his mind halfway?

The real sleuthing was about to begin, but the autopsy had still more clues to reveal. 'I also noted that the lung had an awful lot of froth in it – much more than I would have expected simply from a lung, which had been cut, absorbing embalming fluid,' said Dr West. 'There was a bruise on the back of the right shoulder, quite a superficial one, which the

Spanish had seen, but we also found some bruising on the right side of the neck which they had not picked up. And they also appeared to have missed some bruising around the right ear, which we spotted. It was all beginning to fit in with the pattern of damage we were seeing in the muscles.'

Dawn was breaking over Jerusalem before the exhausted pathologists finally finished their work. It was 5 am on the day of Robert Maxwell's funeral.

An idea was already forming in Iain West's mind about how Mr Maxwell might have suffered the disruptive muscle injuries in his back, but at home in London there was much more work to do. The first thing was to satisfy himself that it was indeed Robert Maxwell's body he had been working on and not the corpse of an unfortunate lookalike caught up in some plan to fake the tycoon's death.

To do this, Maxwell's dental records were obtained from his dentist and Mr Bernard Sims, Britain's leading forensic odontologist, compared them with X-rays Iain West had taken of the body in Israel. There were several points of confirmation, but an identically-shaped root filling in the lower right jaw was the clincher. It was definitely the body of Robert Maxwell.

As the worldwide frenzy of speculation about the cause of death continued, the American authoress Barbara Honegger stepped in to help the investigation. She had written a widely acclaimed book on the Iran-Contra scandal and now sent an urgent fax from California to Alan Lord, the chairman and chief executive of Lloyds in London.

The recent report that Maxwell had a puncture mark or wound on or near an elbow (in addition to the reported puncture mark behind an ear) is the calling card, or M.O., of two other suspicious deaths of men central to the US

Iran/Contra scandal: Cyrus Hashemi, who worked with CIA director William Casey and who died in London on July 21, 1986, and Stephen Carr who worked with the CIA in Central America and who died in Van Nuys, California in December 1985.

Hashemi's autopsy report cites 'Injection sites on both elbows with surrounding bruising' and Carr's autopsy cites 'marks (plural) behind his left elbow'.

Hashemi has been centrally implicated in the genesis of both the Irangate period (1985–6) arms sales to Iran and the earlier 'October Surprise' negotiations of an arms-for-hostages-delay deal with Iran by the 1980 Regan–Bush campaign. Carr was the first whistle-blower on the Contra side of the Iran/Contra affair.

With recent allegations that Maxwell was also deeply involved in illicit arms shipments to Iran through Czechoslovakia, if Maxwell also had a puncture mark behind one or both elbows, that would mean that three men linked to Iran/Contra all died suspiciously, each with puncture marks on the elbows.

This was conspiracy theory gone mad, but the stakes were high and the insurers were determined to leave no stone unturned. Alan Lord sent the extraordinary fax to Iain West who, having himself conducted the autopsy on Cyrus Hashemi (see Chapter 3), was uniquely placed to make sense of it. 'I can't imagine where that idea came from,' he said. 'I did report on injection marks in Cyrus Hashemi's arms, but he died in hospital where he was being treated for leukaemia, so it is hardly surprising. As for Maxwell, I never saw an injection mark either in his arm or behind his ear, though a combination of decomposition and embalming might have obliterated any evidence of such marks.'

In the laboratory at Guy's, a sample of Maxwell's bone marrow brought back from Israel was tested for the presence of diatoms – tiny plankton that are frequently found in both sea water and fresh water. To a pathologist, diatoms, if they can be detected, are an invaluable aid in determining whether or not a body found in water has drowned. Three litres of Atlantic sea water from the spot where the body had been found was flown to London for similar testing. The scientists could find no trace of diatoms in Maxwell's body. Could this mean that he was dead before he went into the water and had not drowned? They turned their attention to the sea water, but there were almost no diatoms present there either.

'At certain times of the year you won't have many diatoms around,' said Dr West. 'The test is useful only if you can identify intact any diatoms in the body as being of the same species as those in the water. There were so few in the sea-water sample that it is hardly surprising we couldn't find any in the bone marrow.'

In December, one month after their Tel Aviv autopsy, Iain and Vesna flew to Madrid to look at the organs and tissue samples retained by the Spanish authorities. 'They wouldn't give permission for us to go until they had completed their investigations and the material was ready to be released,' said Dr West. 'I had taken sections of organs for microscopic examination from Tel Aviv, but they had material taken at the original postmortem which was in a much better state.'

He had been critical of the initial work carried out in Tenerife but now had much more confidence in the scientists in Madrid. 'Where the death involved a prominent person who had died under somewhat odd circumstances I would have expected more than just a standard postmortem examination, which was all the Spanish had done,' he said. 'There were one or two things which had not been looked at properly and the arms, back, face and the areas under the skin had not been examined with any intensity. But when the material was sent to Madrid there's no doubt that all the organs were subjected to a thorough and intensive examination.'

He returned to London with samples of the heart, brain and other organs and a comprehensive toxicology report. Over the next few weeks he and Vesna carried out their own exhaustive tests on all these samples and came to the conclusion that although Maxwell displayed signs of heart and lung disease, the circumstances suggested that the disease was unlikely to have killed him.

By January the Maxwell story was still making headlines worldwide and Iain West was furious when *Paris Match* came out with a story – taken up extensively by the rest of the media – asserting that he had found concrete evidence to prove that Robert Maxwell was murdered. The French magazine had obtained a pirate copy of the video film taken during the Tel Aviv postmortem and had concluded from this that the large number of bruises and abrasions found by the pathologists proved that Maxwell had been brutally beaten up before being thrown into the sea. They published colour stills of the body taken from the video.

Guy's Hospital immediately issued a statement: 'Dr West has not seen the videotape from Israel or the original tape leaked to *Paris Match*. There appear to be some errors of translation and substantial errors of interpretation. Had Dr West felt that assault or murder had been the case he would have reported the matter to Scotland Yard. There are injuries found on the body, some of which are *post mortem* and some of which occurred in life. There are also changes which have been caused during the first postmortem, irrelevant to the cause of death. The release of this material is in appalling taste and most unfortunate for all concerned.'

On Tuesday 12 May 1992 Dr West flew to Nice in the south of France for a very interesting appointment. *Lady Ghislaine* was moored in the harbour there and a team of investigators had assembled to test their theories about what exactly had happened that fateful night in the Atlantic Ocean six months earlier. The man who could help to make sense of it all for them was Iain West.

Armed with drawings and plans from the naval architect who had designed and built the *Lady Ghislaine,* the intention was to reconstruct all Mr Maxwell's known movements and develop a hypothesis on what had happened to him, using a video camera to record the findings. The plan was outlined by one of the lawyers, who wrote in a letter of instruction to a colleague:

Assuming that Dr West agrees that there is only one possible place where he went over, it will be necessary for an individual of Mr Maxwell's height (it is too much to expect you to produce someone of his build!) to demonstrate, under the guidance of Dr West, what he believes Mr Maxwell must have done in order to suffer the muscle injuries which he found.

At the meeting you were understandably not keen on doing this yourself! However, whilst I said that one could perhaps use the video to record someone beginning to clamber over and then resort to sketches or drawings drawn under Dr West's instruction showing what must have happened after that, it really would be a great deal better if an individual could be found who is prepared to hang on to the rail and be videoed. He could of course be roped to the boat so as to reduce the risk of accident.

In the event, Iain West vetoed the unusual scheme as being far too dangerous but the visit to the boat proved to be extremely useful. 'At that stage I had a lot more information about the voyage on the actual night,' he said. 'The stabilisers had been on and it was a fairly smooth trip with no sudden changes of course. I was able to see the general layout of the boat and check the rail, which wasn't very high. There was an area at the sides protected by a simple wire, which went down to the deck. In front of this stood the launches, which made access to the wire railing very awkward. He would have had to manipulate himself into that position quite deliberately, and if he'd grabbed hold of that wire, I don't believe he would have been able to hold on to it. At postmortem I could see no wire-burns on his hands. It was just a thin wire, and I do not believe that it would have held his weight. He would have pulled the wire out of the vertical support if he had fallen while holding it.'

So, straight away, the open area at the sides of the vessel appeared to be unlikely points from which Maxwell went into the water. But what about the torn muscles ? Could he have suffered the injury without hanging on to the side of the boat?

'I looked at the possibility of him sustaining the injury by simply going into the sea and flailing about in the water,' said Dr West, 'but I have never seen that sort of damage produced by such an action. You can tear a muscle by violent movement, but the whole pattern suggests that he had grabbed on to something and was hanging there by the hand when the body came to a sudden halt. There is also evidence of a violent twist whilst he was suspended. Either the sudden jerk tore the muscle, in which case he would definitely have let go, or he was hanging on to some structure and twisting himself, using the shoulder and back muscles. He was so unfit that when the muscles tore, pain forced him to let go.'

So what of the three options: murder, accident, suicide? Dr

West said, 'I can't dispute the possibility of him being murdered. There is no evidence for murder, but clearly if you throw someone in the water there may not be. Some of the injuries on him could have been caused in a struggle. If someone is violently resisting – somebody has got you by the arm, pulling you in, for instance – you could tear muscles. There would be, in such an instance, evidence of restraint marks on his body – none were present.

'But if he were being pulled or thrown in, that obviously would mean complicity among members of the crew because there was no evidence of anyone else being on the boat. Unfortunately no investigation of the boat as a scene of crime was ever done – no fingerprints, footprints, or anything.

'Did he have to be alive when he went into the water? The answer is no. Could he have been killed and then thrown into the water? The answer is yes, but I think it very unlikely.'

But what about the confusion over the length of time the body might have been in the water? If it had been in the sea for almost thirteen hours, shouldn't it have been sunburnt? Should it have been floating at all? If his stomach and lungs were full of water, how could he have surfaced that quickly?

'I couldn't really tell whether the body was sunburnt or not because it had been embalmed,' said Dr West. 'There was certainly no great evidence of thermal burns, and if the body had been in the water at high temperature, the reflection from the sea surface should have caused some mild burns.

'He was found floating face upwards. Whether he was face up for the whole period is another matter. Most people who drown float face downwards, but he was such a large obese man that he had an enormous natural buoyancy. I would not regard him as being a typical example of how a body is going to behave after death from drowning. When it comes to the time at which a body will float to the surface, it depends on the specific gravity of the whole body. If you don't have a lot of body fat, you won't surface quickly. You might find a level of buoyancy where your body floats for quite a long time beneath the surface without reaching the river or sea bed. But if you have high levels of fatty tissue and have only got modest quantities of water in the lungs, often mixed with air, you may well float. The buoyancy of salt sea water is such that an obese body might easily float.'

To this day it has not been possible to give a definite cause of death because the tests on the tissues of the lungs were inconclusive when it came to deciding whether Maxwell drowned or not. It remained the preferred option, but the fluid found in his lungs might have come from the sea or from his circulation.

If Maxwell had been truly dead for thirteen hours when he was found, however, surely rigor mortis should have set in? Dr West considered: 'On dry land a body would be stiff long before sixteen hours had elapsed. One normally sees it in six hours or so, but it is highly variable. Maxwell was not stiff when they examined him after landing but nobody knows how stiff he was in the water. He was lifted up by a net – there were marks on the arms from the netting – and one of the problems when you are lifting a body by a net is that you will move the limbs. And if you move the limbs to the point where you break the rigor mortis, it completely disappears.

'With Maxwell, you have one of three options. Firstly, the body had been stiff but rigor mortis had passed off. Secondly, he had died only a short time before he was found. Or, thirdly, the rigor was broken by manipulating the body during the recovery process.'

Nothing significant had been found beneath the dead man's fingernails to suggest that he had scratched anyone or anything as he fought for life, but if there was a doubt about the time of death, then could it not be worked out from the time taken to digest the last meal? 'That is highly variable and of no relevance,' said Dr West. 'Digestion depends on one's state of mind as much as anything else. It depends on the type of food and, if you are in a very anxious state, food could stay in your stomach for a very long time. People have attempted to use stomach emptying as a means of estimating the time of death, but it is now regarded as potentially very erroneous and one can use it only in very general terms.'

If not murder, then what is the likelihood of Robert Maxwell's death being an accident? There were no bruises on the lower legs or around the ankles to suggest that he had stumbled or tripped over something as he leaned over the side. 'People do fall off boats,' said Iain West. 'People who have been drinking fall off boats. He had not been drinking. People under the influence of drugs may fall off boats. He was not under the influence of any drugs. If the weather was bad, you could pitch over and hang on, but the weather was good. There's always a possibility that he accidentally dropped a towel or a gown over the side and tumbled over trying to retrieve it.'

Maxwell's fractious behaviour in demanding that *Lady Ghislaine*'s air conditioning be turned on and off at frequent intervals in the hours before he went missing might have signalled the imminent onset of a heart attack, but Dr West is sceptical. 'People who have heart problems may well, if they get cold and sweaty, go into shock and have a coronary. Maxwell certainly had heart disease but there was no sign of acute heart attack. If he had a heart attack, how did he get into the water with torn back muscles? He could have fallen backwards or slumped forwards but he would not have been in a fit state to grab on to something firmly enough to have injured all those muscles.

'If his body had been found in the water without those substantial muscle tears, I would have accepted that it might have been related to his heart, but even then I would have been unhappy because it would have been much more likely that he would have fallen onboard and would have been found lying on the deck. There is no area where he could simply have rolled overboard from the deck.

'If he had been having difficulty breathing through the onset of a heart attack, let's say, and that was why he had come out on deck to get some air, he would have been most likely to have braced himself against the rail with both hands and with his arms straight to help the lungs by using the accessory muscles of respiration, which are the shoulder muscles. He would not lean over the side, because he would then be splinting the muscles of respiration. If he collapsed in that position, he would simply fall straight down on deck.'

But what if Mr Maxwell were feeling seasick and fell as he was leaning over the side to vomit? The only traces of drugs in his body were seasickness tablets. 'The weather was calm and the boat was using its stabilisers. There should have been no seasickness problem. In any case why go to the side, why not the toilet?' asked Dr West.

So, if he was not murdered and his death was not accidental, what then is the evidence of suicide? Could the restlessness that he was displaying have triggered a sudden impulse to kill himself? The pathologists had been unable to detect any kind of acute disorder in the tissues of the brain which might have led to a sudden alteration in behaviour, but most alterations in behaviour are not associated with detectable changes in the brain tissues. 'When an individual is in serious trouble you obviously have a situation where suicide could happen,' said Dr West. 'He was not the sort of man who would be likely to carry out such an act with a lot of premeditation. If he killed himself, it would be an impulsive act.'

Most drowning suicides do not simply go in naked, however; they are either fully clothed or they leave their clothes neatly folded behind them. But this was a situation different from the norm. Maxwell was already naked, and naked people do not put clothes on before killing themselves. 'Many people who drown themselves in an act of suicide jump into the water in a public place,' said Iain West. 'They do not take their clothes off; they jump in as they are because they are in public. A classic situation of impulsive suicidal drowning one may see in some mentally ill individuals.'

So are we talking about a depressed man impulsively throwing himself over the side and changing his mind just in time to make a futile grab at the ship's rail? Dr West said: 'Not necessarily. Take the case of somebody who commits suicide by going over the edge of a bridge or coming out of a high building. They are similar situations. One is going to land on land, the other is going to land on water. The common feature is height.

'Some people jump straight off. A paratrooper I dealt with some years ago actually took a running leap straight through a double-glazed window and landed a hundred feet below. But in other scenarios which I have seen, the victim has climbed out of a window and taken a few steps along a ledge or has hung on to the windowsill for a time. They either have no real intention of killing themselves or they are carrying out the act in stages – building up to it. If that latter approach had been adopted by Maxwell, he would have found it difficult, with his bulk, to throw himself over or to clamber quickly over the rail – there were no wire-burn marks on the body, so I don't think he went over in that area.

'A younger, fitter, individual might stand on the top of the rail and just launch himself. But at his age he might have stepped up and over the handrail himself to stand on the top of the curved teak taprail which is smooth and varnished. He might have slipped while he was holding on with one hand or he might have slipped while trying to lower his grip to the rail below the handrail. He might even have changed his mind, having got over the rail, and slipped while trying to get back.

'I never found the alleged perforation behind his right ear, but the bruising and damage to the right side of his head and neck is consistent with his hanging by one hand, falling, and then banging his head against the side of the boat as he went down.'

This scenario developed by Dr West is perhaps more succinctly put by his wife. In her report on the Maxwell case, Vesna Djurovic wrote of the back injury:

The pattern of tearing in these muscles suggests that the deceased had at some point been hanging on to an object with his left hand and with his weight being carried by that hand. This could occur, for instance, in a person who is hanging vertically from a rail with his body freely suspended. There are a number of possible scenarios where these injuries might have been received:

a) If he was hanging on to the rail of the boat and trying to prevent himself falling into the water, it is possible that in such a large and unfit man the muscular effort involved in trying to hoist his body back on to the boat could cause the damage seen here;

b) If he overbalanced and fell over the railings but managed to grab the rail as he fell, it is possible that he would have torn these muscles. One must look at this, of course, in the context of a man of his age, size and state of health being able to carry out this type of action. One must also consider the ways in which an individual could accidentally fall from this boat. It is, we think, difficult to see from the available evidence how such an accident could have occurred on a smooth sea unless the deceased had been leaning well over the rail. The arrangement of the railings suggest that if he had tripped or slipped on the deck, then it is improbable that he would have fallen overboard;

c) These injuries would not be seen if an individual allowed himself deliberately to topple over the side of the boat. If, however, the deceased had climbed over the railings so that he stood on the protrusion of the outer hull at deck level, then it is possible that he could have slipped from this while still holding on to the railing with his left hand. This could well account for him hanging for a short while by that hand and for the injuries that were found.

The great pity in this case is that Maxwell having died abroad and been buried in Israel, there never was a formal inquest at which the family and his insurers could air their doubts and question the expert witnesses.

But what is Iain West's opinion? 'There is no evidence for homicide, but it remains a possibility because I am in no position to exclude it,' he said. 'I don't think he died of a heart attack. Without the background of a man who was in financial trouble, and who knew it, I would probably say accident. As it is, there are probably only a few percentage points between the two main options, but I favour suicide.'

The insurance syndicate gratefully accepted this verdict and refused to pay out the £20m to the Maxwell family, but what might have happened if the case had come before a British court? 'The burden of proof in murder is beyond reasonable doubt,' said Dr West, 'as it is for suicide. I have not got to the point where I could say this is beyond reasonable doubt – I simply don't have enough evidence one way or the other. I could not go into a coroner's court and say: "This man has committed suicide." So if it came to an inquest, you would undoubtedly get an open verdict.'

When the trial of Maxwell's two sons, Kevin and Ian, began in London in the summer of 1995 the principal player had been dead for three and a half years, but there was no doubting who took centre stage in the courtroom drama. From the very first day the prosecution alleged that it was Robert Maxwell, along with his sons, who had fraudulently misused multi-million pound pension fund assets in his media group to help Maxwell companies facing a debt crisis. And it was alleged in court that in the days after his death, Maxwell's sons Kevin and Ian conspired to defraud the pension fund further by misusing £25m worth of shares to prop up their ailing business empire. Those charges were denied by all defendants.

It was in these early days of the trial that Iain West's findings came in for criticism from Kevin Maxwell's counsel, Alan Jones QC, who referred to Maxwell's death having brought about the collapse of the company. It was made worse by 'the perception that his death was caused by suicide by a man who knew the game was up,' he said. 'We do not accept that Robert Maxwell killed himself, but that perception led to a disastrous plunge in the Maxwell Communication Corporation share price.'

When Kevin Maxwell gave evidence, he told the jury that thoughts of accident or murder had gone through his mind but never that his father had killed himself. 'He was a light sleeper,' he said. 'He would frequently get up in the middle of the night. He found it more convenient to relieve himself over the side while the vessel was moving. At the spot where he would have stood, instead of a handrail, there is only a thin wire – not the safest part of the vessel. It occurred to me it might be an accident, it might be murder, it might have been a robbery motive. It certainly never occurred to me that he would have committed suicide though that was a theory that became very popular as the days went by.'

Eventually – on Friday 19 January 1996 – after 131 days, 76 witnesses, and £20m of taxpayers' money the most expensive trial in British legal history ended. To the enormous relief of their families and friends, both Ian and Kevin Maxwell and their co-accused Larry Trachtenberg were unanimously found not guilty – a decision which cast doubt on the long-term future of the Serious Fraud Office which had brought the charges.

But the trial had not thrown any further light on the death of the tycoon himself. So in death, as in life, Robert Maxwell seems set to remain an enigma – the central figure in an enduring mystery. He would have liked that.

CHAPTER 2

INTERNATIONAL TERRORISM

Dr West has undertaken postmortems on the victims of many of the IRA terrorist outrages in recent years and has spent hours helping juries to understand the full horror of the killings. As Arab terrorism, too, has spread to Britain he has learned a great deal about the ruthless and cunning methods of Middle Eastern terror groups. With his special skills and wide experience he has often been able to give detectives crucial evidence to assist in solving such crimes.

WPC Yvonne Fletcher

From the age of three, Yvonne Fletcher had always wanted to be a policewoman. As she grew up in a tiny Dorset village, her parents tried to dissuade her, gently explaining that at 5 feet 2 inches she was really too short to become a constable. But behind her twinkly smile and sunny disposition lurked a young woman of steel with an unswerving belief in herself and a determination to realise her ambition. Before she turned nineteen, Yvonne had written to a dozen police forces and was thrilled when London's legendary Metropolitan Police accepted her as a recruit.

By the time she was twenty-five, WPC Yvonne Fletcher's life could not have been sweeter. A fully-fledged constable, she was posted to the world-famous Bow Street police station in central London and engaged to marry a fellow officer, PC Michael Liddell. She was in love with her job and in love with her man. But then came a tragic incident which would forever engrave the name of Yvonne Fletcher on the nation's memory and give her a proud place in the lexicon of police heroics.

It was 17 April 1984, a sunny spring day in the capital. For Yvonne, Michael Liddell and several dozen of their colleagues on 'early turn', there was a routine task to perform. They were to ensure that rival demonstrations outside the Libyan People's Bureau in St James's Square went off peacefully.

As she strolled the three-quarters of a mile from Bow Street to the quiet square where the demonstration was to take place, Yvonne chatted happily to her sergeant. Attachment to a central London division meant that they were both used to such duties, for chanting, banner-waving protestors of all races and creeds from all over the world are a familiar sight in London. And the freedom with which they are allowed to launch their political protests and make their voices so publicly heard is a source of pride to the British. This demonstration was to be no different, or so everyone thought.

Libya, at that time, was in the grip of political unrest. Its dictator, Colonel Muammar Gaddafi, had ordered that all opposition to his régime was to be crushed. That included the large and growing army of dissident refugees living abroad. Several dissident Libyan leaders had been murdered in Europe, and anti-Gaddafi student leaders in Britain had been the target of several, largely unsuccessful, bomb attacks. It was these outrages that were to be the subject of a demonstration outside Libya's London embassy, now renamed the People's Bureau in accordance with Gaddafi's views.

Coaches had been hired to bring protestors from all over the country, and mobile metal barriers had been erected around the square to keep the demonstrators on the pavement and permit the free flow of traffic. Fearing reprisals on their families back in Libya, many of the protestors wore balaclava helmets or makeshift masks to prevent themselves from being identified by security cameras mounted on the Bureau or secret photographers in the crowd. An almost equal number of Libyans loyal to the régime had been rounded up by the pro-Gaddafi faction to try to drown out the chants of the protestors with cries of support which would be filmed and broadcast on television back home later that night.

A loose police cordon was keeping the two groups apart, but the atmosphere, while not exactly friendly, was not as menacing as it had been on many similar occasions. The shouting was hostile, but everyone seemed to understand that what they were there for was political posturing. There were, however, a couple of danger signs.

This was a routine, unremarkable, demonstration of the kind seen in London dozens of times every week. Only a handful of protestors was expected, yet already a small press corps was assembling, including several international TV crews, all apparently summoned to the scene in advance at the invitation of the People's Bureau, who were promising an interesting story.

An hour before the scheduled start of the protest, labourer John Sullivan got a chilling foretaste of what was to come. He was erecting barriers to keep demonstrators away from the building when an Arab man came out of the Bureau and tried to prevent him from doing his job. 'This little guy came to me and said: "Look, I am not taking responsibility for you or the barriers because we have guns and there is going to be shooting here today,"' said Mr Sullivan. This conversation was relayed to a female security officer in a nearby building, who thought she had seen weapons being taken into the Bureau earlier. According to evidence later given in a coroner's inquest, these sinister developments were conveyed to the local police hierarchy but not acted upon. They could not be taken seriously, surely? Diplomats would not use guns. Not in the West. Not here in the birthplace of democracy in the heart of London. Could they?

The time was 10.20 am. WPC Yvonne Fletcher was standing directly in front of the People's Bureau about fifty yards away on the other side of the street. She was following the usual crowd control procedure by facing the demonstrators so as to spot any trouble and nip it in the bud. This meant that her back was turned to the target of their hatred, the Bureau itself.

Suddenly there was a burst of automatic gunfire from the first floor of the Libyan People's Bureau – a staccato rat-a-tat like firecrackers, the tell-tale sign of a sub-machine-gun – and people were dropping like flies in the street below. Yvonne Fletcher was the first to go down, groaning in agony and clutching her stomach as she lay in a pool of blood. Within seconds the scene was one of utter carnage. Eleven protestors had also been hit in the hail of bullets. Several policemen, among them Michael Liddell, rushed to Yvonne's aid. Others tended to the stricken demonstrators while the remainder frantically tried to clear the square. The Libyan demonstrators, accustomed to violence, were the first to take cover and flee the scene. But British bystanders could not believe their eyes and remained transfixed until bellowed warnings from desperate policemen galvanised them into flight.

Although mortally wounded, Yvonne Fletcher remained conscious throughout the journey to hospital, taking oxygen and bravely telling the ambulancemen where the pain was. As they lifted her gently from the ambulance, a single bloody bullet fell from her uniform tunic to the floor of the vehicle. Despite a desperate battle by surgeons to save her, she died an hour later – the first police officer in the Western world to be killed by a bullet fired from within an embassy.

For Iain West it was to prove a busy day. After dealing with a heavy caseload of routine mortuary work in the morning, he had to drive down to Sussex to give evidence at an inquest. 'At lunch-time I heard a rumour that there had been a shooting in the West End,' he recalled. 'I kept in touch, and it soon became clear that a woman police officer had been shot.'

By early evening he was back in London and preparing to carry out the postmortem. The first thing he noticed, on examining the X-rays taken in the mortuary, was the absence of bullets or bullet fragments within the body. But he quickly spotted four firearm wounds on the surface of the body which indicated the passage of just one bullet through the young policewoman's back, abdomen and left arm. This, he reasoned, was going to be crucial evidence at a later stage, so he ordered photographs to be taken which would indicate precisely the angle at which the bullet had struck. Dr West's postmortem report then tells the precise story of that devastating missile.

The entry wound was on the right side of the back of her chest, 45¾ inches above the right heel, 10 inches below the top of the right shoulder, 5½ inches to the right of the spine and 3¼ inches behind the back fold of the right armpit. The wound was situated over the position of the sixth and seventh right side ribs.

The entry wound was almost round, measuring 7mm by 7mm, and was surrounded by an elliptical rim of abrasion set obliquely upwards and to the right. The rim of abrasion measured 4mm at its upper end and 1mm and 1.5mm wide around the lower end and sides of the bullet hole. There was very slight splitting of the margins of the hole itself.

Beginning to follow the path of the bullet, the report continues:

The bullet track passed downwards, forwards and towards the left, travelling sharply downwards in the tissues of the chest wall at an angle of 60–70 degrees to the horizontal plane of her body. It penetrated the rib cage between the tenth and eleventh ribs in the right side, some 2½ inches below the entry wound on the skin. The track splintered the lower edge of the tenth rib, 3 inches from the side of the spine.

This was the point in its split-second journey at which the bullet began to do its fatal damage. Dr West reported:

The bullet then passed through the right lobe of the diaphragm and immediately entered the right lobe of the liver just above the outer extremity of the bare area of the organ. It then penetrated through the right lobe, extensively lacerating it, to exit from the liver just below and to the right of the neck of the gall bladder. The exit wound in the right lobe of the liver was 3 inches in diameter.

The bullet then penetrated the inferior vena cava below the liver and was deflected upwards against the side of the spine, which showed a small area of bruising. The right adrenal gland had been lacerated by the bullet prior to its entry into the vena cava.

After deflection, the bullet passed through the head of the pancreas and then re-entered the left lobe of the liver, bursting it upwards and outwards.

Having described such devastating internal injuries, Dr West then turned his attention to the exit wound:

The bullet then left the chest by passing through the left lobe of the diaphragm and notching the lower edge of the left lower costal margin and produced a 12mm by 8mm exit wound on the front of the lower left chest. This wound was almost rectangular with one rounded end and was surrounded by an almost bullet-shaped rim of abrasion laid obliquely upwards and to the right.

Giving measurements of the exit wound, the report concentrated on its odd shape. 'The shape of the wound appeared to have been caused by the bullet tumbling as it left her body,' Dr West wrote, going on to describe how the bullet re-entered the stricken policewoman's left elbow, which:

appeared to have been held in contact with the side of her left chest, with her elbow bent at right angles, at the moment she was shot. The re-entry injury was kidney-shaped . . . and was surrounded by bullet-shaped abrasion mirroring the abrasion surrounding the exit wound on her chest and consistent with the entry of a tumbling bullet.

The killing of Yvonne Fletcher brought worldwide condemnation and sparked off a furious diplomatic row between Britain and Libya. Within minutes of the shooting, the square was sealed off by armed police and an eleven-day siege followed, while Britain demanded that the murderer be handed over and Libya claimed full diplomatic immunity for everyone in the building at the time.

While this drama was being played out in front of the world's television cameras, Scotland Yard's Anti-terrorist Squad under Commander William Hucklesby were painstakingly piecing together the evidence which would be needed to convict the gunman should he ever come to trial. But the detectives had first to contend with wild rumours, claims and counter-claims coming from all sides involved in the débâcle. 'One of the initial allegations was that she had been shot by Israeli agents on the roof who were trying to foment trouble between Britain and Libya,' said Iain West. It was a ludicrous suggestion, of course, but coupled with equally vehement claims that WPC Fletcher had been shot by anti-Gaddafi factions in the crowd or in nearby buildings, it had to be addressed and Commander Hucklesby turned to Iain West for the proof he needed. He recalled the pay-off in the last paragraph of the pathologist's postmortem report:

> The angle of the bullet wound track indicates that she was shot in the back by a person who was situated at a considerably higher level. Assuming that she was standing upright at the moment she was shot, the track would indicate that she had been shot from one of the adjacent floors of an adjacent building. Again, assuming that she was standing when she was shot, it would have been impossible for the bullet wound to have been caused by a person situated nearby at ground level. I could see no

evidence of any other conditions or injury which could have caused her to fall to the ground prior to being shot.

Encouraged by this opinion, the Commander asked West to do more work on the trajectory of the bullet. 'We badly needed evidence to corroborate the fact that the bullets had been fired from the Bureau itself,' said Mr Hucklesby, now retired from the police service. 'We had plenty of witnesses whose evidence was very convincing on this point, but the matter was so politically delicate that we needed to be certain beyond doubt.'

'From the body, we already had the angle of the wound reasonably accurately', said Dr West, 'and when we looked at film footage taken moments before the shooting, we could see precisely the direction in which she was facing. In fact this film showed that she had her arms folded across her chest at the moment she was shot, which accounted for the exit wound from her chest directly into and out of her elbow.

'We then looked at the angle at which the bullet passed through her tunic. I had been up to St James's Square while the siege was still on and had a good look at the building from behind an armoured Land Rover. In the Forensic Science Laboratory with Brian Arnold and David Pryor, we used an inclinometer and worked out a maximum angle. It indicated that the shot had come from the first floor of the building or, a lesser possibility, from the second floor. In any event, the shot could not have come from street level or from the roof,' he insisted.

While this work was going on, the wounds of the nine other victims of the shooting were carefully tabulated. Four had been shot in the leg or foot, two had been shot in the thigh, two had been shot in the hip area. There were three wounds in the forearm, one had a wound in the upper arm and one man had been shot in the chest and the back. 'The police gave me a chart relating to the injuries of the other victims,' said Dr West. 'I went and looked at some of them in Westminster Hospital, but their injuries could not help me in terms of positioning the shot which killed Yvonne Fletcher.'

Mr Hucklesby said: 'Iain's work on proving that the shooting did take place from the embassy and nowhere else was invaluable and most convincing. He went to extreme lengths, even going to the scene whilst we were still holding the ground and in a situation where they could have opened fire again at any time. I remember him doing his calculations at the precise spot, standing me there, drawing a line through my body and showing with his finger how the bullet had come out of the window – which tied up beautifully – and gone into her body to do that terrible damage which his post-mortem report showed.

'That sort of work was so professional and he was so committed. There was no stone left unturned. Not only on that occasion but on numerous other occasions I worked with Iain, he showed himself to be a forensic medical investigator, not just a pathologist trying to prove cause of death. He went way beyond that, and his enthusiasm was awe-inspiring – being willing to put himself on offer to prove the point.'

Eventually the impasse was broken when Britain broke off relations with Libya and expelled all her diplomats, including thirty people holed up in the Bureau, Yvonne Fletcher's killer among them. It later emerged that only twenty-two of those released from the Bureau had diplomatic status sufficient to protect them from prosecution.

At the inquest into Yvonne Fletcher's death held a month after the shooting, a number of interesting facts emerged. There had apparently been two gunmen. Police scientists revealed that deposits from firearms and discharge residues were found beside two windows in the ambassador's first floor waiting-room. Of the twelve bullets collected from the roadway outside, microscopic examination revealed that all were fired from 9mm Sterling sub-machine-guns, but nine were fired from one weapon while three others came from a different gun. A four-day police search of the building produced 4,367 rounds of ammunition, four .38 revolvers, three self-loading pistols with loading magazines, Sterling sub-machine-gun magazines, body armour and bomb blankets. One of those guns was found to be the one which, four years earlier, had been used to assassinate a Libyan journalist outside the Regent's Park mosque. Five witnesses, including four police officers, each told the inquest that they had seen a gun barrel pointing out of the embassy window.

A decorator, David Robertson, was crossing the square from a nearby bank to put money in a parking meter when the shooting started. 'I looked at the window directly to the left of where the flag was flying and saw a man,' he said. 'He had a short-barrelled gun with a long stock in his hand, and he was left-handed.'

PC Simon Withey, a police motorcyclist, said: 'I looked up at the Bureau because I saw someone shaking his fist from the window. He had thick wavy hair, was clean shaven, and was wearing lightish clothing. I looked to one side of me and saw a group of police officers, WPC Fletcher was with them. I looked back at the window and saw, to the left of the man who had been waving his hands, a small barrel. It was a very sunny day and the sun was glinting off it. I couldn't believe that something like that could appear at the window. Next I saw the gun open fire in a short static burst.'

In giving evidence to the inquest, Iain West told the jury that WPC Fletcher's injuries were so severe that no medical intervention could have saved her. She died, he said, from an abdomen wound, having been shot in the right side of the back by a bullet striking her from a 60-degree angle. The bullet – the one found on the floor of the ambulance, he surmised – entered her liver, struck her spine, severed the pancreas, re-entered her liver and started to 'tumble' before emerging at the junction of her chest and abdomen. It had ruptured the main vein in her abdomen. The bullet finally pierced the lining of her tunic as it came to rest. Dr West gave evidence as to the angle of the wound, which led him to determine that it was fired from the Bureau's first floor. It was fired from a 9mm sub-machine-gun, and WPC Fletcher was probably the first victim to have been hit.

Commander Hucklesby narrowed down his list of suspects for the murder to two names. The British Foreign Office pressed the Libyans to take action, and eventually Gaddafi, desperate to get back on good terms with the West, leaked a story to the effect that he had ordered the summary execution of the gunman responsible for Yvonne's death. Nobody really believed this, and when Mrs Queenie Fletcher went to Libya ten years after the killing all she got was a half-hearted apology from Gaddafi for the loss of her daughter.

Film director Michael Winner was so shocked by the death of Yvonne Fletcher that he determined to erect a monument in her honour. He established the Police Memorial Trust to commemorate police officers killed in the course of their duty. Ten months after the shooting, Yvonne's parents Tim and Queenie, together with her sisters Sarah and Heather, met the prime minister, Margaret Thatcher, as she unveiled a plaque at the spot where the policewoman fell.

To this day, people strolling through St James's Square pause to read the inscription and admire the bouquet of flowers still constantly replenished by local residents grateful for the sacrifice of her young life.

The Brighton bomb

It was at 2.54 am on Friday 12 October 1984 that the IRA came closest to murdering the British prime minister and wiping out most of her cabinet. Mrs Thatcher was working on the final draft of the keynote speech she would deliver to the closing session of the Tory Party conference in Brighton later that day when a massive explosion shook the Grand Hotel where she and most of the government were staying.

The terrorists had been extremely cunning. Weeks earlier, posing as a businessman, Patrick Magee had booked into the hotel and stayed on the sixth floor in Room 629. Carefully he had unscrewed a panel on the side of the bath and planted a suitcase filled with 20lb of explosive, a detonator, and an electronic timer from a video recorder before replacing the panel and checking out of the hotel.

The video timer could be set to activate weeks in advance and had been programmed to go off at the height of the Conservative conference, in the small hours of the last morning when the hotel could be guaranteed to be packed with dignitaries asleep in their beds. The explosive was Czech-made Semtex, odourless and virtually impossible for the sniffer dogs which searched the hotel before the conference to detect. The terrorists knew that the prime minister's suite was on the second floor almost directly below Room 629 and reasoned that the blast would bring the upper storeys of the old building crashing down.

In the event, their deadly plan failed by a matter of a few feet. The blast, when it came, did bring all the rooms down but only in the central section – like a slice from a cake. Mrs Thatcher's suite was in the adjoining section of the building, protected from the devastation by a narrow dividing wall. Although her drawing-room was covered in broken glass and the suite was filled with dust, Mrs Thatcher and her husband escaped unscathed and were hurried away down a rear fire escape and off to a place of safety by anxious bodyguards.

Others were less fortunate. Sir Donald McLean, the Scottish Tory President, and his wife Muriel were staying in Room 629. He was trapped, but escaped with a badly shattered heel. She was blown into the next room and died a month later. The Tory chief whip John Wakeham lost his wife Roberta in the blast and was himself unconscious for several days, having to spend many painful months while doctors worked to save his legs which had been badly crushed. Sir Anthony Berry, MP for Southgate, also died. The Trade and Industry Secretary Norman Tebbit was trapped in the rubble for hours, and his wife Margaret has been paralysed from the neck down ever since. It was Lord Tebbit's cry of 'Get off my bloody feet, Fred' televised live around the world as he shouted at the fireman leaning across the rubble to free him that came to symbolise the courage of both victims and rescuers that night.

'I remember waking up and hearing on the first early morning news at 6.30 that there had been something going on in Brighton,' said Iain West with his customary understatement. 'I tried to phone the police but couldn't get through, so after about twenty minutes, having some work to do in London, I set off, keeping my bleeper with me – in those days there were no mobile phones. When I got to London I kept trying, but the lines were permanently engaged so I waited until the police contacted me about an hour and a half later. Then I went to Brighton by train – there seemed little point in trying to drive – and stayed there for the whole weekend until we'd finished.'

His job was to organise the examination of those killed,

supervise their removal to the mortuary and then perform postmortem examinations. It was exhausting and potentially dangerous work with detectives working in pairs as they gingerly searched through the remains of the crumbling building for the last missing victims. 'The building was very unstable,' said Dr West, 'Certain floors were dangerous, so we worked on the basis of no more than two people on the floor at any one time. The fire brigade and the borough engineer had more or less excluded everybody.'

By the time Saturday arrived, there was only one person still unaccounted for – Mrs Jean Shattock – and it was her body that was to prove the most important in terms of the forensic investigation. But by the time she was found and removed from the tottering Grand Hotel it was 11.30 at night, almost forty-five hours after the explosion.

Dr West recalled: 'We still had not found her by the Saturday afternoon, so I suggested to one of the Anti-terrorist Squad chaps that a reconnoitre might be useful. At that stage I thought we would probably become aware of the body because it would be starting to decompose.

'The fire brigade were convinced they knew where she was and we were sure that they were wrong. We had an idea where she might be, and this detective went up there and returned within half an hour, having located her. She'd been blown through several walls, across a corridor, and was in the remains of a wardrobe in another bedroom towards the centre of the building on the sixth floor. We then went up in pairs and excavated the body. We weren't too pleased when a very senior police officer brought up twelve uniformed officers just to give them a look at the scene, particularly as at that stage the floor was actually bouncing up and down when you walked. So they were politely asked to leave.'

The postmortems on three of the victims, Roberta

Wakeham, Sir Anthony Berry and the 54-year-old chairman of the North West Conservative Party, Eric Taylor, were relatively straightforward. All the signs of traumatic asphyxia were present. 'They had been crushed and you could tell immediately from the discoloration of the skin – the areas of pallor – how their bodies were compressed by the rubble,' said Dr West. 'There is a general compression of the trunk preventing respiratory movement and it also prevents blood returning to the heart, so the face may become enormously distended. It's a scenario one sees in certain types of explosions which take place in buildings and in rail crashes, for instance.'

Some weeks later Dr West was to carry out a postmortem on Mrs Muriel McLean, who unfortunately died of pneumonia after the shrapnel wounds to her legs became infected. But for the time being he turned his attention to the body of Mrs Shattock, which displayed all the devastatingly disruptive injuries so familiar to a pathologist used to dealing with the victims of bomb blasts. The examination took many hours on the Sunday following the explosion. But it began to yield so many clues that Dr West had the body removed to his own mortuary in London so that he could carry out a second examination the following day.

'The examination of Mrs Shattock proved to be crucial in terms of where the bomb was placed,' he said. 'We knew where she had been the night before. Her husband was able to say, though I don't think his recollection was totally accurate, that he remembered her being in bed with him in Room 628 at the time of the explosion. But the direction in which she had been blown and the injuries on her body made it clear to me that she had been in the bathroom at the time of detonation and not in the bed.

'She had a pattern of flash-burning and a pattern of shrapnel injury, including pieces of ceramic material from the sink – not

just from the tiles on the wall but from the bathroom furnishings – which placed her in relation to the bomb. In other words,
it put the bomb in the adjoining bathroom on the seaward side
of her bathroom. The pattern of flash burns indicated that she
was actually leaning over something. Now the baths were cast
iron and there was a gap in the wall between the bathrooms at
the heads of the baths. So the question arose, where was the
bomb? Was it in the front or the rear bathroom? The detectives
couldn't find any bits of cast iron going outwards, but they
started finding them on going up into the building. The flash-
burns showed that she had to have been very close to the
bomb, but there were burns on her body which looked as
though she had possibly been in contact with a fireball.

'I used a technique we have developed over the last decade
or so for looking at small areas of a body, where death has
occurred from a bomb, in order to find pieces of the device
itself. At Brighton the detectives were working on a hunch,
later proved correct, that this bomb was on a long-term timer.
So I was keeping my eyes open for a circuit board from the
timing device. I was removing pieces of tissue from likely
areas and everybody got very excited when I actually got a
circuit board from the remains of tissue. Unfortunately it had
nothing to do with the bomb; it was from a watch.'

The Commander of Scotland Yard's Anti-terrorist Squad at
the time was William Hucklesby and he made full use of Dr
West's skills. 'Iain West was vital to us in two respects,' he said.
'Firstly in determining the location of the bomb in the hotel
and secondly in searching for fragments of the bomb itself.

'His postmortem on Mrs Shattock was very important in
corroborating what we thought was the case – that the bomb
was put in a bathroom, but not *her* bathroom. The marks on
her body, as Iain explained it to us, clearly showed that she
was bending down over the basin at the time the bomb went

off, and the injuries to her were consistent with that. But they were also consistent with the fact that the bomb wasn't in her bathroom.

'Having located where that bomb was, as a result of its having been corroborated by Iain, we were then able to move our search procedures outwards from that bathroom. The operational importance being that once you locate the site of the bomb it is within the location of the detonation that you will find the most important evidence – how big the bomb was, what it was made of, what the timing device was. In this case, the timing device was very important if we were to prove the theory we were working on.'

Some eighteen months after the Brighton outrage, when the bombing team had been arrested and charged, Dr West was unexpectedly plunged into controversy when he made a formal statement to be given in evidence at the trial. It was the first time he had set out fully what his findings were in the case of Mrs Shattock:

The body of Mrs Shattock showed a pattern of disruptive injury, indicating that she was close to the site of explosion. She had many pieces of shrapnel driven into her body, including pieces of cast iron and ceramic material. The ceramic material had not been the result of contamination of the body surface but had been driven into her body tissues as a result of the explosion.

From the position of her body, as found at the scene and seen by myself, appearances would indicate that Mrs Shattock was near to the bath at the wall adjoining the two bathrooms and that the explosion occurred in the adjoining bathroom, causing fragments of the tiles from the party wall to be driven into her body.

The extensive flash-burning which had resulted from radiant heat injury and the direct burning of her left hand would be consistent with the fireball caused by the explosion spreading under the bath in the adjoining bathroom towards the front of the building, passing through the gap in the wall between the heads of the baths in the two rooms, and thereby providing a source of intense heat fairly close to her body.

If Mrs Shattock had been sitting on the toilet at the time of the explosion, I would not have expected her to be found in the position at which I saw her shortly after her body was discovered. I would also not expect the flash-burning to be as severe.

When they read this statement, the defence lawyers were incensed. Why had they not seen this detail before? Why had Dr West never said these things before? They demanded to know. Where did his allegiances lie?

'I did not really give any conclusions in my initial report,' admitted Dr West. 'That was a report to the coroner and didn't require extensive conclusions. Nobody had been charged at that stage, and the conclusions were added following a conference with the prosecuting authorities at a later stage when I was asked to state my opinion. The coroner does not require me to go into such depth, obviously, but it is required for the purposes of a trial. Eventually the question came up as to why I had not included these opinions in my initial report. Didn't this appear a bit strange? Wasn't I being motivated by a desire to assist the prosecution?

'The row all died down finally when I explained that it has always been my practice. If no one has been charged, then I tend to leave the conclusions relatively brief.'

Mostaghimy Tehrani Gholam Hossein

In the Spring of 1980 the public was absorbed for six days by a siege at the Iranian embassy in London which had been occupied at gunpoint by a gang of terrorists. The dramatic live TV pictures of hooded Special Air Services commandos storming the building to rescue the hostages were flashed around the world and quickly established a swashbuckling reputation for British special forces. But as talk of the invincibility of the SAS and the bravery of one of the hostages, PC Trevor Lock, continued for weeks afterwards, another violent act in the heart of the nation's capital passed virtually unnoticed.

Some two weeks after the ending of the siege, late in the afternoon of Saturday 17 May, there was a massive explosion in the Queen's Gardens Hotel in Bayswater, west London, not far from the now destroyed Iranian embassy in Prince's Gate. On the fourth floor of the hotel, Room 21 was devastated with the adjoining wall being blown through into Room 20 next door, which was also badly damaged.

When the police and rescue services arrived, they found one man dead in Room 21 and another seriously injured. But who were they and why were they victims of a bomb?

Detectives soon discovered that two men had arrived at the hotel five days earlier and had checked into Room 21, describing themselves as uncle and nephew. They were apparently Iranian and spoke little English. The elder of the two, forty-four-year-old Mostaghimy Tehrani Gholam Hossein, was now dead. A guest in the room at the time of the explosion was critically ill under armed police guard in hospital. And the 'nephew', twenty-eight-year-old Ebadollah Nooripour, was under arrest. He had been in the foyer of the hotel making a telephone call when the bomb went off.

Just days earlier Iain West had been completing his post-mortem examinations on the victims of the Prince's Gate siege – the hostages killed by the terrorists, and the terrorists gunned down by the SAS. Now he was asked to apply his skill to determining exactly what had happened on the top floor of the Queen's Gardens Hotel.

He began his postmortem, as usual, by examining X-rays taken of the body and was immediately puzzled by a most unusual sight:

I found multiple small opaque fragments to be present in the head, neck, chest, left side of the pelvis, left thigh, and in the calves and feet. Similar fragments were also present in the hands and forearms.

The opaque bodies included tiny 'V'-shaped opacities which were present in large numbers in the left thigh, left side of the pelvis, chest and neck. Larger fragments were present in the left thigh around the left hip and on the lower part of the neck in the region of the left collarbone.

The X-rays showed the anticipated multiple fractures caused by an explosion, and it was also not unusual to spot fragments of débris in the bodies of bomb victims. But Dr West had never seen anything like the tiny 'V' shapes before. Putting these inexplicable objects out of his mind for the time being, he pressed on with the autopsy. The dead man's clothing was charred, tattered and bloodstained, but the trousers yielded the first possible clue as to the victim's proximity to the device because they were torn mainly down the front of the legs.

Moving on to the body itself, Dr West reported:

There was extensive destruction of the lower part of the face, front and sides of the neck and over the region of the upper breastbone with only tattered remnants of skin remaining on the sides of the neck and lacerations of the skin of the forehead and upper cheeks. There was blackening of the skin around the whole area and on the underlying exposed tissues, particularly over the front of the neck. The damage was particularly severe on the right side of the face, where it extended on to the temple with destruction of the right orbit. There was laceration and partial destruction of the left orbit.

The postmortem report continued to describe horrific blast injuries, but in doing so threw up two more significant clues on the dead man's location relative to the bomb when it exploded. First, the pathologist reported:

> . . . partial traumatic amputation of the left hand in the region of the palm. There were multiple fractures of the lower forearm and of the remaining bones within the hand. There was extensive blackening of the exposed surfaces and small fragments, mainly of grit, were embedded in the hand. There was some flash-burning and laceration on the inside of the left forearm . . . Blackening of the left upper arm.

Secondly, when he came to the lower limbs Dr West recorded:

> Extensive laceration of both feet and both shins with marked blackening and superficial burning of the skin in this region. On the inside of both calves there were multiple round and oval puncture wounds consistent with explosive injury with a deep laceration of the right upper inner shin. The direction of both groups of wounds on the shins was upwards and backwards. Along the

inner aspects of both thighs were multiple similar punctures surrounded by extensive blackening and superficial burning. They extended from just above the knees to just below the groin and were much more prominent on the left thigh.

There were deep horizontal lacerations on the inner parts of both upper thighs just below the groin. If the knees were flexed to 30 degrees then the wounds on the insides of the thighs were in a line with the wounds on the inner upper calves.

When he began to dissect the body, Dr West soon discovered what the 'V' shapes he had seen on the X-ray were. 'I dug some of them out of the body tissue and found little "V"-shaped pieces of yellow metal – dozens of them all over the body,' he recalled. 'We racked our brains as to what they were and eventually one of the police officers at the postmortem came up with the suggestion that they could be the teeth from a zip. And, of course, that's exactly what they were. They were the teeth from the zip of a bag. They were every-where except in the left hand, which was badly damaged. So obviously the bomb had been in a bag and his left hand had been in the bag at the time of the explosion.'

That discovery, together with the injuries on the lower limbs, head and chest, told its own story. This was no innocent tourist. This was a terrorist bomber at work. Hossein had been squatting on his haunches over the bomb, probably priming it with his left hand, when it had blown up literally in his face.

To use the more formal language of the postmortem report:

The pattern of the injuries received by the deceased indicates a seat of explosion situated at or near floor level, between his feet and just in front of his shins. The appearances suggest that the deceased was partially crouched over an explosive device which detonated whilst he was handling it. I give as cause of death: explosive injuries to the head and limbs.

As if Iain West's evidence was not damning enough, it was also revealed that forensic experts combing the wreckage of the hotel room had found a second explosive device containing two batteries and a detonator.

As Scotland Yard's Anti-terrorist Squad set to work, it quickly emerged that the two Iranians had slipped quietly into Britain just hours after the end of the embassy siege. Both were from Tehran, and both were skilled electronics technicians. They had been booked into their £14-a-night room by a third Iranian, twenty-seven-year-old Mohammed Abcou, who returned daily to visit them. It was he who was in the room with Hossein at the time of the blast, and he was now permanently blinded.

Throughout the week leading up to the explosion the pair had made repeated phone calls to an unlisted number in London. It was the Iranian Cultural Attaché's office in Kensington Square just a quarter of a mile from the hotel. This was the number that Nooripour had been frantically ringing when the bomb went off. Abcou was evidently a clerk who worked in the Cultural Attaché's office. So, according to the prosecution, the official Tehran régime was closely implicated in the attempt to plant bombs in London – an attempt, it seemed, although the intended targets were not known, to exact some kind of revenge for the recent events in Prince's Gate.

Nooripour and Abcou were charged with conspiring, along with Hossein, to cause explosions 'liable to cause danger to life'. The prosecution said they had turned the hotel room into a bomb factory and were assembling two car bombs when one accidentally exploded.

Abcou argued that he was not a terrorist. He did not know the other two men and had been lured to the hotel by a telephone call. 'His story was that he had been lying on the bed reading a newspaper and Hossein was pacing up and down very concerned about the wardrobe for some reason,' said Iain West. 'Apparently at some stage he bent down, pulled the wardrobe door open and everything went black. Abcou had flash burns on him, which indicates that he was not the 10 feet away he claimed. He also had some shrapnel damage and the characteristic blackening of somebody who is in close proximity to a bomb. He's lucky to be alive, and I don't believe his story.'

The jury did believe him, however, and he was cleared of the charges. But Nooripour was jailed for twelve years.

The incident led to an immediate souring of relations between London and Tehran – a situation which continued for a further eight years while the Iranians, who were holding two Britons prisoner for minor indiscretions, argued vehemently for compensation for damage caused to their London embassy by the SAS firebombs. Ironically it was the early release of Nooripour, after serving two-thirds of his sentence, which put an end to the dispute and re-opened diplomatic links between the two countries.

Kenneth Howorth

'Well, here we go again, lads,' joked Ken Howorth cheerily as he walked to his death.

For the brave forty-nine-year-old bomb disposal man it was 'just another day at the office' as he marched confidently into the Wimpy Bar in London's Oxford Street. But moments after his wisecracking departure from the group of anxious policemen in the street outside the front of the burger bar, it seemed to swell and then burst with a terrific blast.

The time was 3.43 pm. The date was Monday 26 October 1981. The outrage represented one of the most callous acts ever perpetrated by the IRA during their bloody terror campaign against Britain. For the bomb that killed Kenneth Howorth was aimed at innocent schoolchildren. It had been planted behind the washbasins in the downstairs toilet of a popular burger bar in the centre of the capital's busiest shopping street. As it was the middle of the half-term school holidays, the area was packed with mothers and children doing early Christmas shopping.

Within hours of the explosion, the IRA issued a chilling statement in Dublin. It read: 'The Irish Republican Army claims responsibility for planting bombs in Oxford Street today. Let the British people take note that Irish children, the victims of plastic bullets fired by their soldiers, do not have the luxury of receiving warnings. In future, when we give warnings, respect them.'

The terrorists had, indeed, given a warning, telephoned to Reuters news agency some twenty minutes before the blast. There were bombs in the Wimpy Bar and in Debenhams and Bourne & Hollingsworth department stores, said a man with a cultured Irish accent.

As police hurriedly evacuated the buildings and cleared the area outside, two of Scotland Yard's most experienced bomb disposal officers, Peter Gurney and Kenneth Howorth, raced to the scene. Pausing outside the Wimpy Bar, they agreed that Howorth would tackle that device while Gurney would deal with whatever was found in the department stores.

As Peter Gurney walked purposefully towards Debenhams he heard the explosion behind him. Turning momentarily, he knew instinctively that his colleague and friend was dead. With the cool courage that only bomb disposal men possess, he marched on straight into the shop and calmly defused a 5lb bomb, thereby not only saving lives but also preserving vital evidence about how the device was made – evidence which later was to help convict the bomb-makers.

'Postmortem examinations in victims who have been close to bomb explosions, particularly those close to the seat of the explosion, must be very detailed and very prolonged,' said Iain West, 'because there is an awful lot more to be gained than simply discovering why someone has died. In terrorist bombing cases it helps to know what the victim was doing at the time, and the postmortem can help us to reconstruct that.

'It is also vital to recover from the body as many fragments as possible in case any of them came from the device itself . It is clearly a major boost to the successful criminal investigation of the case if you can reconstruct the bomb with all its component parts, for instance.

'I heard about Ken Howorth's death the night before, and carried out the postmortem the next day. It was obvious from the pattern of injury, given the size of the bomb, that one of his hands and forearm must have been in contact with it. In other words, it must have been moving at the time he had handled it. It simply was not the sort of cleavage damage that one normally sees in those in close proximity to a bomb – much more than that. This strongly suggested that we were dealing with a device with an anti-handling circuit in it, so I put a lot of effort into seeing whether we could detect fragments that might have come from such a source.'

The postmortem report sets out the details of a human body torn apart by a bomb. Most of the head and face, for instance, had been blown away, but Dr West discovered that before entering the Wimpy Bar the unfortunate bomb disposal officer had made a futile gesture towards personal safety.

'On an attempt at reconstruction of the head, it was clear that there were symmetrical areas of undamaged skin on both sides of the face and temples extending downwards just in front of the angles of the jaw,' he wrote. 'The ears and parts of the neck adjacent to the ears were also undamaged. The undamaged areas corresponded to the position of the protective helmet which had been worn by the deceased. Outside the protected area, there was extensive laceration and burning of the skin and underlying tissue with flash-burning present and many small particles embedded in the skin of the face and neck.'

It was these particles which might prove crucial in reconstructing the bomb for the Anti-terrorist Squad detectives, so Dr West set about recovering as many of them as he could. 'The particles included pieces of grit, silvery material resembling silver foil, pieces of hardwood ply, small pieces of soft wood, white coloured laminate, pieces of glass, pieces of fibre, pieces of white metal and small pieces of blue and green plastic,' he reported. 'Pieces of what appeared to be black cotton were also found within the wound.'

Both the victim's arms had been blown off, and, by a careful study of the remains of the arms and hands, Dr West was able to conclude: 'The pattern of injury indicates that the deceased was crouched partially over and very close to an explosive device when it detonated. The degree of destruction of the left forearm and hand indicates that this part of his body was very close to the device when it exploded and he could, in fact, have been handling the device with his left hand at the time of detonation.'

Kenneth Howorth, a family man with two children, was a veteran of the IRA bombing campaigns in Northern Ireland, having served in the Royal Army Ordnance Corps and defused many bombs before joining Scotland Yard as one of their small team of civilian explosives officers.

But the 5lb device which killed him and blew a massive hole in the pavement outside the restaurant had, as Iain West surmised, been cunningly booby-trapped. The charge and the detonator had been separated and fitted with an anti-handling device – something not previously seen on the British mainland.

Almost four years later two twenty-nine-year-old Belfast men, Thomas Quigley and Paul Kavanagh, were convicted at the Old Bailey of mounting a number of terror attacks in London, including the murder of Kenneth Howorth. They were both jailed for life with a recommendation that they each serve a minimum of thirty-five years – the longest life term ever handed out in a British court.

The Hyde Park bombing

One minute it was gentle British pageantry, the next it was awful carnage on a beautiful summer day in London. It was precisely 10.40 am on 20 July 1982 when the IRA unleashed perhaps the most shocking outrage of their twenty-five-year reign of terror.

As a troop of the Queen's Horse Guards, the Blues and Royals, rode through Hyde Park on their way to the daily changing of the guard ceremony in Whitehall, they were ripped apart by a car packed with gelignite and nails.

While passing tourists marvelled at the spectacle of dancing plumes and burnished breastplates gleaming in the sun, an apparently innocent young couple sat on a park bench directly in line with the car bomb which had been parked earlier. When the pair spotted that the Blues and Royals' standard-bearer, who always rides in the centre of the troop, was directly in line with the car, they pressed the button on a radio-controlled detonator. The explosion was enormous, hurling the majestic horses, so beautifully groomed moments before, up into the sky to come crashing down as misshapen masses of flesh.

Public horror was intense. To think that such a tragedy could occur in the heart of the capital!

Four soldiers, including the troop commander twenty-three-year-old Lieutenant Anthony Daly, died, and seven horses were killed or had to be destroyed. Seventeen civilians and more horses were injured. The now legendary Sefton later became a national hero after recovering from his injuries.

Just over two hours after the attack a second bomb, hidden under a bandstand, killed seven men from the Royal Green Jackets regiment as they gave a lunchtime concert in Regent's Park. But within two days of the atrocities, sixteen men of the Blues and Royals resumed ceremonial duties. It was a fitting show of defiance from a regiment whose motto is 'Evil be to him who evil thinks'.

Iain West was conducting postmortems on the victims of a fire at a Vietnamese gaming club in Soho (see Chapter 12) when the first bomb went off. The first he knew of the tragedy was when the bodies of two troopers were brought to the Westminster mortuary where he was working. It was cramped temporary accommodation while the mortuary was being rebuilt.

When the Regent's Park bomb went off, it was obvious that the facilities at Westminster were going to be insufficient, so a neighbouring local authority was persuaded to make its mortuary available and Dr West's colleague Hugh Johnson agreed to take on the task of performing postmortems on the dead Green Jackets, leaving Iain free to concentrate on the Hyde Park victims.

The sight which met his eyes when he entered the post-mortem room was not only tragic but it was an affront to the dignity of the Queen and her loyal soldiers who had been so cruelly ripped apart. The evidence of this outrage lay before him in the shape of the once proud uniforms of the Blues and Royals.

There was a nail embedded in the riding boot of Lieutenant Daly, and his gleaming breastplate was split almost in two. The scabbard which had contained his officer's sword was bent and buckled and his white buckskin breeches and gauntlets were ripped to shreds. On his tattered tunic he still wore the Northern Ireland medal – a grim reminder of why this carnage had been wrought.

Trooper Simon Tipper, just nineteen, was still wearing his full uniform with the breastplates still in place over a torn tunic and his trooper's cape draped loosely over the body. His injuries were horrific. Dr West reported:

Extensive laceration of the scalp extending across the back of the head, over the top of the head and down on to the right cheek. The upper third of the right ear was burnt and part was missing. The hair on the right side of the back of the head was singed, as was the hair on the left temple.

There was an extensive comminuted fracture of the vault and base of the skull with a large gaping defect to the right side and back of the head, exposing brain which was spilling free. The brain was extensively lacerated.

I removed pieces of metal from the scalp, skull and brain. I removed a piece of black thread-like material from the substance of the brain.

There was a compound fracture of the jaw with metal fragments in the jaw, a fractured tooth, and loose fillings inside the mouth. There was bruising to the tip of the tongue.

So the catalogue of dreadful injuries went on, but essentially the young man had died from head injuries.

In the case of Daly, the young officer appeared to have been killed by projectiles hurtling through his chest. 'There was a large gaping lacerated wound on the back side of the right chest about 3 inches below the armpit,' wrote Dr West. 'It exposed ragged black underlying muscles and subcutaneous tissue.' The wicked nature of the bomb was also illustrated by Lieutenant Daly's body. 'A nail transfixed the skin on the back of the right calf and pieces of nail protruded from either side of the right ankle,' reported the pathologist. 'I removed two pieces of nail from the ankle.'

The other two dead soldiers had not died immediately, but their injuries were equally severe. Lance-Corporal Vernon Young, also nineteen, had died of head injuries. 'The vault of the skull was fragmented with pieces of bone missing. Most of the floor of the front section of the base of the skull was fragmented with numerous bone fragments missing. The eyeballs were exposed and displaced,' wrote Dr West. He went on to describe damage to the brain before making the key discovery: 'I removed yellow metal fragments from the scalp and front section of the skull.'

Corporal Young had been killed by his own ceremonial

helmet. 'An object had struck his helmet, fragmenting it and propelling it into his brain in the right forehead region', said Dr West. 'One wonders what would have happened if he hadn't been wearing a helmet of that type because I found no fragments of other shrapnel. The only articles I found were fourteen pieces of yellow metal from the helmet. Had he been wearing a soft helmet, for instance, it might well not have been a lethal injury.'

Corporal Major Roy Bright, the thirty-six-year-old standard-bearer on whose erect body the bombers had taken aim, died, along with his horse, Waterford. He was perhaps the unluckiest of the four fatalities. Dr West recorded the presence of a 'projectile entry wound on the skull just above the right ear with radiating fractures across the top of the vault of the skull and into the middle section of the right side of the base of the skull. The brain has been traversed by a bent nail which appears to have travelled horizontally through both cerebral hemispheres cutting a path from the right to the left, the nail terminating in the left parietal region,' he reported. 'On another occasion the nail might have gone in and come out and damaged part of the brain, but not necessarily lethally,' said Dr West. 'On this occasion the nail actually turned and did irreparable damage.'

Early on, the Anti-terrorist Squad detectives approached Iain West with their concerns that vital evidence might be lost in the bodies of the dead horses. 'So I made tentative arrangements with the Royal Veterinary College to use their large animal postmortem facilities to examine the horses,' he said. 'But the next thing I knew, the horses had been taken away by the army, who did their own postmortems.

'They produced bucketfuls of nails, but the police weren't interested in the nails that surrounded the bomb, they wanted shrapnel from the device itself. It would have been a laborious and quite painstaking endeavour to have examined the horses and it probably wouldn't have been possible to examine them all. But I would at least have liked to have looked at them to identify the general type and pattern of injury involved and point out areas where shrapnel from the device might have penetrated.'

He went on: 'The thing that always strikes me about the Hyde Park bomb is that when you look at the fairly limited number of fatalities and injuries to others, there is no doubt that the bodies of the horses were enormously protective as far as the people were concerned. They absorbed quite a lot of the débris which could quite easily have killed other soldiers or passers-by.'

In fact, the most devastation to the horses came in the very centre of the troop, which was riding in pairs apart from a three-abreast formation containing the officer and the standard-bearer. Nearest to the car itself when the bomb exploded was Lieutenant Daly's mount, Falcon. To his left was Corporal Major Bright on Waterford, with Lance-Corporal Young riding Rochester on his outside. Immediately ahead of them were troopers riding Yeastvite and Epaulette. To their rear rode trooper Tipper on Zara and his partner on Cedric.

These were the seven horses which either died instantly or had to be put down on the spot where they lay.

A crime against Christmas – the Harrods bombing

Prime minister Margaret Thatcher called it 'a crime against humanity and a crime against Christmas' when the IRA bombed the world's most famous department store in December 1983.

It was lunchtime on 17 December, the last Saturday before the yuletide holidays, when a massive car bomb ripped through Harrods of Knightsbridge. As a Salvation Army band played Christmas carols a few yards away, six people, including three police officers, were killed and seventy-seven injured. A warning had been given in a call to the Samaritans an hour earlier, but it was vague and deliberately designed to dissipate police resources and cause confusion. The 15lb bomb went off just as three police officers approached to check the car in which it was hidden, giving rise to suspicions that it had been detonated by remote control.

The three police officers who died – all from the nearby Chelsea police station – were twenty-two-year-old WPC Jane Arbuthnot and Sergeant Noel Lane, aged twenty-eight, killed instantly, and thirty-four-year-old Inspector Stephen Dodd who died a short time later in hospital. The three dead shoppers were twenty-four-year-old Philip Geddes, Caroline Cochrane-Patrick aged twenty-five, and an American tourist from Chicago, thirty-one-year-old Kenneth Salveson, who had been buying Christmas presents to take back to his friends and family.

When it came to the postmortems, which were to take two days, Dr West began with the body of WPC Arbuthnot. Of the many catastrophic wounds she had suffered from flying pieces of metal as the car disintegrated, the most devastating appeared to have been caused by a lump of shrapnel which had pierced her stomach, and one which had passed through her chest and transfixed her left lung. Dr West counted forty-five separate fragments in her body large enough to detect on the X-rays. She had also suffered flash-burning, which enabled the pathologist to conclude: 'The pattern of injury suggests that WPC Arbuthnot was facing the device when it exploded and that she had direct line of sight when the detonation occurred. The pattern of flash-burning indicates that her line of sight was unobstructed.'

Next he dealt with the body of the young journalist Philip Geddes, who had been shopping in Harrods and had left the store to find out what the commotion was about. Among his many wounds Dr West noted: 'There was a huge defect on the front of the chest wall measuring 9 by 12 inches, with exposure of broken ends of ribs, breastbone and lacerated remains of the chest and abdominal organs.' He went on: 'The heart was shredded and two pieces of thin wire were removed from the remains of the heart. One piece of wire was removed from the right lung.' The body of Geddes, too, was packed with fragments of shrapnel and débris. 'The deceased was facing the device when it exploded and he was struck by several large pieces of shrapnel. He was situated further from the bomb than was WPC Arbuthnot,' concluded the pathologist.

Sergeant Noel Lane had clearly been closest to the car when it went up. Among the police accoutrements found on his body were the burnt remains of a truncheon – symbol of his authority under the law but a poignant reminder of human frailty in the face of a bomb.

As with the other victims, Dr West was determined to retrieve as much potentially useful forensic evidence as he could from the bodies and paid particular attention to the sergeant's uniform. 'Adherent to the surface of the deceased's clothing were pieces of solidified white metal, pieces of copper wire, white metal fragments, red and white fragments, blue fragments and a screw nut and washer,' he reported. 'I removed the tunic, pullover and shirt in two sections together with the burnt remains of the aerial from the personal radio. I cut the clothing down the top of the right shoulder and down the front of the chest and removed the whole of the clothing of the chest area together with adherent fragments.'

Once again the body was packed with shrapnel, and there was 'extensive burning of the body surface with severe charring of both lower limbs. The appearances indicate that the deceased was close to the seat of the explosion when the bomb detonated and that he received both primary burns as the result of radiant heat damage caused by the explosion itself and secondary burns caused by the ignition of flammable material after the explosion.' Fortunately all of the burns were *post mortem*, and Sergeant Lane had died almost instantly.

When he came to the body of Kenneth Salveson, Dr West made a pathetic discovery. In the pocket of the American tourist's jeans he found three dress circle tickets for a performance of *Snoopy* at the Duchess Theatre the following Tuesday – a Christmas treat for the family, perhaps, which would now never be enjoyed. Once again there was extensive destruction of the body by bits of flying metal and a good deal of burning and charring. Dr West reported that there were 'heat contractures in all limbs with the body adopting the pugilistic attitude . . . The deceased appeared to have been fairly close to the bomb when it exploded – close enough to receive blast damage to his lungs,' he concluded. Salveson, too, had died instantly from a shrapnel projectile in his brain.

On the Monday morning Dr West was back in the mortuary examining the body of Caroline Cochrane-Patrick, whose injuries told a slightly different story. Her shredded blue and white sweater gave the first clues because it was covered in glass and Christmas decorations. She had been thrown through the Harrods store window.

'There were multiple punctate and round grazes and lacerations over the whole of the back of the body,' wrote Iain West, 'with multiple deep lacerations on the back of the arms and thighs with slicing lacerations passing through the upper right thigh, mid left thigh and through the mid left calf where there were extensive compound fractures.'

Most of Mrs Cochrane-Patrick's injuries were to the back and to the left of her face, leading Dr West to conclude: 'She was close to the seat of the explosion when the device detonated and her back was towards the bomb when it exploded. It would appear that the left side of her face was also turned towards the bomb. Most of the injuries had been received by fragments striking her from behind, but there were other injuries on the thighs consistent with injuries produced by broken glass caused when she was thrown through the broken display window at Harrods.'

Inspector Stephen Dodd had survived for a few hours with dreadful brain damage but was now dead, and his body was the last to be examined. The injuries were similar to those seen before, and Dr West concluded: 'Inspector Dodd was near to the seat of the explosion when detonation occurred and appeared to have had the right side of his body facing the bomb when it exploded.'

There was a sad footnote to the pathologist's work that morning when he performed a postmortem on the police dog, Queenie. His report simply says: 'There were surface and internal injuries on the dog entirely consistent with injuries received from shrapnel during an explosion. There were also two bullet wounds in the head.' With her handler lying critically injured nearby, a merciful policeman had put the mortally wounded animal out of her misery. The dog-handler lost a leg by amputation following the tragedy and this limb, too, was examined by Dr West in a further bid to recover elements of the bomb itself.

'The time taken to do the postmortems will stay in my memory,' he said. 'On the X-rays we saw an awful lot of wires and other pieces of possible electrical material. We obviously needed to retrieve as many pieces of the bomb as possible, but there were bits of car and pieces of electrical circuitry from the Harrods window also in the bodies, so it made the sorting out very difficult.

'The postmortem examination in a death by explosion is very detailed and can be very time-consuming. The longest I have ever spent on bomb victims – just two bomb victims – was three days, time consumed in removing bits of metal. In the Harrods case it became fairly obvious that what we were seeing in the X-rays was not fragments of bomb but the débris of the car and wiring from the windows.

'The other thing I noted was that the Metropolitan Police had just changed from natural fibre clothing to synthetic. And it was apparent that when one was exposed to flash burns, material made of nylon, for instance, was melting on to the body surface. I thought it was important to mention this from a safety point of view – not for the people who were close to the explosion, but for the people who were a surviv-able distance away and might suffer unnecessary burns.'

Ali El Giahour

While the killing of Yvonne Fletcher was still fresh in every-one's minds and relations with Libya remained bitter, another murder with connections to Tripoli was discovered in London.

On Monday 20 August 1984 a woman living in Bickenhall Mansions – an exclusive block of flats in Marylebone – com-plained of a strange smell coming from an adjacent apartment. She telephoned the head porter, who was baf-fled. The apartment had been rented a week earlier by a middle-aged Arab-looking man who had paid a deposit of

£100 and a weekly rent of £350. As far as the porter was aware, the flat was still unoccupied.

When the police broke in, they found the decomposing body of a middle-aged Arab-looking man in the bath. He was fully clothed. After a few hours detectives were able to identify the dead man as forty-five-year-old Ali El Giahour, a wealthy Libyan haulage contractor who was on bail charged with organising a terrorist bombing campaign. They had been searching for him since the previous Friday when he failed to make the second of two daily reports to Paddington Green police station – a strict condition of his bail.

'We had a pretty good idea that he had been shot,' said Iain West, 'because there was a gun and silencer dropped in the bath beside him, obviously washed over to remove any prints. He'd been shot in the head, but we had the devil of a job finding the bullet wound and the bullet because of the decomposition. The scalp was swollen and the wound had more or less sealed itself shut. We X-rayed him but found the bullet only after we put the voltage up enormously to penetrate the layers of gas which had built up in the scalp.'

The state of decomposition is graphically described in the first paragraph of Dr West's postmortem report:

The deceased was in an early state of decomposition with gross gaseous distension of the face, neck and upper chest. The mouth was open and the distended tongue protruded through it. There was green/black discoloration of the face, neck, trunk and arms, with marbling of the left leg and shoulder areas. The upper eyelids had been swollen shut due to a combination of gaseous decomposition and bruising. Blood emanated from the left nostril.

He followed this with a textbook description of the bullet wound, recording:

> There was a perfectly circular, single, non-contact, firearm entry wound on the back of the crown of the head situated 6 inches above the nape of the neck (seventh cervical vertebra). The wound was situated in a horizontal plane 1 inch above the top of the right ear and was 6 inches behind the tops of either ear. It was fractionally to the left of the midline.

Giving precise measurements of the hole itself he went on:

> Gas bubbled through the firearm wound. There was no compression of the overlying hair and I could see no gross bruising surrounding the entry wound and no evidence of muzzle mark. There was no singeing of hair or stippling of the scalp in the region. On the undersurface of the scalp the entry wound contained a small triangular piece of bone.
>
> The bullet track immediately entered the skull through a triangular defect measuring 6 by 8 mm. The entry hole in the skull was bevelled on its inner surface and the bullet track passed through the underlying dura and arachnoid and pierced the left occipital lobe of the brain, passed through the left parietal lobe and through the superior longitudinal sinus to exit from the skull via a fragmented exit wound on the frontal region of the skull just to the right of the midline.
>
> The exit wound was bevelled on its outer surface and a slightly distorted jacketed bullet lay sideways within the exit wound in the skull. The exit wound measured 23 by 19mm and was situated 19.3cm above the entry wound.

The bullet was still held inside the head because, although it had made an exit hole in the skull, it had not gone right through. The eye sockets had been shattered by the impact and the eyes had partially collapsed inside the skull. Two other significant clues remained to be found – bruising on the left side of the face and bruising on the right knee – before Iain West could deliver his analysis. When it came to the conclusions, he wrote:

> The deceased had been shot once in the back of the head with a bullet traversing the back of the skull and through the left side of the brain to ultimately lodge high in the forehead region of the skull. There is no evidence to suggest that the weapon had been held in contact with the deceased's head when firing took place.
>
> The subcutaneous bruising on the left side of the deceased's face is consistent with at least two blows being struck to the face. The appearances are consistent with injuries produced by a clenched fist. Because of the state of decomposition, I could not exclude a blow from a weapon such as the side of a gun.
>
> The bruising on the tissues in front of the right knee are consistent with either the deceased being struck on the knee or being forced into a kneeling position with his knee coming into firm contact with the floor.

So that was it. El Giahour had been punched in the face, perhaps even pistol-whipped, and then forced to kneel with his head bowed, before being shot once in the back of the head. 'It was quite clear that this was a cool, very careful, highly professional execution,' said Dr West. 'A classic terrorist hit.'

But there was one more piece of the forensic jigsaw to fit in. Was the murder bullet fired from the gun found in the bath? The task fell to Scotland Yard's ballistics expert David Pryor, who had been present at the autopsy to pick up as much information as he could and remove the bullet found inside the dead man's head. The next day, he took away from the murder flat a .32 cartridge case found lying on the sofa, and a slightly rusting Walther pistol, loaded magazine and silencer from the bath.

Back at the Forensic Science Laboratory, Mr Pryor began his tests. The .32 bullet was rifled 'with eight grooves having a right-hand twist'. The gun was a Walther PPK .32 self-loading pistol in fair condition. 'The original barrel had been removed and a replacement fitted being rifled with eight grooves having a right-hand twist,' reported the scientist.

After an exhaustive series of test firings, made more difficult because of the rusting of the gun and bullets in the magazine, Mr Pryor was able to report: 'It is my opinion that the bullet had been fired in the pistol and I am satisfied that the cartridge case had been fired in the pistol.' Further tests on the gun showed that it could have been fired as close to the victim's head as 6 inches without leaving any of the contact markings that had been absent at the postmortem.

'The gun had been a German police weapon which had reached the end of its natural life and been sold,' said Dr West.

Gradually the full story of El Giahour began to emerge. He had fled to Britain in 1978 when the régime of the dictator Colonel Gaddafi began to confiscate property. But two years later when the Libyan leader announced that exiled opponents would be hunted down and eliminated, El Giahour returned to Tripoli and made his peace.

In return for his own safety he agreed to work for Gaddafi and along with other businessmen living in Western capitals was soon supplying intelligence about opponents of the régime. According to other Libyan exiles, El Giahour was a weak and greedy personality whose vulnerability made him an ideal target for Tripoli to enrol in its terror campaign.

He was staying at the Hilton Hotel when Anti-terrorist Squad detectives arrested him for complicity in a series of explosions in Mayfair. One bomb had damaged a newsagent's shop frequented by anti-Gaddafi exiles. Another went off under a table at the Blue Angel club also used by opponents of the Tripoli régime. Twenty-three people were injured.

He had three London bank accounts, lived in Maida Vale, and spent £21,000 at the Hilton on one visit. When magistrates refused him bail and rejected his offer of a £20,000 bail bond, he broke down in tears and beat himself about the face and chest. It was this public indication of weakness and vulnerability which probably sealed his fate. A short time afterwards, in spite of strong police objections, he was bailed with the approval of a High Court judge after the intervention of a mystery third party who deposited sureties of £200,000 as well as the £20,000 bond in cash. El Giahour, who was married and had six children living in Libya, was forced to surrender his passport, keep a midnight to 7 am curfew, stay in the London area, not enter nightclubs and report to police twice daily.

But in Tripoli his court outburst had been noted by his spymasters and a hit squad was despatched on Gaddafi's personal orders to kill him before he could give away the secrets of the terror campaign. After making his 9.30 morning report to the police station, the flamboyant millionaire had been lured to the luxury flat with the promise, no doubt, of a lucrative business deal.

When the police arrived, they found that absolutely everything the killers had touched in the flat – right down to cigarette butts and tissues – had been put in the bath along with the body to hamper forensic tests. In their haste, the only item they had missed was the bullet cartridge on the sofa. El Giahour's shoes had been placed neatly alongside the body. Nearby lay a note, written in Arabic, which simply said, 'This is the punishment for the one who is employed to do a job and who does not succeed in doing it.' It was signed 'Al-Fatih, the Conqueror' – a reference to Gaddafi himself.

On the Friday of the murder, the daily Libyan Airways flight from Tripoli to London was mysteriously delayed by engine trouble. It should have arrived at Heathrow Airport at 1.35 pm for a departure on the return leg to Libya at 2.30. In the event the plane did not arrive in London until 4.15 pm, when three young Arab men, who had only just arrived at Heathrow, were able to board. Clearly Colonel Gaddafi had arranged an escape timetable for his hit squad which would give them plenty of time to do the job and leave the country unhurried and undetected.

The day the body was discovered, Libya made a formal diplomatic complaint to London, blaming Britain for the killing. There was no response and the killers were never brought to justice.

Abdullah Rahim Sharif Ali

Dinner in the Cleopatra Taverna in London's trendy Notting Hill Gate on 6 January 1988 was a noisy affair. Three Iraqi businessmen were sorting out a problem over their meal, and in the usual manner of Middle Eastern trading the exercise involved much gesticulation and gabbling in Arabic. Eventually the deal was done, and the company director Abdullah Ali proposed a toast to his two countrymen.

It was 2 am and the trio had eaten well, but from the

moment the forty-three-year-old Ali downed his large vodka and orange he was dying – a slow agonising death. The three men smiled, shook hands, and arranged to meet later that day but by the time Mr Ali woke feeling unwell at his Kensington apartment, the other two had been airborne for 30 minutes on their way back to Baghdad.

Mr Ali took himself to hospital suffering from flu symptoms, but was not admitted. It was only after severe stomach pains persisted that friends took him to the Cromwell private clinic, where he was diagnosed as suffering from thallium poisoning. Thallium is a metallic element widely used as a pesticide but banned in Western countries. It is a favourite assassination weapon of Arab criminals and intelligence agencies.

Moved to St Stephen's hospital, where he was given massive doses of the only known antidote to thallium, Mr Ali made a statement to police naming the two men with whom he had dined and a third who was their leader. They had poisoned him by slipping the colourless, odourless, tasteless liquid into his vodka when he got up from the table to go to the toilet, he insisted. The statement proved to be a dying declaration, for Mr Ali lost his battle to live twelve days after the fateful dinner.

The Ali case was an uncommon experience for Iain West in one particular respect. It was the first and only time, as a pathologist, that he was asked to carry out an examination *before* the subject was dead. With the stricken Mr Ali's inevitable death rapidly approaching, Scotland Yard's Anti-terrorist Squad called Dr West in to familiarise himself with the case so that he could make an early start on what they rightly assumed was going to be a tricky and politically sensitive investigation.

'They phoned me up to ask me to have a look at him in the old St Stephen's Hospital at Chelsea,' recalled Dr West, 'and I remember going in there just as the magistrate was taking down his dying deposition. He died the next day.'

In fact, most unusually, the postmortem report begins with an ante-mortem passage which reads:

> . . . I examined Mr Abdullah Ali and studied his case notes.
>
> It was clear from a visual examination Mr Ali was suffering from respiratory infection. I noted that both the head and body hair was being shed with ease, a sign typical of thallium poisoning. I was made aware, by my examination of the notes, of the high thallium levels found in Mr Ali's blood. The neurological pictures seen clinically were quite typical of the effects of thallium poisoning.

Sixteen hours later Dr West was in the mortuary beginning an autopsy. The case was so unusual that he was accompanied by three colleagues from Guy's Hospital, including his deputy Dr Dick Shepherd, and his wife Dr Vesna Djurovic. The British medical world was going to take full advantage of such a rare opportunity to see the effects of thallium at close hand.

The first tell-tale sign they spotted was the hair. 'The head hair was grey with a temple balding pattern and slight balding over the crown of the head,' wrote Dr West. 'The hair in the central frontal and upper temporal regions was more sparse than when examined on the previous evening, and plucked with great ease.' He added, 'The body hair was grey and plucked with relative ease.'

The doctors treating Mr Ali had managed to acquire a rare

supply of the only known antidote to thallium from the Poisons Unit at New Cross Hospital in south London. It is a purgative substance known as Prussian Blue, and evidence of its use became quickly apparent to the pathologists. 'There were blue-stained secretions in the mouth and nose,' reported Dr West, later noting: 'the air passages contained purulent blue-stained secretions,' and the stomach 'contained blue-coloured fluid'.

Apart from these two observations, there was nothing startlingly unusual about the body except that several of the main organs were congested. The brain appeared slightly swollen. 'The lungs were firm and congested showing confluent areas of pneumonic consolidation in both lungs with formation of microabscesses in the right middle and lower lobes,' wrote Dr West.

A larger number of body samples than usual was taken for testing in this case and sent to the Metropolitan Police Forensic Science Laboratory, where they were analysed by the pharmacist, Dr John Taylor. He found huge concentrations of the poison, which he tabulated with the terse comment: 'The above findings are consistent with the subject's death having been due to thallium poisoning.' Later, in his court statement, Dr Taylor added a chilling description of the effects of thallium salts. 'Those which are more soluble in water – for example the sulphate, acetate, nitrate and carbonate – are the most toxic, and the minimum single fatal dose has been estimated at about one gramme. Thallium is a cumulative poison and a toxic level can be built up in the body by several smaller dosages over a period of time. With a single fatal dosage, the symptoms normally appear within eight to twenty-four hours of ingestion and initially are burning sensations, severe and spasmodic abdominal pain, vomiting and diarrhoea, later followed by painful sensations in the extremities, lethargy, fumbled speech, tremors, coma, respiratory failure and death.'

While Dr Taylor's work was proceeding, another branch of the medical establishment was taking a close interest in the case. One of Britain's leading neuropathologists, Professor Peter Lantos of the Institute of Psychiatry at the Maudsley Hospital had asked Iain West for the brain and spinal chord of Abdullah Ali so that he could dissect it and study the effects of thallium.

Dr West was not able to take part in this fascinating research because he had, ironically, flown to Iraq himself at the invitation of the British Parliamentary Human Rights Group to investigate poison gas attacks on Kurdish villages (see Chapter 4). In an exchange of letters with Professor Lantos, he wrote: 'I have had to dash off to the Middle East to look at some civilians who have got innocently involved in the Iran/Iraq conflict. I will contact you as soon as I get back, always assuming of course that I do not end up keeping Terry Waite company.'

Two weeks later he was safely back in Britain and, having studied Dr Taylor's reports, gave his conclusions for the coroner:

> Abdullah Ali was a well-nourished man who has died as the result of thallium poisoning. Natural disease has played no part in his death. The deceased has toxic levels of thallium salts within his body. The levels are detectable both in the ante-mortem and postmortem samples. The neurological symptoms, the hair loss experienced by the deceased, is typical of thallium poisoning. The bronchopneumonia found at postmortem is a direct consequence of thallium poisoning.

Mr Ali's dying declaration was read to the inquest, which

decided that his death was an unlawful killing. The court heard that he died from one of the highest blood levels of thallium ever recorded.

As the Anti-terrorist Squad began to probe the sinister killing, they unearthed a great deal of information about Mr Ali. He had entered Britain in the early 1980s and was an intelligence officer for the ruling Ba'ath régime in Iraq. He was sent into the Iraqi community to report back on dissidents, but he was also suspected of illegal financial dealings as a representative of an Iraqi printing business.

Ali acquired great wealth at the expense of his company, but by then he was in dispute with Baghdad. The business was failing and he was ordered to return. He refused. Just weeks before his death, the company's managing director flew to London in a vain attempt to persuade Mr Ali to see sense. When this mission failed, the two Iraqi secret agents arrived to make an example of him. They succeeded in a spectacular and devastating fashion.

To this day no one has been arrested for the crime.

CHAPTER 3

ESPIONAGE AND INTRIGUE

In fiction the high-octane world of international politics is always played out against a sub-plot involving sinister power-brokers, glamorous secret agents and, inevitably, death gloriously depicted. In real life the power lust is just as sinister but the espionage is rarely glamorous and the death is frequently sordid. But for Iain West all this is routine business as he sets out to discover exactly how each victim died.

Robert Ouko

As Kenya's foreign secretary, Dr Robert Ouko was internationally respected as a politician of integrity, a skilful diplomat and a determined critic of corruption in his country's ruling circles.

In February 1990 he was a member of the team of ministers and senior civil servants who accompanied the Kenyan President Daniel Arap Moi on a private visit to Washington. He had strongly advised the President against the trip, warning that Kenya's human rights violations had provoked hostility in the United States, and he predicted unpleasant scenes.

During the visit, there was an angry argument between Ouko and the Kenyan energy minister, Nicholas Biwott. It was to prove a costly outburst for the fifty-eight-year-old foreign secretary. Ouko criticised the foreign bank accounts held by Biwott and other ministers, saying that the huge sums of money in them should be repatriated to Kenya to help pay for economic development. Their existence, which was known to the international aid authorities, was hindering Kenya's applications for foreign assistance. Biwott, widely suspected of being the most corrupt of Moi's ministers with overseas investments and cash sums alleged to top $200m, was furious and went to the President, a member of the same minority Kalenjin tribe and his closest political friend.

Ouko's position within the entourage was already precarious because he had been welcomed with open arms by President George Bush and the US administration while Moi and the others had been treated with cold disdain. President Moi told Ouko that the foreign accounts issue was none of his business, ordered him to leave the government entourage and fly home on a commercial flight, and had his passport seized when he arrived in Nairobi.

In this atmosphere of hostility and suspicion Ouko sought a meeting with the President, but instead of a reconciliation found himself banished to one of his three homes – a farm at Koru forty miles from the western Kenyan provincial capital of Kisumu on the shores of Lake Victoria. There he began an anxious wait, telling friends and family that he feared for his life because of his threats to expose a network of corruption within the government.

Robert Ouko disappeared from his country house on the night of Monday 12 February. He was due to fly back to

Nairobi the following morning and had arranged to meet his bodyguard – whom he had temporarily discharged – at Kisumu airport. However, his wife Christobel had left for Nairobi the day before in a state Mercedes and there was no car to take Ouko to the airport. On the Monday evening he asked his watchman for the keys to the front gate and to the farm storeroom. He said he was planning to leave very early in the morning.

At 3 am the housekeeper was woken by the sound of a door slamming and later saw a white or light-coloured car driving away down the main road. In the morning she was surprised to discover that Dr Ouko had not locked the door as usual and had left his reading glasses and briefcase on his bed.

Three days later Ouko's badly burned body, with a bullet through the brain, was found in undergrowth only four kilometres from his house. Despite government claims to have mounted a massive search, the corpse was discovered by a seventeen-year-old herdsboy. Beside it lay a jerrycan from Ouko's storeroom, the minister's Somali sword-cum-walking-stick, his own .38 revolver and a neatly folded pile of his clothes. The grisly discovery was puzzling. Ouko, a former teacher and father of seven, was a fastidious man with set habits. He did not usually ask for his servants' keys and he certainly never left the house unlocked. It seemed that he had an appointment and left the house voluntarily. But why would he remove a can of diesel from the store; why should he leave his briefcase behind?

The Kenyan authorities were quick to provide a solution.

Local police visited the scene where the body was found and expressed the belief that the minister, depressed by his banishment from Presidential favour, had carried out a carefully prepared suicide plan. The uncharacteristic discussion with his servants the previous evening had been a ruse designed to make them believe that he was indeed leaving early for an appointment and the need for the storeroom key was to enable him to take the jerrycan full of diesel with which to set fire to his body .

The police opinion was backed up by Kenya's top pathologist Dr Jason Kaviti, who carried out a postmortem on the body and declared that Ouko had set fire to himself while sitting on the ground, hoping that all trace of his body would be removed by incineration, and had then killed himself with a single shot to the head. Kaviti's story was supported by the fact that a single chamber of the minister's .38 revolver had been fired. Four other bullets were found in a jacket nearby along with the pile of freshly pressed clothes.

But if the Kenyan government thought this explanation would be good enough for the people, they were sadly mistaken. The incident plunged the country, until then one of the most stable in Africa, into its worst crisis since independence in 1963.

For the first time President Moi's administration was questioned publicly and there were calls for his resignation. The government was accused of covering up a murder with the suicide story and bloody street battles broke out between students and riot police, leaving at least four protestors shot dead. Moi banned all demonstrations and gave police the power to arrest and charge anyone deemed to be rumour-mongering – defined as alleging a political motive for Ouko's death. A reward of £30,000 for information leading to the conviction of the killers was offered, but the unrest continued to worsen.

For a country heavily reliant on tourism, the case – the fourth unsolved death to make headlines in a year – was devastating. There had already been the bungled inquiry and cover-up of the death of the British student Julie Ward, the killing of the father of the singer Roger Whittaker and the shooting of the naturalist George Adamson.

In this tense situation President Moi personally turned to Britain for help, and Detective Superintendent John Troon of Scotland Yard's International and Organised Crimes Branch was dispatched to investigate Ouko's death.

For Iain West it was an important time. He had just married his second wife, Vesna, also a pathologist, and the pair had managed to snatch a twenty-four-hour honeymoon break in Germany between work commitments. Flying into London from Hamburg on the Monday morning, Dr West was not surprised to be plunged back into the hurly-burly of police investigation immediately.

'John Troon called and said he was going to Kenya to investigate the suspicious death of the foreign secretary whose body had been discovered three days after he went missing,' he said. 'So I flew out the following day with John and two other officers and we went straight to work when we arrived in Nairobi at seven in the morning.'

Before Dr West could begin his painstaking inquiry there were irritating diplomatic formalities. He had to meet the permanent secretary in charge of the Health Department and a number of doctors, one of whom, a professor of biochemistry at the University of Nairobi, had been appointed to report on West's work direct to President Moi. There was also a senior orthopaedic surgeon who had been at the original postmortem and was to prove an unlikely and rare ally in the difficult days that lay ahead.

Meetings with the internal security chief, the police commissioner and Dr Ouko's widow followed before the postmortem, which was to last several hours, could begin in the afternoon. In common with modern practice, the post-mortem was not only photographed but also videoed with Detective Sergeant Sandy Sanderson assisting Dr West.

Dr Kaviti, whose findings of suicide in the Julie Ward case had been proved totally wrong, had undertaken the first post-mortem examination of the minister's body. He was now present, looking over Dr West's shoulder, no doubt anxiously hoping that the more experienced pathologist from Britain would agree with his findings.

What was to follow proved to be a classic piece of forensic detective work. 'Despite the riots that were still going on when we arrived, my assumption, looking at the reports that morning, was that Dr Ouko probably had killed himself,' said Dr West. But his ten-page autopsy report makes fascinating reading and gives early pointers to the thoughts he was already formulating. To the layman, the report is a baffling mass of clinical terminology. But amid the precise, almost pedantic, detail, the doctor picked out, one by one, the significant clues:

> I could find no evidence of radiant heat or flame burns on the face. Dried blood stained the upper lip and appeared to have tracked across the left cheek on to the left lower eyelid with a separate track of dried blood running horizontally across the inner left cheek just above the level of the mouth. There was a faint track of dried blood running from the right upper lip on to the cheek adjacent to the right nostril.

Later, after several pages of detail on the burn destruction, including a reference to the main fire damage being in the abdominal and lumbar regions, Dr West turned to a detailed description of the bullet entry and exit wounds in the skull, adding significantly, 'I could see no evidence of propellant tattooing or smoke soiling of the surrounding skin. No evidence of singeing of the adjacent hair.'

The body also showed a broken right ankle. Dr Kaviti was insistent that this had been caused by the intense heat of the fire. But Dr West reported, 'Although there was charring of some of the exposed parts of the fracture, the proximal end of the tibial fracture showed little heat damage and protruded through adjacent remaining soft tissue, indicating that this had been a compound fracture and was not a heat-related injury.'

To his everlasting gratitude, the local orthopaedic surgeon backed him up on this diagnosis. 'At that stage I did not reveal my thinking to Kaviti, who was present at my postmortem, other than to say "I don't think this is suicide,"' said Dr West. 'He replied: "But you can't exclude suicide", and I agreed, because at that stage we didn't know what the tests on the firearm residues were going to show.'

'Iain was very meticulous over the postmortem,' recalled John Troon later, 'and he found things that appeared to have been missed either through incompetence or on purpose because of fear or under orders. Iain found primarily the broken ankle which he believed had been caused in life and he found other bruising to the arms which suggested violence to the body before death.'

That night the Scotland Yard team had a tense meeting with Hezekiah Oyugi, the internal security chief, who was later to become a prime suspect in a political intrigue which rocked the nation. 'I gave him my preliminary conclusions that this must be treated as a homicide, but he seemed more interested in keeping suicide as the main option,' said West. 'We actually expected the government to announce a full-scale murder inquiry at that stage. But they didn't, and the riots went on, with bricks flying through our hotel windows and the local people blaming us for colluding at the suicide suggestion and seeing us as part of the cover-up.'

Back at their hotel West and Troon, friends of long standing, went to the superintendent's room for a private conference with Sandy Sanderson and Detective Inspector Graham Dennis which lasted almost five hours while they demolished a bottle of whisky. 'We discussed his findings in minute detail,' said John Troon, 'and we were both of the same view that this was homicide. I was relying entirely on Iain's evidence at this stage of my inquiry.'

The following day the British investigators flew up to Kisumu and were driven in convoy to Koru to examine the dead man's house and inspect the scene where his body had been found.

The scenario that followed was reminiscent of old black-and-white Hollywood whodunnits where the outline of the body is chalked on the floor and cigar-smoking detectives pace around it looking for the angle from which the fatal shot might have been fired. Blown-up photographs taken of the body when it was first discovered showed Dr West the position in which Ouko had been lying. Using these and precise measurements of the dead man's height and build taken at the postmortem, he and Sandy Sanderson made a plastic cutout of the body. This was then carefully positioned on the ground within the burned outline and scorch-marks which were still present on the grass. Dr West's report goes on:

The scene adjacent to the body was marked out using string, and a systematic search made of the area in an attempt to find any bullet fragments.

Damage on the branch of a guava tree adjacent to the position where the deceased's body was found was noted.

The damaged area of the branch had some marking on its surface. Using string, we fashioned a line showing the direction through which the branch appeared to have been damaged. This was done by passing the string through the line of the groove in the branch, placing the string within the groove and parallel to the edges of the groove. Extending the string backwards towards the position of the body gave a line which passed through the position where the deceased's head had been found.

Det. Sgt. Sanderson measured the relative distance of the damaged branch from both the ground and the body. I photographed the branch and noted that the damaged area was at the level of the deceased's head or shoulder area.

In my opinion, if the deceased had been shot whilst seated in the position where his head was found, the branch could have been damaged by that projectile. It is also my opinion, however, that if the deceased had been seated with his buttocks in the same position as when his body was found, then a bullet passing through his head in the trajectory seen at autopsy would not have struck that part of the tree.

'I asked Iain and Sandy to home in on that scene and spend as long as they could there,' said John Troon. 'For someone in my position out there, I could not have had any better support professionally or forensically than those two combined: Iain with his expertise as a pathologist and Sandy with his experience as a scenes of crime man. They found things there that the Kenyans appeared to have missed. We spent three weeks searching for that bullet and never found it. But Iain's discovery told me what I was looking at and set me off on the right footing.'

Although it seemed like a lifetime, Iain West was in Kenya for only four days, leaving his police colleagues behind to set up headquarters in the Sunset Hotel at Kisumu, where they were to remain for a further three gruelling months. 'By the time I left, suicide was looking more and more improbable but I got the impression that the government desperately still wanted it to be the official outcome of the injuries,' said Dr West.

Back in London, with a host of samples and exhibits for examination by Scotland Yard's Forensic Science Laboratory, Dr West was able to jot down his preliminary conclusions:

> The discovery of flammable liquid near to the body and other circumstances may suggest suicide, but in my opinion there are a number of inconsistencies which indicate that death was not suicidal. The movement of the head, the position of the gunshot wound, the absence of flame burns on the face and the position of the damaged branch in relation to the deceased's body strongly indicate that the fatal injury was caused by another person.

Now it was the turn of a team of forensic scientists in London to carry out a series of tests on the samples and exhibits Dr West had brought back from Africa.

First, the scientists devised a test to see if it was feasible for Ouko to have set himself alight before he shot himself. Using a dummy dressed in clothes made of the same fabric as Ouko's, they doused it in diesel around the waist area where the damage to the body indicated the seat of the fire had been.

Noting that Ouko's face had shown no sign of burning, the fire expert Andrew Douglas reported on his tests:

> The liquid-soaked fabric was difficult to ignite but once it was lit the flames spread very quickly up the front of the

coat and reached the face in about five seconds.

A metal tray was inserted and the fabric rested on it to simulate a man in the sitting-up position. A flame was placed on the lap close to the vertical front of the material. This fire developed slightly slower than in the first test and reached the face after about ten seconds.

The liquid used in the tests was decanted from a container labelled 'Cooper's Cattle Dip' found at the scene. This liquid was a mixture of diesel fuel plus the original contents of the container.

After discussing several other tests the report concluded:

Dr Ouko was lying on his back [for] either all or most of [the duration of] the fire. His clothing and the surrounding area was soaked in diesel fuel. In my opinion the clothing was ignited with a flame around the waist/stomach area where the most severe fire damage had occurred.

Another scientist, Geoffrey Warman, found a particle of firearm-cartridge discharge residue on a swab taken from Ouko's right hand but nothing on the left hand. But in case the casual reader might assume this meant that Ouko, who was right-handed, had fired the single shot which killed him from his own gun into the right side of his head, his report went on to explain: 'These discharge residues originate from the percussion primer and may be deposited on the skin and clothing of the firer and on surfaces within the immediate vicinity. In addition they may be transferred to other surfaces by direct contact or through the air.' Tests were also carried out on a sock, a handkerchief and a sample of urine which showed traces of an antihistamine drug.

The ballistics tests on Dr Ouko's gun, the ammunition

recovered at the scene, the skull and several branches were carried out by Kevin O'Callaghan, the senior ballistics and firearms expert at the laboratory. He discovered that an empty cartridge case recovered from the scene had been fired from Dr Ouko's Smith & Wesson five-shot revolver. He could not, however, determine precisely where the lead fragments recovered from the victim's brain had originated. He went on to examine the skull, reporting: 'The entry hole in the skull showed no signs of blackening around its margin, indicating that the shot had not been fired with the muzzle of the weapon in contact with the victim. Examination of the skull also revealed that the bullet had struck the victim on the right side of the head and had travelled at a slight angle forward to exit from the left side of the skull'. He concluded, 'The indications were that the shot had not been fired from a distance greater than 10 feet. The branch to the left of the victim had probably been damaged by the passage of a lead bullet.'

It was this piece of evidence which was to have a devastating and quite unexpected effect at the official inquiry into the case the following year. For when Kevin O'Callaghan told the Kenyan Judicial Commission of his findings, there was a near riot which brought the proceedings to a halt for two days.

It was not what the findings indicated about the probable cause of death that caused the uproar but the revelation that part of the dead man's skull had been removed from Kenya. Under Luo tribal law and tradition, every part of a body must be buried together, and coffins have glass lids to ensure that this rule is adhered to. In the case of Ouko, John Troon had helped Dr West to take the skull vault through the airport by persuading the authorities that the usual X-rays might damage vital samples being taken back to England. When it came to the state funeral, an imaginative and innovative mortuary assistant had simply covered the discrepancy by creating a convincing death-mask to attach to the top of the body for the benefit of those wishing to view the body.

By May of 1990 with all the scientific tests completed, Dr West was sufficiently sure of his original conclusions to confirm them in writing:

I could see nothing which has altered my opinion that Robert Ouko was shot by another individual and that his body was subsequently set on fire. Bizarre suicide attempts do occur and I have seen a considerable number of such, but I found nothing to indicate that his death was suicidal.

The position of the apparent bullet damage to the branch of the tree adjacent to the deceased's body is such that the upper part of the body must have been in the relatively upright position. In other words, he was seated or kneeling when shot so that the bullet, after passing through his head, struck the branch. He then could have collapsed into the position in which he was found, indicating that his body was moved after death. This is confirmed by two distinct trails of dry blood on his face.

If he had been shot in the head in such a way that he would have fallen back into the position in which he was found, then I would have expected that the bullet, after passing through his head, would have struck a different part of that tree and at a different angle. This, of course, assumes that the bullet responsible for his death was the one that struck the tree.

There was bruising on the deceased's right upper arm. The bruising was recent and could have been caused by either a firm grip to the arm or by a blow.

The total absence of any apparent bloodstaining on the grass immediately surrounding the area of burning could indicate that he was shot at another site and his body subsequently moved into that position where it was set on fire. I could not exclude, however, any small traces of blood being obscured as a result of climatic conditions or by the footwear of the individuals who attended the scene.

Eighteen months after the killing, Iain West found himself back in the stifling heat and dusty parched surroundings of Kisumu and at the centre of controversy once again. 'I gave evidence for half a day at the Judicial Commission of Inquiry, which had already been sitting for seven months when I got there,' he said. 'The Director of Public Prosecutions was leading for the Kenyan government side and he was still pushing for suicide at that stage. There were representatives of Ouko's tribe – the Luo – and the family asking questions.'

It was under this questioning that West dropped his bombshell. The government had refused to publish Superintendent Troon's report and had been censoring foreign newspaper coverage of the case, so the Kenyan public still believed that the official version was suicide.

But the morning after Dr West gave his testimony, the Kenyan nation woke to screaming headlines proclaiming 'Pathologist says Minister was Murdered'. Court reports quoted West as saying, 'I have excluded suicide. The indications are, from pathological findings, that the deceased was shot by another individual after breaking his right ankle, possibly as a result of a fall while trying to escape. In my opinion, his body was subsequently set on fire in an attempt to destroy it.' And, worse, the newspapers also reported that Iain West and Jason Kaviti were at loggerheads, with the British expert accusing Kenya's top pathologist of lying and incompetence.

'By this stage, Kaviti had been thoroughly discredited,' said

Dr West. 'Half the questions I was asked were designed to do a hatchet job on him. "Would you be surprised, Doctor, to learn that some of this was written before the body was even seen?" was the kind of question for instance.'

An even more crushing blow was soon to be dealt to the Moi government's attempts to sweep the Ouko killing under the carpet when John Troon, by now retired, entered the witness box. Courageously the former Scotland Yard officer told the three presiding judges that Ouko's sister had told him that, just before his murder, her brother lived in fear of his life after he had called for a probe into corruption at the highest levels of government. 'Ouko mentioned the industry minister Nicholas Biwott as one of the corrupt members of government . . . He said Biwott was blocking progress,' said Mr Troon. He added that he had repeatedly tried to interview Mr Biwott, but the minister always failed to turn up. Mr Troon said that he was treating the case as one of murder, and named Hezekiah Oyugi, the head of internal security, as the man who refused to announce that fact.

With Biwott and Oyugi publicly named as being implicated in a conspiracy to murder, President Moi was forced to act. He sacked both men, stopped the inquiry, and ordered that the two men, along with three other Troon suspects, should be arrested.

'I went back to give evidence at the trial, and by that stage the prosecution were no longer pushing suicide,' said Iain West with a grin. But by then Biwott and Oyugi had been released without charge.

Looking back, he now regards the Ouko case as one of the most interesting foreign jobs he has ever encountered. 'It was fascinating because it was so complicated,' he said. 'We got there after the initial examination had taken place and you've lost so much of the evidence in terms of the scene because the body had been moved, the scene's been disturbed, all the evidence had been taken away. Whereas here one would have taken a long time considering things, as everything would be left *in situ*. For obvious reasons in this case we had to rely on photographs in order to assess the scene.

'It wasn't until I started the postmortem that my suspicions began to be aroused,' he said. 'Apart from the position of the shot, the angle, and the fact that it would be an extremely awkward place to shoot oneself, there was the absence of burns to the face.

'While the work done by the Forensic Science Laboratory showed that there could be a delay of a few seconds before flames engulfed the face, you have to say that the first thing that happens is that you've got to set yourself on fire. You can't set yourself on fire after you've shot yourself; although there are recorded cases in America of that happening, I've never seen it, and it must be exceptionally rare. And in order to immolate yourself, you've got to be in a seated position. You couldn't shoot yourself while lying on the ground like that. If he had shot himself, you would expect that by the time he'd got everything organised there would be flames rising and burning the face.

'There's heat damage, obviously, because the body has been subjected to a smouldering fire for many, many hours. Another inconsistent thing was that the matchbox was beside him but *closed*. Would he have had time to close the box after setting fire to himself? His torch was there, too, but *switched off*. Bearing in mind this was happening in the middle of the night, where was his light coming from? The container of diesel was some distance away.

'The scene was a couple of miles from his home down a rough track which would have been difficult to negotiate at night carrying his change of clothing, his stick and all the other paraphernalia. Why carry a change of clothing if you are going to kill yourself? He would have also been carrying a container of diesel fluid. A pair of shiny wellington boots were found some distance away. Apparently no fingerprints on them; they'd been removed by the time we got there. The gun was found by his right-hand side.'

Perhaps the most satisfying piece of sleuthing came at the scene. 'Sandy Sanderson and I spent an awful lot of time on our hands and knees looking for the bullet,' said Dr West. 'Whether the lead bullet which made the mark we found on the tree is the fatal bullet, I have my doubts. It certainly is not in a position you would expect a bullet to strike a tree if it's been fired through the deceased's head. It's really impossible for it to hit that branch at that angle unless he was in a different position. We couldn't see any traces of blood or brain on the ground, but there had been so many people trampling all over the scene that it was no surprise. We know he was set on fire in the position where he was found because of the scorch pattern on the ground, but it doesn't preclude the possibility that he was moved after being shot. He may have been shot at a different site entirely.'

Summing up, he added: 'The key elements to convince me that it was murder, not suicide, were the general area where the body was found, the angle of the shot and the awkwardness of holding a revolver at that angle, and the distance from which it was fired. Also, evidence that the face was not burned. Someone intending to set themselves on fire would douse themselves with diesel or petrol from the head downwards. In this case the fire was in the belly area and was moving upwards from there. People intending to immolate themselves will normally immolate the whole body, and I've seen it on a number of occasions. I've never seen this pattern except where others have tried to dispose of a body.'

It was more than two years after the murder that the real danger in which Dr West and the Yard team had been working began to emerge through sinister reports from within Kenya itself. A former Kenyan intelligence officer fled to Britain and told Home Office immigration officers an astonishing tale. According to him, Kenyan Special Branch officers had tapped the telephone of a senior political figure and had overheard him plotting to kill Mr Troon with poison.

That chilling threat had an uncanny echo for John Troon when he heard it, because to this day he can find no satisfactory explanation for a mystery illness which caused him to be rushed to hospital in Kisumu. The illness, which was diagnosed as pleurisy, displayed many characteristics of poisoning. 'When you hear allegations such as these, it makes you wonder,' said Mr Troon. 'We always knew the consequences of our investigations, and took precautions.'

John Troon is generous in his praise for Iain West's contribution to the successful outcome of the inquiry. 'Because of his expertise and his experience, he found things that the people out there never could have imagined he would find. They thought they'd destroyed anything which would give it away as a murder, but they'd reckoned without Iain West.

'Iain's evidence was the turning-point. I'd always had my suspicions while keeping an open mind. But Iain's way of finding out the cause of death, then actually saying it, sticking by it, making a written statement to that effect and giving evidence twice was crucial. His evidence was never ever disputed by anyone. He was spot on and supported by toxicology and all the other tests. A superb piece of work. Forensic pathology at its best.'

Ludmilla Klimova

Early in the morning on 20 March 1984 Iain West was called to a block of flats in Hyde Park Square – a secluded enclave in the Bayswater area of London a quarter of a mile west of Marble Arch.

In the basement well of the block was the body of a young woman. She was dressed in a red top and grey skirt and her face, though ashen in death, displayed the high cheekbones and full lips of a classic Eastern European beauty. Forty feet above, in a third-floor flat, an urgent conference was going on. Senior London detectives were in heated discussion with officials from the Russian embassy.

The difficulty was that the apartment belonged to the Russians and the dead woman, who had lived there, was a Russian citizen. The Soviets were insisting that the flat was diplomatic property and, as such, constituted Russian soil. They wanted to remove the body to the Soviet embassy where, they said, a Russian doctor would perform an autopsy before the dead woman was flown back to Moscow for burial. If diplomatic immunity applied, a British coroner would have no jurisdiction.

The earlier summons from the police to Dr West had been mysterious. They had refused to discuss the details over the telephone. So, while the bizarre negotiations continued, he began to acquaint himself with the circumstances.

The young woman was Ludmilla Klimova, the twenty-nine-year-old mother of six-year-old Alina. Witnesses had heard a scream and a bang at 6.45 that morning and had found the body, which had apparently fallen from the window of the flat where the Klimov family lived. Had she jumped, had she fallen, or was she pushed?

The family had arrived in Britain just a year earlier and the dead woman's husband, Alexander Klimov, had diplomatic immunity. He was the senior member of a three-man Russian 'technical' translation team working at the London head-quarters of the United Nations-run International Maritime Organisation, a body which deals with multi-million-pound insurance claims relating to accidents or pollution at sea.

The story he was telling the police was a little odd. The day before, he said, his wife had telephoned him at work to say that she had fallen on her way to the Soviet embassy, where she worked as a cipher clerk, and her stomach felt strange. When he had arrived home, he found his wife depressed and nervous, wringing her hands and grabbing at her clothes. She seemed afraid, and told him she had done something which would be bad for their daughter. She had committed a crime, for which she blamed herself. Later that evening she repeated that she was to be blamed and punished for something she would not reveal to her husband.

According to Mr Klimov's account, that morning while his wife was preparing breakfast for the child, she suddenly went into the lounge. He followed, and found her squatting on the window ledge. He went to her and grabbed at her skirt, but she was already falling.

With the British police contingent holding their ground, the Russians were beginning to back off and it was clear that Dr West would be permitted to carry out a postmortem on the deceased. But before that could take place, a few diplomatic courtesies and formalities had to take place. He was approached by the senior Soviet official, a dapper man in his fifties, who introduced himself as Arkadi Gouk, a first sec-retary and liaison officer at the embassy. He spoke faultless English and was scrupulously polite. He asked if Dr West had everything he needed and inquired if he would be required to attend the postmortem. When this offer was declined, Mr Gouk asked whether his Russian doctor could assist in the autopsy and another embassy official attend as an observer. This request was delivered with such firmness that it was clear Moscow was insisting on it, and any refusal would be met with a diplomatic complaint to the Foreign Office.

The first thing to do was to examine the scene. The lounge window had been closed, but Dr West noticed a number of scuff-marks on the stone ledge outside. Directly below, he could see a black-painted railing which bordered the pavement and surrounded a flight of steps which led from the street down into a basement area. To the right was a concrete-roofed outhouse. The body was lying just to the right of this building. He reported:

> There were flakes of paint on the concrete roof and on the top step of the flight of steps. There were flakes of paint missing from the top of the iron railings . . . and there was an imprint on the surface of the paintwork of the handrail such as might be left by impact from a fine-weave fabric.
>
> The deceased was lying on her back with her head about two feet away from the wall of the outhouse. Her arms lay beside her, her legs outstretched with the right leg bent at the knee, where there was an obvious compound fracture of the right upper tibia which appeared to extend through the knee-joint. Clear fluid, apparently from the knee joint, stained the ground under the knee. There was a visible laceration of the right side of the chin with some dark grey staining of the skin surrounding it. A trickle of blood ran down the side of the face.

'The Russians were obviously very concerned and taking a close interest in everything,' Dr West recalled later. 'I noticed that Gouk, for instance, got down close to the body with the Russian doctor and they had a few anxious words in Russian before Gouk made his suggestion that they should be represented at the postmortem.'

When it came to the autopsy, in the presence of Mr Ippolitov and Dr Razoumov from the Russian embassy, the body showed all the classic signs of death as the result of a fall from a considerable height. The body was still warm. Rigor mortis had not yet set in. There were lacerations and friction marks, with numerous fractures of the ribs and chest area and a massive rupture of the heart. The pathologist paid particular attention to the neck and throat area to ensure that no attempt had been made to strangle her. He took a number of samples for forensic testing and gave some to the Russian doctor also. Later, the results showed that she had no alcohol, carbon monoxide or drugs in her system.

When it came to his conclusions, Dr West reported:

The pattern of fresh injuries is entirely consistent with that received following a fall from a considerable height. It would appear that the deceased had fallen from the window on the third floor of the block of flats, initially struck the iron railings surrounding the steps down to the basement and then bounced on to the courtyard outside the basement . . . I found nothing on her body to indicate that she had been involved in a fight or struggle immediately prior to her death.'

But there were indications that Ludmilla had been roughly treated recently. 'There were a number of old bruises on her body,' he wrote. 'These were of varying ages, some being between three and five days old, others between seven and ten days old. Many of the bruises had the appearance of grip-marks.'

It all looked very curious, but if the young mother had taken her own life, there was a possible explanation which had nothing to do with the sinister world of espionage and international diplomacy. 'She was menstruating at the time of her death, and the relationship between a mild mental disturbance and menstruation is well recognised.' She also had two ovarian cysts, one of which had recently been haemorrhaging. 'In my opinion there could be considerable lower abdominal pain as a result of this,' West concluded.

A month after the death of Ludmilla Klimova a sensational treason trial took place at the Old Bailey. At the end of it a thirty-four-year-old MI5 secret service agent, Michael Bettaney, was jailed for twenty-three years for selling Britain's secrets to the Soviets. He had been exposed by a double agent, a British banker called Dennis Skinner, who travelled regularly to the Soviet Union and had close links to both the KGB and MI6.

The previous summer, three months before the arrest of Bettaney, Skinner had died in an incident which chillingly foreshadowed the manner of Ludmilla's end. He fell out of the window of his eleventh-floor flat. Three weeks after the end of Bettaney's trial an inquest was held into the death of Dennis Skinner. John Burnett, the first secretary in charge of security at the British embassy in Moscow, flew from Russia to give evidence. He said Skinner had reported to him the fact that Bettaney was a spy who was supplying information to a senior Soviet diplomat. That diplomat was none other than Arkadi Gouk. The inquest returned a verdict of unlawful killing and, a week later, Gouk was expelled from Britain. In a tit-for-tat retaliation the Russians immediately expelled John Burnett from Moscow.

Soon the true role of Gouk was exposed. He was not a humble diplomat, but General Arkadi Vasilyevich Gouk of the KGB, the Soviets' espionage mastermind for the whole of Western Europe. The spymaster in the Savile Row suit had been so good at evading British Intelligence 'watchers' that Bettaney had been able to deliver information to the door of his home in London's Holland Park without arousing suspicion. It was only when Skinner's information came in that his part had been discovered.

When it came to the inquest on the death of Ludmilla Klimova, the coroner, Dr Paul Knapman, declared that he could give no satisfactory reason why she had died. But he recorded a verdict of suicide anyway.

To Iain West, the case remains a mystery. 'The story was that she worked for Gouk's section of the embassy and there were rumours that she may have had a relationship with someone else. The Russian did not treat it as a straightforward suicide jump. I don't think we would have ended up with someone like Gouk if they had. Their concern was that somebody else had been involved in her death. Obviously one is never able to exclude the possibility of something else happening in a fall, because if you push somebody off, there are no marks left. The only other finding of interest was the presence of a fresh chocolate cyst in one of the ovaries. This had bled recently and would have caused a lot of pain. Whether that was a factor, I don't know.'

Dr Cyrus Hashemi

The curious case of Cyrus Hashemi will live long in Iain West's memory as one of the strangest he has ever investigated.

Dr Hashemi, a forty-seven-year-old Iranian banker living in London's Belgravia, hit the world's headlines in the spring of 1986 when he was revealed as the central figure in what has been described as the most elaborate 'sting' operation ever carried out. The trick he pulled off foiled a £1.7 billion weapons deal and smashed the biggest arms-smuggling conspiracy in American history

The illegal plan was to sell to Iran vast quantities of American weapons held by other countries, mainly Israel. More than 100 fighter aircraft, transport planes, helicopters, air-to-air missiles, anti-tank missiles and tanks were included in the package – all the sales in direct contravention of the American arms embargo at that time in place to prevent Iran from replenishing its supplies in the bloody war with Iraq. Had the deal gone through, it would have been Iran's largest arms purchase since the fall of the Shah and would have tilted the balance in the war.

The sting operation involved setting up a fictitious Iranian purchasing company with a US bank account of $2 billion – funds provided by the US government. An Iranian national, Hushang Mehran – a pseudonym – was co-opted to pose as an Iranian diplomat attached to the United Nations in New York and empowered to negotiate on behalf of Tehran. He was given a team of 'advisers' – US Customs investigators in disguise – and Dr Hashemi, known for his close ties with revolutionary Iran, was recruited to front the whole phoney operation.

It was the culmination of years of turbulent dealings between Dr Hashemi, chairman of the Gulf Trust and Credit Bank, and the United States government. He had first come to official attention during 1980, when fifty-two hostages were seized at the US embassy in Tehran. Hashemi, claiming to be a cousin of the Iranian prime minister Hashemi

Rafsanjani, offered to help negotiate the hostages' release.

Although nothing came of his offer, the incident allowed him to open contacts in Tehran through whom he sold American arms in 1981 and 1982. All this clandestine activity was to come to an abrupt end, though, when he attempted to offer his services to the CIA. The US spy agency was suspicious, and asked the FBI to check him out. This produced evidence leading to a 1984 criminal indictment against Hashemi and two of his brothers, Reza and Djamshid, for sanctions-breaking. Because of this background, some officials expressed reservations about using Hashemi to set up the sting operation when he first approached the Americans to report two contacts, in London and Paris, from a consortium of arms dealers offering a package for sale to Iran.

Hashemi was anxious to have the charges against him for earlier sales of embargoed items to Iran dropped in return for working the sting. Eventually he was able to strike a deal with Rudolph Giuliani, a thrusting young US attorney from Manhattan, who was brought in to direct him personally, and the operation got under way. After months of shuttling across the world conducting high-powered negotiations, Hashemi tipped off the US government that the trap was ready to be sprung, and ten men were arrested in New York and Bermuda – among them Avraham Bar-Am, a former Israeli general, and two of the country's leading arms dealers. Charges filed in Manhattan named seventeen Israelis, Europeans and Americans in the conspiracy.

The collapse of the arms deal made Hashemi an instant army of powerful enemies. Many of the biggest names in the Middle Eastern arms business and influential figures in the Israeli defence industries were reported to be furious at the loss of what was to have been an immensely lucrative transaction. Although the Israeli government denied involvement in the affair, it soon became clear that the supply of false end-user certificates and the shipment of such vast quantities of arms from Eilat to Bandar Abbas could not have been arranged without the approval of government agencies. The Israeli radio, in its Persian service, immediately denounced Dr Hashemi as a criminal and a US spy. But Hashemi, a familiar figure in financial and gambling circles in London where he once owed a casino £1.5m, was unconcerned, merely saying: 'I am taking security precautions.'

Three months later, long before he could give evidence against the co-conspirators, he was dead, the victim of a mystery illness. The multi-millionaire businessman with homes on both sides of the Atlantic was apparently in robust health just a week before his death. He was a regular jogger and keen tennis player and, according to his family, had undergone a thorough medical examination by Swiss doctors just weeks earlier. That health check, including a blood test, had confirmed that he was fit.

On Wednesday 16 July 1986 he collapsed in his London office and was rushed to the Cromwell private clinic with a suspected heart attack. When it was established that there was nothing wrong with his heart, he was moved to the hospital's neurological department. Bone-marrow tests indicated that he was suffering from leukaemia. Treatment started on 19 July, but two days later he was dead. The death certificate put the cause of death as accidental brain-stem damage due to a stroke and leukaemia.

The Americans were hugely suspicious about the suddenness of Hashemi's death, and Scotland Yard's Serious Crimes Squad was called in to investigate. They turned to their top pathologist to conduct the postmortem. 'The Americans suggested that they send somebody over to do the PM,' said Iain

West, 'but that was declined, so I did it the next day. I was given the background that this man was an important witness for potential prosecutions in the Irangate affair and there were people he had upset who had not only the motive but the means to have done something to him.'

Iain West's postmortem, at which a senior US Customs official was present, looked at every possible way in which dirty tricks could have been played. 'The Americans wanted to know if there were any injuries on him; if we could confirm leukaemia; and whether leukaemia could be artificially induced,' he said. 'The leukaemic process had altered cells – cells which were important to blood coagulation. When you have a deficiency of these cells, sometimes you have a spontaneous bleed and he had had a small spontaneous bleed in his brain. It is unusual, but not necessarily unexpected.' Turning in his report to the question of foul play, Dr West concluded:

> Leukaemia can be induced by a number of predisposing factors, of which radiation injury is the most important. An interval of some years will, however, be present between the time of exposure to radiation and development of acute leukaemia. Deliberate induction of leukaemia by radiation would not be a practicable method of homicide, as the time required is too great and the induction could not be guaranteed.
>
> A number of chemicals may be leukaemogenic. Some, such as benzine, are related to occupational exposure and require exposure over a considerable period. Others include alkylating agents used in the treatment of Hodgkin's disease, for instance. The risk appears to be much greater in this instance where the patient has been exposed to radiation. There was no evidence to suggest

that the deceased had been exposed to any such agent. Although viral transmission of leukaemia will occur in some animals there is no evidence of transmission of myeloblastic leukaemia by viral infection

There are a number of conditions which may superficially mimic leukaemia, some of which may be induced by chemicals. There is, however, no evidence of any disorder, apart from acute leukaemia, in the deceased.

All in all, his postmortem was tending to knock down the idea of murder. But he was not completely sure and still inclined to keep an open mind. He said later: 'Hashemi had first become involved in the Irangate business about eighteen months earlier. Realistically, the timescale was too short to have induced leukaemia by the use of drugs and/or radiation, even assuming that his enemies had decided there and then to start carrying it out. They would have to take time to plan it, which would further shorten the timescale.

'Leukaemia was certainly confirmed by microscopic examination and I checked it out with a number of specialists. I also took advice from other experts, and they said, "We don't know of any way in which this could be done."

'The thing which makes me think this was a case of plain straightforward leukaemia was the fact that we have not had any other examples that I have become aware of either in this country or in the States. If they had occurred, there would have been people knocking on the door, saying "What about Hashemi?"'

At the end of the day he gave the official cause of death as 'acute myeloblastic leukaemia'.

This was not good enough for Dr Hashemi's brother Mohamed. He maintained his brother had been poisoned by introducing toxic substances through a spray, a drink or an injection which could produce symptoms similar to leukaemia. 'Certain Middle East intelligence services are known to use this method,' he claimed. He was doubtless referring to the Israeli secret service, Mossad, whose ruthless and unscrupulous methods are legendary and whose complicity in the illegal arms deals was strongly suspected.

Commander Ronald Dowling of Scotland Yard quickly went on record, closing the case and declaring Dr Hashemi's death to be natural and not murder. The Americans, however, were not so sure. By November the first inklings of the Iran-Contra scandal, which was to so embarrass the Reagan administration over secret arms supplies to Iran, were beginning to emerge. As an early precaution, the Department of Justice sealed Hashemi's file on national security grounds.

But by early 1987 the Americans were calling for a full-scale murder inquiry after Hushang Mehran – the man who had played a key role in the successful sting the previous year – came forward to claim that Hashemi had been killed because he 'knew too much' about what was now being dubbed 'the Irangate affair'. Mehran told a British newspaper that US Customs agents had told him on three occasions that Hashemi had been 'got rid of' by an unidentified US government agency. He claimed to have recorded the telephone conversations in which this sinister development was revealed, fearing that his own life was in danger. 'This has played on my conscience,' he told journalists. 'It makes me very angry that this man was killed for nothing. I hardly knew Hashemi, but I was shocked when I was told two days after his death that he had been murdered.'

Mehran's claims caused Rudolph Giuliani to order the inquiry reopened. By June 1987 the Hashemi case was right at the centre of the Irangate scandal, with Mehran's story being taken very seriously indeed in Washington. Congressional committees investigating the controversial arms-for-hostages trade were told that Cyrus Hashemi had sought, unsuccessfully, to become a key middleman in the Iran-Contra deals.

Mehran's suggestion that Hashemi was eliminated to protect the then secret Iran Initiative were supported by documents filed in a Federal court. A senior Senate investigator made two trips to London to meet government officials, police and medical authorities – including Iain West – to raise questions about the accuracy of the postmortem findings. By now the Americans were inclined to believe the suggestion that chemical or radiation injections or sprays could have produced similar symptoms. 'There are lots of sophisticated methods of assassination these days,' said one Committee member. 'Given all the circumstances, we'd be ignoring our responsibility if we didn't follow up what is, at the very least, a mysterious death of an important link in the Iran arms affair.'

The mystery was to be raised again almost five years later when rumours began to circulate about the death at sea of the newspaper tycoon Robert Maxwell (see Chapter 1). Maxwell's death came within a fortnight of allegations linking him to Israel, its secret services and the international arms trade.

International observers began to question how it was that so many people connected with arms deals between Israel and Tehran had died. Six mysterious deaths in particular – among them the Hashemi case and that of Senator John Tower – were highlighted. Senator Tower, who died in a light plane crash, was the head of a three-man board of inquiry into the Iran-Contra affair and took to his grave a number of unpublished secrets about arms sales to Iran.

Although British officials always maintained that Hashemi's death was caused by leukaemia, Iain West sent body-tissue samples to the government top-secret germ and poison warfare laboratory at Porton Down for analysis. The results of those tests have never been made public.

In January 1989 Federal prosecutors dropped all charges against eleven people, including General Avraham Bar-Am, for trying to sell advanced weapons to Iran. The lawyers said they could not go ahead with the case because Cyrus Hashemi's death robbed them of the only witness who could rebut the defence claim that the eleven defendants proceeded with the multi-billion-dollar deal in the belief that it had been sanctioned by a top official in the administration of President Ronald Reagan.

CHAPTER 4

WAR CRIMES:
Saddam's chemical warfare atrocities

The date of 17 March 1988 represents an ugly blemish on the shamefully scarred and disfigured face of Iraqi history. That was the day when the northern Iraqi city of Halabja was attacked by the forces of the brutal dictator Saddam Hussein, using poison gas. More than 5,000 of the local Kurdish inhabitants, men, women, and children, died in agony within a matter of minutes. But for two days the aircraft continued to spray the area with nerve gas, and a further 10,000 people were injured from the effects of mustard gas.

It was the most deadly use of the banned weapons in the eight-year Gulf War, causing more civilian casualties than at any time since the weapons were first used by the Germans at the Battle of Ypres in 1915.

The attack led to tens of thousands of Kurds fleeing over the border into Iran and Turkey amid accusations by human rights groups of widespread torture and executions. The government of Saddam Hussein was charged with committing genocide under the 1948 UN Convention on Genocide as it pursued a policy of forced assimilation of the Kurdish minority living in Kurdistan. Whole Kurdish communities were

119

reported to have been sent to concentration camps in the western desert, from which few were expected to emerge alive. Mass political executions were said to be taking place in the country's prisons and about 500 Kurdish homes in the city of Kirkuk, at the heart of the country's oil industry, were simply demolished.

The West was kept up to date about these tragic developments by clandestine Kurdish and Arab political parties within Iraq. They reported Saddam's use of chemical weapons against Kurdish villages months before the Halabja catastrophe hit the world's headlines.

It was into this volatile and extremely dangerous situation that Iain West was asked to step by the British Parliamentary Human Rights Group. He arrived within days of the Halabja débâcle, and the report he produced is a fascinating document which details the history of military poison-gas usage, spells out the types of chemical weapons currently available, and details the effects of Saddam's cruel attacks. It also illustrates the astonishing variety of tasks the modern pathologist is called upon to undertake. The report, entitled *Chemical Warfare in Kurdistan*, is worthy of being reproduced in full.

Chemical agents, directed against troops, were extensively employed, by both sides, during World War I, but despite considerable expenditure on research and production, these weapons were not used in any major conflict during the next seventy years.

Occasional reports of the use of blister agents have been received during the intervening years, usually from isolated areas of the world, and with all indications suggesting the usage was on a very limited scale.

During the current war between Iran and Iraq, however, numerous reports of attacks involving the use of chemical weapons have appeared. All of the early incidents involved the deployment of blister agents of the mustard gas type against Iranian troops. Many of the survivors were sent to various European cities, including London, for treatment.

Since those early attacks, many further allegations have been made indicating the use of weapons of this type against military personnel from both sides of the conflict, although the great majority of the reported incidents suggest their use by Iraq against the Iranian army.

There have, however, been two extremely sinister changes in the pattern of chemical attacks during the past two years. In the first instance, whilst the military have continued to be targeted, with the majority of incidents pointing to Iraq as the aggressor, there is now irrefutable evidence of the deployment of chemical agents, of varying types, against the unprotected civilian population of Kurdistan and a neighbouring province in Iran. The second, and potentially more serious, development has been the employment of far more lethal chemicals, nerve agents of the organo-phosphorus type, against some of the recent targets, culminating, during March 1988, in the attacks on the town of Halabja and on other populated areas in the adjacent parts of Kurdistan.

The chemical weapons deployed during the majority of this conflict have been of the blister agent group and it is probable that the primary weapon used was sulphur-mustard, a gas or liquid which was widely used during World War I and which was responsible for large numbers of battle casualties. Sulphur-mustard, or mustard gas, is not effective because of its capacity to kill, the mortality following exposure being no more than 1–3 per cent, but due to the agent's ability to seriously injure and thereby incapacitate many of those individuals who come into contact with it in either gaseous or liquid form.

Exposing troops to a blister agent will severely handicap any enemy's capacity to wage a war by placing heavy demands on his support facilities, particularly the medical and transport units. The use of this type of agent has also been found to be profoundly demoralising to troops who have been or who might expect to be exposed to its effects. Properly designed, well-fitting protective clothing will prevent the more serious consequences of blister agent exposure but, because of its capacity to persist in the environment, much care must be taken, even by protected individuals, to prevent potentially serious and incapacitating injury.

Nerve agent exposure carries a very high mortality in unprotected individuals, owing to its capacity to cause paralysis of the nervous system. The use of protective clothing, particularly a well-fitting mask and NBC suit, will be more effective against a non-persistent nerve agent than against the heavier and more persistent blister agent.

The population at the greatest risk following nerve agent exposure must, therefore, be the totally unprotected civilian inhabitants. Any instigator of such an attack would be aware of the devastating effects on civilians compared with the more limited effects on military personnel, even if the latter wore less than ideal standards of protective equipment.

A chemical agent may be defined as one which is intended for use, in military operations, to kill, seriously injure or incapacitate man due to its physiological effects.

A substantial number of chemicals have been tested,

and in many cases developed, for use as an anti-personnel weapon. They can be classified into the following groups:

1. Nerve Agents: These were developed before and during World War II and are all organo-phosphorus compounds related to a number of insecticides. Two main types exist: more persistent compounds known as 'V' agents and the more volatile 'G' agents. The persistence and skin penetration of the latter can be increased by thickening with other compounds. The principal agents are: Tabun, Sarin, Soman and VX

Contact may be in the form of liquid or vapour and absorption may result from inhalation, through intact skin, through wounds and by ingestion.

All show high toxicity, and ordinary clothing gives no protection; butyl rubber and polyester are of some use.

They act by blocking the cholinesterase group of enzymes, which results in the transmission of nerve impulses in both the central and peripheral nervous systems.

The rapidity of effect depends upon the dose and the route of administration. After heavy exposure, the inhalation of vapour leads to almost immediate signs and symptoms. Death may result in a few minutes. Absorption through skin is often followed by a delay period of an hour or more before symptoms appear. The oral route is followed by a delay period between the two. Nerve agents are cumulative in their effects and the signs and symptoms may persist so that full recovery of cholinesterase function can take up to three months.

Prophylaxis, utilising pyridostigmine or pralidoxime, will confer a degree of protection against exposure; this will be much more effective if combined with proper protective equipment.

Treatment must be very rapid, and in the field would involve the administration of atropine, an oxime, either pralidoxime or obidoxime, together with an anti-convulsant drug of the benzodiazepine group, preferably diazepam.

Early decontamination is important, utilising Fuller's earth or, if unavailable, soap and water. Chlorine-containing compounds like bleach or certain sterilising compounds will help to deactivate nerve agents. Severe exposure frequently requires assistance with respiration – the use of a resuscitator or, in a decontaminated individual, mouth-to-mouth ventilation as an initial measure.

The diagnosis of nerve-agent poisoning is made by testing the levels of cholinesterases in blood. The tests will remain positive for a variable time after exposure.

2. Vesicants or Blister Agents: There are three main groups of chemicals which act in this manner.
A) Sulphur (HD) and nitrogen mustards (HN1, HN2, HN3). HD and HN3 are the most dangerous of this group.

Absorption of these agents, through their effects on DNA, cell membranes and body proteins, will lead to the death of a small proportion of those exposed. The main purpose behind the use of this type of chemical is the effectiveness with which the mustards cause incapacitation through their potential to damage the eyes, skin and the mucous membranes lining the respiratory system.

They are persistent, particularly in cold and temperate climates; a persistence which can be augmented by thickening them with non-volatile solvents. Penetration of many materials occurs with ease; even the NBC suit will not give complete protection against mustard in its liquid form.

The compounds are hydrolysed rapidly by water but, because of poor solubility, this process is slow when there has been heavy contamination by liquid mustard, which leaves stagnant water hazardous for up to several months. Mustard in vapour form is much less persistent; both the liquid and the vapour forms are less persistent in hot climates although the vapour concentrations will be significantly higher in this type of climate.

The mustards act by combining with various chemical groups in tissue proteins and in the nuclei and membranes of cells. They are particularly hazardous to rapidly dividing cells, such as those of the blood-forming elements in the bone marrow and the intestinal lining cells. The group is known to be carcinogenic and possibly to be teratogenic for pregnant women who have been exposed.

After a delay period of between one hour and several days, chemical burns appear on exposed skin, followed by blistering, which commences after some hours but may continue for many days.

Exposure to high doses can lead to rapid death from cardiac or cerebral damage. The most important acute physiological changes relate to the effects on DNA, producing results very similar to those of ionising radiation.

Healing is slow following injury by mustard. Long-term complications include chronic lung disease, scarring, visual damage and malignant disease.
B) Lewisite.
A blister agent derived from arsenic and developed during World War I. It is rapidly absorbed through skin

and produces the changes of arsenic poisoning.
Immediate injury to the unprotected eye occurs, skin
irritation appears rapidly and blisters appear on the first
or second day. Respiratory injury similar to, but more
rapid in development than, mustard occurs, and damage
to the intestines, liver and kidneys results.
C) Halogenated oximes.
The most important is phosgene oxime. It is a severe
irritant causing intense pain. Its action is immediate with
irritation and swelling of skin followed by blisters on the
first day. It may damage eyes and lung tissue.

The only prophylaxis against blister agents is to wear a
respirator and special protective clothing

The first principle of treatment is decontamination of
clothing and exposed skin using water, and absorbing
powders containing chlorine, although the latter are not
effective against phosgene oxime. Further treatment is
symptomatic and based on the principles of treatment for
burns, the use of antibiotics and specific remedies for
complications such as bone-marrow failure. Sodium
thiosulphate may reduce the effects of mustard gas on the
body, but must be given within a few minutes of
exposure; its efficiency is very doubtful.

3. Lung-damaging Agents (Choking Agents).
The most important is phosgene, which caused 80 per
cent of the gas deaths during World War I.

The agent acts by combining with chemicals in the air
spaces within the lungs causing fluid derived from the
circulation to flood the lungs (pulmonary oedema). After
a period of respiratory irritation during and after
exposure there follows a short symptomless interval
before severe pulmonary oedema develops.

Treatment employing extremely high doses of steroid drugs given at a very early stage combined with, if necessary, oxygen and antibiotics may prove effective.

4. Cyanogenic Agents (Blood Agents).

The most important are hydrogen cyanide and four cyanogen halides. They have been used since World War I. Cyanides are highly toxic and readily absorbed through the eye and skin, but the usual route is by inhalation.

Cyanide acts by poisoning cellular enzymes, leading to asphyxia. Following massive exposure, the chemical will be rapidly fatal but its volatility makes it disperse quickly.

Treatment of cyanide poisoning may be successful except when the attack has been substantial, where death is likely to occur very rapidly. Respirators may not be effective against cyanide unless metal salts are included in the filter canister. Even then, the protection is limited and much less so when the cyanogen halides have been employed.

5. Other Agents.

A number of other chemicals have been developed for use as incapacitating agents, as riot-control measures and for creating smoke and flame. No persistent or lethal effects would normally result from their usage, although some carry serious acute effects. Military use of herbicides appears to carry little risk to man except for the dioxins which may contaminate – 2,4,–D and 2,4,5,–T.

Delivery of a chemical weapon may be effected in a number of ways including: from aircraft as a spray; by rocket or by bomb, including cluster bombs; by artillery shell; and hand delivered, such as by a grenade. It is not uncommon for a chemical attack to be preceded by one involving conventional high explosives.

The environmental contamination which follows a chemical attack varies from agent to agent and the duration of such contamination depends upon a number of factors, including the nature of the targeted ground, rainfall, wind and humidity. In open areas, agents such as unthickened organo-phosphorus compounds and cyanide are rapidly dispersed and the risk to the population diminishes very rapidly.

Chemicals of the blister type, such as mustard gas or thickened nerve agents, are considerably more persistent in terms of surface contamination. Clothing soiled with a compound of this nature provides a particular hazard for those who survive a chemical attack, for the rescuers and for medical and nursing personnel.

Dry soil may retain blister agents for a number of days, producing a hazard for anyone sitting or kneeling on it even if they are wearing protective clothing

There are situations where even unthickened nerve agents may place rescuers at risk, even days after an attack. Groups of bodies found in enclosed spaces, for example a cellar, may retain sufficient undispersed chemical to cause danger to an unprotected individual. Bodies stored in small rooms or sheds may constitute a similar problem. Open deep wounds, such as a shrapnel wound, may become heavily contaminated during a chemical attack. Bodies displaying such injuries should not be handled by persons who are not wearing proper protective clothing, including a respirator and heavy rubber gloves.

The measures to counter the effects of a chemical attack have been developed, and whilst they may be widely known by military personnel, the civilian population and – with the possible exception of Iran – the medical profession are largely ignorant of the effects and possible methods of treatment of the victims of chemical warfare.

Although reports of chemical attacks have emanated from Iran for a number of years, and indeed many of the victims have been seen in hospitals in Europe during that period, allegations of Iraqi chemical attacks against the unprotected civilian population of Kurdistan appeared earlier this year.

The attacks appear to have escalated, culminating in more than twenty gas attacks taking place against the Kurds between the 16th and 30th of March 1988. This phase began with the bombardment and subsequent chemical attack on the Kurdish town of Halabja, which resulted in a devastating carnage of the unprotected population.

I was approached by the Parliamentary Human Rights Group and asked to visit Iran to investigate the alleged attacks in an attempt to establish some scientific proof of the use of the chemicals suspected of having been used. Weapons of this type have not been employed in Europe since World War I, although accidental exposure to mustard occurred during World War II. First-hand experience of these agents has, therefore, been extremely limited except for those doctors involved in research into the medical effects of chemical warfare and those who have dealt with the Iranian soldiers who were sent to Europe during previous attacks.

I arrived in Tehran early in the morning of 28th March 1988, where I had some difficulty in contacting the Kurds who were supposed to meet me in Iran. Eventually it was arranged that I should contact the Iranian authorities the following day. I was met by representatives of the Iranian Foreign Office and their Minister of War

Propaganda and was given access to the hospitalised victims of the chemical attacks, and it was arranged that I visit Kurdistan to examine sites where chemicals had been used.

The United Nations team were in Tehran at that time and I arranged to visit the hospitals and Kurdistan with their party.

During my stay in Iran I had discussions with doctors who had treated the victims, with officials of the Iranian government and with journalists who had been taken to the front a few days earlier.

On the afternoon of 28th March I attended at Lochlan Hospital in Tehran, where we were briefed by Dr Jalali, director of the hospital, regarding the admission over the previous few days of some 140 patients, all of whom were suffering from varying degrees of injury caused by chemical attacks.

Dr Jalali appeared an experienced physician and had undertaken training in the Poisons Unit at Edinburgh Royal Infirmary.

The majority of the victims were admitted on and following the 18th March subsequent to attacks on Halabja, and all but a few were reported as showing the effects of blister agents with a small number admitted with signs of nerve-agent poisoning

Of the 140 patients, 40 were children ranging in age from 2 months to 10 years. Six of the children subsequently died. Seventy of the victims were Iranian soldiers, mainly members of the Revolutionary Guard. The remaining patients were Kurdish civilians, many of whom could only communicate in Kurdish.

I was shown around and given an opportunity to examine all of the patients in the hospital.

Almost all had been burnt, due to the effects of a blister agent. Burns varied from minor, almost healed, injuries to instances where substantial deep burns affected much of the body surface. The stage of blistering had passed in all instances and varying stages of healing had been achieved. The majority of the victims showed the classical reactive pigmentation which surrounds healing or healed burns caused by blister agents of the mustard gas group.

Respiratory symptoms were present in a small number of the adults and in some of the children, indicating damage to the respiratory tract caused by inhaling the gas.

Some of these victims had been injured during the attack on Halabja and the surrounding villages. Other victims, who all appeared to be soldiers, had been injured in an attack on the Kurdish town of Morivan. These individuals had evidence of chemical burns consistent with mustard gas, but some showed additional symptoms and signs indicating that they had been subjected to an attack by a nerve agent. Visual disturbance, striking muscular weakness and respiratory difficulties resembling asthma were seen in several.

All the surviving victims had been given in varying degrees the standard treatment for chemical attack. The mustard gas victims had been generally treated using water and other first aid measures such as removal of clothing. Calamine lotion and sodium sulphadiazine, when available, was applied to the burns. Affected military victims were given sodium thiosulphate, more commonly associated with treatment of cyanide poisoning, in an attempt to bind the mustard gas and prevent it from damaging tissues. Cystine was also used in a similar manner, and the doctors treating the patients reported some limited success with these agents in preventing extension of chemical burns.

The victims who had been exposed to nerve agents had been given atropine in high doses, pralidoxime and diazepam. Some required artificial ventilation and the eye symptoms were treated with cyclopentate. I was told that some individuals had recovered with surprising rapidity from nerve-agent-induced coma using these measures.

None of the victims had been wearing effective protective clothing, although some of the military personnel were equipped with light anoraks and respirators which did give some measure of protection – mainly against nerve agents – but had little effect where heavy concentrations of mustard gas were met.

The Iranians reported that many of the Halabja deaths were due to cyanide. I was shown no victims who had been subjected to cyanide attack. The diagnosis of cyanide poisoning was based on the response of some of the comatosed patients to the administration of the cyanide antagonists sodium nitrate and sodium thiosulphate. I am somewhat surprised at this, as the stage of cyanide poisoning when coma is induced is usually rapidly followed by death.

I enquired as to whether any chemical tests had been performed to substantiate the use of either cyanide or organo-phosphorus nerve agents, but was told that none had been done on this occasion although tests for nerve agents had been positive for attacks which had occurred in the past. The doctors treating the patients felt that their clinical experience was sufficient to substantiate the diagnosis of nerve-agent exposure.

Later that afternoon I was taken to a second hospital where chemical attack victims were being treated, but no

medical staff were able to conduct us around the wards
so we were unable to gain access.

The next morning we were taken by military jet and
helicopter to Kurdistan, where we were shown some of
the victims of a chemical attack which had taken place on
28th March. We were then taken to two villages near the
Iran–Iraq border which had been subjected to chemical
attack seven to ten days previously.

The victims of the attack, on the town of Nusud,
which took place on 28th March 1988 were in hospital in
Bakhteran. The party were conducted round the hospital
by a Dr Phorotan, who had been treating the victims of
chemical attack both in hospital and in the front line. Dr
Phorotan, although no burns were visible, displayed
respiratory symptoms which suggested that he had
inhaled a small quantity of blister agent, presumably the
result of treating patients who were contaminated with
the agent, whilst not wearing a respirator.

Outside the hospital I was shown a large pile of
clothing said to be contaminated with chemical agents.
This appeared to be a mixture of military fatigues and
civilian clothing

Within the hospital we were shown 35 patients, all of
whom showed varying degrees of mustard-gas-type
injury. All the victims were Revolutionary Guards and
none showed signs of nerve agent poisoning. They
demonstrated blistered burns, mainly on the limbs, and
with some showing blistering of the buttocks. All
appeared to have been wearing some form of protective
clothing, and the lack of respiratory symptoms suggested
that all had been wearing properly fitted respirators.

The pattern of burns suggested that the injuries had
occurred due to contact with surfaces contaminated with

a blister agent rather than due to a direct attack. It would appear for instance that the victims with burns on the buttocks had been injured by sitting down on ground contaminated with mustard gas. Others showed the pattern of burns which suggested that the agent had penetrated through the protective clothing at points where the clothing was firmly pressed against the skin, i.e. around the ankles and wrists and around areas where webbing might be worn, particularly in the shoulder area.

It is likely from discussions with those treating these patients that all of these soldiers had become contaminated whilst rescuing the victims who had been subject to attack in Nusud. We were shown none of the victims of the initial attack and we were unable to visit the town.

We were then taken to a large village called Nowdesheh, near the Iraqi border, which had been subjected to chemical attack seven days previously. The village was situated between 4,000 and 5,000 feet above sea level on a hillside and had been attacked by two aircraft which appeared to have dropped nine bombs.

We were shown the site where five of these bombs impacted, together with the remains of a number of bombs including what later were found to be shape charges (devices designed to pierce armour-plating) dropped from aircraft.

On the mountainside above the village there were two craters containing torn, rusty, metal. The craters had been caused by the detonation of high explosive, not by simple impact with a chemical bomb containing no explosive. The Iranians tested one of the craters and showed that the soil was still positive for traces of mustard gas.

We were next shown a house further down the same

hillside. The roof had been largely destroyed by impact from above, but there was no sign of high-explosive damage. A number of deaths had occurred from chemical explosion to both the occupiers of the house and to their immediate rescuers.

In line with the house and just below was a small building which we were told was a hospital. Here we found a number of bomb fragments including the rusty tailfin of a bomb. Adjacent to this was a hole in a stone retaining wall which proved, on chemical testing, to be positive for the presence of mustard gas. In the same line as the other impact sites but at a lower level we were shown a house with holes in the roof where another bomb was said to have landed. The room into which the bomb fell showed no sign of high explosive damage but in an adjacent room I was shown a piece of metal which was said to have been damaged by shrapnel during the attack. I am not clear as to whether that piece of metal had been moved into that house from another part of the village, but it did show characteristic shrapnel damage.

This house was approached through a narrow alleyway and in the alleyway were the nosecones and the tailfins of two bombs, neither of which showed signs of high explosive damage. Two small finned bomblets were shown to me, together with a number of steel discs which appeared identical with the nosepieces of the bomblets. I could see no sign of high explosive damage in any of the houses surrounding the alleyways in which these items were found. The intact bomblets and the remains of the larger bombs carried Cyrillic characters. The bomblets proved to be shape charges, of foreign manufacture, designed to penetrate armour. They could not be used to carry any chemical weapon.

Near to the floor of the valley we were shown a further impact site on the edge of an embankment. No high explosive damage could be seen, but the ground around the site showed some white discoloration and much of the vegetation was dead. The soil proved positive for mustard gas. No fragments were found here.

Through an interpreter, the villagers talked about the attack and indicated that it had involved two aircraft making two passes along the valley in which the village lay, both passes being made at low level.

I was shown one villager who had been injured during the attack. He had minor healed mustard-type burns on the back of his neck. The burns were surrounded by the typical increased pigmentation associated with mustard gas damage.

Later that afternoon we were taken to a second village, Nejmal, which had been subjected to a chemical attack eight days previously. Following the attack, 22 villagers had died and more than 100 had been injured

The attack had taken place from two aircraft which had passed low over the village from a northern direction, i.e. from the direction of Iraq. There were two craters on the southern edge of the village, both caused by high explosives and containing rusty twisted metal. From both craters the soil débris was thrown to the north, i.e. towards the village. Normally, following the detonation of a bomb dropped by an aircraft, the soil débris would be thrown in the direction in which the aircraft is travelling and not in the direction from which the aircraft has come.

Witnesses described the victims of the attack as showing the classical signs of organo-phosphorus nerve agent poisoning with visual disturbances, excessive salivation and excessive secretions from the respiratory tract.

We were shown no surviving victims from this attack. Following the visit to Nejmal, the party returned to Tehran.

I had an opportunity of discussing the findings with the United Nations team and saw some of the reports which had been submitted to them by the Iranians regarding the attacks on Halabja and surrounding areas. I was also shown photographs of some of the victims who had been treated for nerve agent poisoning following attacks on Halabja which took place between 16th and 18th March, when there was clear evidence of attack employing both nerve agent and blister agent of the mustard gas type. Cyanide was allegedly used on the 16th March and, according to one report, also on the 18th March. It is clear that there was a heavy chemical bombardment on the 16th. But there was no evidence to substantiate the use of cyanide.

The victims of Halabja had been substantially cleared from the town when I arrived in Iran and I was informed by journalists that the state of the remaining bodies was indicative of fairly advanced decomposition. Examination of these bodies would have been of no value at the time of my visit.

I have seen photographs of many of the victims found after the chemical attack, together with a video recording taken of the town before and after the attack took place.

It is clear that many of the victims died fairly shortly after the attack, and death can only be explained in terms of the use of some rapidly acting agent such as a nerve agent or cyanide. The photographs show bodies in vary-ing states of decay. Some appear to be fairly fresh, others appear to have been dead for more than 24 hours. Some of the bodies showed evidence of excessive secretions from the mouth and nose, which would be in keeping with the use of an organo-phosphorus nerve agent.

A precise estimate of the numbers killed in the attack on Halabja and surrounding villages was impossible to obtain. Figures of between 5,000 to 8,000 dead out of a total population of 70,000 were given to me in Iran.

I was also informed that during the period of 16th–30th March thirteen separate towns and villages had been attacked. Nerve agents had been used in seven of these areas: blister agents in seven areas and cyanide in one area. There certainly is substantial evidence for the use of blister agents, and nerve agents are frequently used in combination with these agents, whether in the same attack or in sequential attacks.

Conclusions

There can be no doubt that parts of Iranian Kurdistan and a section of Kurdistan within the border of Iraq were subjected to attack using chemical weapons during the latter half of March 1988.

The majority of surviving victims exhibited the signs of blister agent exposure typical of the effects of exposure to sulphur-mustard but there were significant numbers of survivors who also showed signs of exposure to organo-phosphorus compounds. In previous attacks with organo-phosphorus agents, the chemical weapon Tabun has been identified in a canister which did not erupt on impact.

There is no direct evidence as to the nature of the chemical nerve agent used currently, but the response to the main method of treatment, i.e. pralidoxin, suggests that the agent was more likely to be Sarin as opposed to Tabun. Tabun exposure is not thought to respond well to pralidoxin but to respond more favourably with the drug obidoxin. Pralidoxin is the drug of choice following exposure to Sarin and to a lesser extent Soman.

There is no evidence to substantiate the use of cyanide. Cyanide may sometimes be detected following a chemical attack with some agents, as it is produced as a by-product of their manufacture.

The attack on Halabja and the surrounding areas indicates the use of a substantial concentration of lethal nerve agents directed primarily against the civilian population who were totally unprotected against such an event.

Other attacks appear to have been directed against military personnel of the Iranian army who had a limited level of protection – protective clothing and respirators – against these weapons. The level of protection would have been poor against agents of the blister type but, for those wearing their respirators, some degree of protection would have been gained against nerve agent attack although none of the soldiers was taking any prophylatic drug which could have protected them against known nerve agents.

There was nothing to indicate the use of any sophisticated chemical agents; for instance thickened nerve agent or any of the dusts containing blister agents.

While there is no doubt that the Iranian government could provide a much greater degree of protection for their soldiers, it is difficult to see what significant protection could be given to the civilian population in the isolated areas of Kurdistan or, for that matter, in the more densely populated cities or towns.

The Iranian government have issued guidelines via the

national press to assist the general population in coping with chemical attacks, but these measures will do little to protect against the death which would follow the concentrated usage of either blister agents or nerve agents. The use of respirators would decrease the absorption, but there is little that can be done that will prevent skin contamination and absorption by this route. Both protective clothing and respirators are extremely uncomfortable to wear, especially in a hot climate, and it is unlikely that untrained wearers, even those who would be issued with these items, could tolerate them for any appreciable period.

Despite Iain West's damning report, which proves the devastating effects of the poison gas bombing – not only illegal but also a clear breach of human rights – the United Nations Human Rights Commission allowed Saddam Hussein to escape all criticism.

A year after the massacre of Halabja, the UN dropped the matter when Iraq played a skilful game of backroom diplomacy among the forty-three member nations at the commission's annual meeting. Saddam Hussein's diplomats successfully used the support of African, Asian and Arab countries to block attempts by the Western nations to raise the subject.

The 'absolution' of one of the world's most notorious violators of human rights before the world body that is supposed to investigate such abuses caused 'outrage and disbelief' among Western governments who had tried to bring Baghdad to account.

But it was all to no avail, and the world must wait in apprehension for Saddam or another tyrant like him to turn again to these dreadful weapons.

CHAPTER 5

DISASTERS

The main job of a pathologist is to determine the cause and the means by which death has occurred. It is extremely important work, and never more so than in the case of major disasters where large numbers of people meet an untimely end. For it is frequently from the forensic evidence that the roots of the disaster can be discovered and structures put in place to ensure that such a tragedy never happens again. Dr West has been asked to probe some of the worst disasters to strike in recent years.

Hillsborough

Liverpool and Nottingham Forest had played just six minutes of a crucial FA Cup semi-final at Sheffield Wednesday's Hillsborough Stadium when a supporter, dressed in the red and white of Liverpool, broke free from the packed terracing and ran on to the pitch.

Sprinting up to Ray Houghton, the Liverpool midfielder, the fan gesticulated wildly towards the Leppings Lane end of the ground.

'Ray, Ray, they are dying in there,' he yelled. It was 3.06 pm on 15 April 1989, and the first indication any of the players had of what, within minutes, was to become Britain's worst sporting disaster.

Before anyone had the time to react, ninety-five Liverpool fans had been literally crushed to death against security fencing designed to stop hooligans invading the pitch. They were pinned against the bars by the sheer weight of thousands of bodies pressing down the overcrowded terraces behind them.

Quite simply the Leppings Lane end at Hillsborough was divided into three sections by high metal fencing – three large cages. It was standing-room-only terracing, and tickets admitted spectators to that area without specifying where they were to stand.

Early arrivals had made their way to the front of the three sections and were standing behind the bars at pitch-level behind the goal. As more and more fans began to arrive, the terraces began to fill up from front to back in an orderly manner. But when the roar of the crowd announced the arrival of the teams on the pitch at 2.54 pm, there was a sudden stampede by Liverpool fans still outside the turnstiles or just leaving the local pub. Most had been drinking heavily, and hundreds of them stormed through a gate and made for the nearest available entrance. It happened to be the central section, which was already full, but the latecomers continued to push until the whole crowd in that section toppled forward trapping those in the front and suffocating them.

The recriminations and repercussions from Hillsborough went on for years, leading to stricter controls on drinking in football grounds, improved policing arrangements, and the accelerated introduction of all-seater stadia. The cost in human terms was enormous, and the litigation which followed heaped bitterness and distress on to the already grieving families of the victims. A £4.5m police inquiry concluded that there was insufficient evidence to bring criminal charges against any of the police or officials involved in the tragedy. An inquest jury returned verdicts of accidental death.

But the families wanted scapegoats. They wanted someone punished. They wanted compensation. The argument was that the coroner had conducted mini-inquests into each death, using summaries of eye-witness statements that could not be properly questioned.

These statements raised controversial issues of whether the deaths were instantaneous. Could those who remained alive for some time after sustaining crush injuries that ultimately proved fatal have been saved by a better response from the emergency services? The coroner's decision not to examine events after 3.15 on the fateful day effectively prevented a proper examination of this question in at least four cases where there was evidence that the crushed fans were still alive after the time the coroner said they should have died.

The stage was set for Iain West to employ his special skills and make use of the experience of crush-injury deaths that he had acquired from the Brighton bomb and the Clapham rail disaster, among others. In April 1992, three years after the tragedy, Liverpool Council's Hillsborough Working Party wrote inviting him to re-examine the cases of eight victims. They sent the postmortem reports and a full set of colour photographs of each body.

The letter included a detailed summary of findings from the official inquiry into the disaster which had been carried out by Lord Justice Taylor – later to become the Lord Chief Justice – and then went on to explain precisely what it was the families wanted from Dr West:

It is plain that Lord Justice Taylor found some serious deficiencies in the police response to the plight of the injured once they had sustained their injuries at some time between 2.52 pm and 3.05 pm, or even later. It is true that he had concluded that many of the injuries and deaths were probably inevitable once the fatal crush had built up. But he recognised that a quicker response to the emergency by the police to ensure the early attendance of the emergency services might have saved at least some lives.

It is clear that he did not rule out the possibility that some lives might have been saved by calling the emergency services in earlier, and his conclusion that in most cases the injuries would have been fatal in any event after a very short period of crush asphyxia depended on a particular pathological premise (namely, that fatal crush injuries were due to a continuing pressure which made death inevitable in a matter of minutes) which has subsequently been challenged and is inconsistent with the fact that some of the dead appeared to have been revived briefly and many of the injured who got medical attention promptly did survive.

At the mini-inquest on 18th April 1990 into the deceased, the cause of death was stated to be traumatic asphyxia. In particular Professor Alan Usher testified that once a person is asphyxiated they may lose consciousness within 10 to 15 seconds and then brain death would occur between 4 to 6 minutes. He further propounded a 'death theory'. At the subsequent mini-inquest into Kevin Daniel Williams, a Dr Slater and a Dr Gumpert appear in their evidence to consolidate Professor Usher's theory.

At the resumed inquests the coroner, in the light of the above evidence, decided that he would not hear evidence as to what happened after 3.15 pm on the day of the disaster as he was satisfied that each of the deceased would have been at least brain dead by that time.

This cut-off time has caused grave concern to some families as they have evidence that their loved ones showed some sign of life after that time and longer, perhaps, than had been said to be possible by the pathologists.

Probably the most controversial of those cases is the death of Michael Kelly. Evidence shows that he was left breathing on his own some time after 3.15 pm. He was later certified dead at 3.59 pm without having received any medical assistance. His postmortem report details reveal no evidence of brain damage, and the relevant pathologist agreed that Mr Kelly's asphyxial changes were relatively mild.

The families of the first six of the deceased named above now seek to obtain a new inquest and for this purpose require an independent review of postmortem details. They need to know whether details in the postmortem reports correspond with the evidence and pathological theories propounded at the inquest.

In the case of Gary Church, his family is seeking to establish that Gary suffered physical harm and pain before he died. This would appear to be borne out by the fact that his postmortem report shows that he suffered a dislocated right sternoclavicular joint. Your comments on this would be welcome.

In his comprehensive report, delivered some four months later, Dr West began by setting out at some length the key issues of the case both from a clinical and a pathological perspective. It is a learned treatise on the subject, and worthy of some study. It begins as follows:

It is clear from postmortem appearances that we are dealing with two different patterns of injury, namely a number of victims who showed the classic appearances of traumatic asphyxia and others where the classic signs of traumatic asphyxia were absent or slight. The difference is relevant in respect of the precise mechanism by which each individual died. It may well be that some confusion has developed over the use of the term 'traumatic asphyxia'.

In the classic sense, traumatic asphyxia is taken to imply injuries caused by the application of mechanical pressure to the chest and, in some instances, the abdomen, so that death results from asphyxiation. The mechanism of asphyxiation in the classic case is thought to be twofold. First there is a mechanical impedence of the movement of the chest wall and diaphragm, thereby severely restricting inspiratory respiratory movements.

The second mechanism, and one which accounts for the most striking findings in cases of traumatic asphyxia, is compression of the chest and abdomen resulting in direct compression over the superior vena cava causing a sudden dramatic rise in the pressure within this vein resulting in engorgement of the blood vessels in the head and neck. It is this displacement of blood and the failure to drain blood from the superior vena cava which accounts for the swelling of the facial features and the gross petechial haemorrhages so regularly seen in the face, neck and chest above the level of constriction.

Where no obstruction to the venous circulation occurs, then the usual signs of asphyxia are present but not those of the classic traumatic asphyxial death. The face may be suffused and cyanosed and there may be fine petechial haemorrhages, in some instances scanty or even absent.

The facial features do not appear strikingly swollen and the coarse petechial haemorrhages are not present.

Unfortunately it has become a habit for pathologists to call all such deaths traumatic asphyxia, and it may well be correct in one sense inasmuch as trauma to the chest has resulted in the mechanical obstruction of respiration. In pathological terms, there is probably little relevance in distinguishing between the two mechanisms as the term merely implies that death has resulted from a mechanical obstruction to respiration resulting from pressure being applied to the torso.

In clinical terms, however, there does seem to be a difference between the two types of traumatic asphyxia with a much graver prognosis for those where there has been a sudden and acute rise in the venous pressure in the upper part of the body. In fact, most of the individuals who suffer from this classic form of traumatic asphyxia do not survive if they are not rescued rapidly.

Where the individual suffers primarily an obstruction to his movements of respiration, death will occur as a result of hypoxic damage to the brain. This may take a much longer time than in individuals who have been crushed so that impedence of the venous return to the heart has occurred. Indeed some individuals will survive but remain permanently neurologically damaged as a result of suffering severe anoxic cerebral injury.

It is probable that a period of at least ten minutes would be necessary before one would be able to state categorically that the absent respiratory movement would lead to death. Consciousness may be lost quite rapidly but, where the obstruction has not been complete, consciousness may take a considerable time to be lost.

I have experience of cases where individuals have died

through anaesthetic accidents whereby no oxygen was being supplied to the lungs while they were paralysed during surgery. In two of the cases, in excess of ten minutes elapsed before the surgeon noticed that the heart action was in the terminal stages of failure.

It is also known that individuals who have suffered severe hypoxic damage may not die immediately. They may be recovered unconscious with an active circulation which rapidly fails, despite all attempts at resuscitation. This may represent concomitant damage to the heart muscle leading to what is in effect a heart attack (anoxic myocardial infarction).

Severe hypoxia of several minutes' duration would be necessary for this to occur. It is therefore possible that a young man who had been asphyxiated by being crushed would be capable of some conscious activity after being removed from danger, but could still die as a result of hypoxia in the ensuing minutes.

Anoxic brain damage could also be aggravated by the failure to maintain a patent airway in individuals who were unconscious but still capable of respiration when retrieved from the crowd. The failure to place the individual in the recovery position, for instance, could lead to subsequent respiratory obstruction.

Experience from a number of instances where individuals have died from traumatic asphyxia has also demonstrated that not all individuals appear to have been affected at the same time. Some could have been affected by movement of the crowd in the minutes after the disaster occurred. Others could have had only partial or incomplete respiratory obstruction initially and then either suffered complete mechanical obstruction of respiration or died as the result of prolonged incomplete respiratory obstruction. This could take many minutes to cause death, and it is entirely possible that death would occur more than fifteen minutes after the incident began.

Perhaps the most interesting of the Hillsborough cases with which Dr West had to deal was the story of fifteen-year-old Kevin Williams. The record showed that he died at 3.15, but a woman Special Constable, Debra Martin, insisted that he died in her arms at 3.55. Miss Martin's story was a compelling and heartbreaking one.

The boy had been dragged out of the crush and carried across the pitch by men who knew that he was still alive. The policewoman tried to pump his heart and gave him mouth-to-mouth resuscitation. She worked on him for at least twenty-five minutes. She recalled later: 'I said to him, "You are not going to die. You can't die." I remember holding him, and he actually opened his eyes and stared at me. He made a noise, and I thought: "I've got him. I have actually got him alive." He opened his eyes again and looked straight ahead at me and said: "Mum." Then he just slipped back down into my arms and died.' She initially recorded the time of death as 3.55, but the problem was that she had changed that to 3.15 some weeks later when members of the police inquiry team interviewed her and persuaded her that she must have been mistaken.

Now it was up to Iain West to find evidence to either support or refute her story – the distraught family were counting on him. He began with a careful review of the first pathologist's findings. 'Kevin Williams was examined by Dr Slater, who described the external features of classic traumatic asphyxia, with cyanosis of the face extending on to the chest with numerous petechial and larger haemorrhages on the face and neck.' This was the first area of disagreement between the two pathologists for, having studied the photographs taken at the postmortem, Dr West immediately concluded: 'they do not indicate the classic signs of traumatic asphyxia. There is no swelling of the face although there is some cyanosis.' He went on:

> The most prominent findings that can be seen on the photographs are the injuries over the undersurface of the chin and left jawline just below the prominence of the larynx (Adam's apple). Dr Slater found bilateral fractures of the hyoid bone and of the superior horns of the thyroid cartilage on both sides of the larynx. These appear related to the linear abrasions over the front of his neck and beneath the chin.
>
> In my opinion there has been substantial damage caused by local pressure to the front of Mr Williams's neck. It is possible that when he was crushed in the crowd the front of his neck was pushed against some rigid structure. It is also possible that he could have been trodden on during the panic subsequent to the incident occurring.
>
> The deformity seen in the photographs and the fractures found by Dr Slater strongly suggest that damage to the upper airway was an important contributory factor in the death of Kevin Williams. Whilst death may occur rapidly following such laryngeal injuries, this is not inevitably the case and death may be delayed for a considerable period.
>
> Although he had suffered injuries to the neck, these are by no means invariably fatal and can be seen in those surviving strangulation. Quite striking signs of classic traumatic asphyxia can also be seen in individuals who survive crush incidents, because they are removed from danger in time to prevent death.

Dr West added significantly:

> This type of injury is amenable to treatment in the form
> of an emergency tracheotomy or a crico-thyroidotomy.
> An emergency tracheotomy is a relatively major
> procedure, but crico-thyroidotomy is a simpler procedure
> which involves the passage of a tube through the
> membrane between the thyroid and cricoid cartilages.
> *It is possible that if one of these procedures had been carried*
> *out at the scene, then he would not have suffered from the*
> *fatal asphyxia which led to his death.*
> *I could find nothing from the postmortem report or from the*
> *photographs to refute the realistic possibility that this young*
> *man was still alive after 3.15 pm on the day and may well*
> *have survived for a considerable period.*

So Iain West concluded that Kevin Williams *did* survive long
enough to have been saved had the emergency services
attended to him earlier. His report continues:

> The evidence of Special Constable Martin is difficult to
> refute in some respects. Whilst it is possible for an
> individual examining a dead body to mistakenly feel an
> apparent pulse, it is usually difficult to be mistaken over
> whether somebody is making breathing movements or
> not. I am, of course, making the assumption here that
> when the term 'breathing' is used, we are referring to
> movements of respiration and not merely sounds.
> Sounds frequently emanate from the air passages of a
> recently dead body when it is being moved. I do accept,
> however, that he is unlikely to have spoken the word
> 'Mum' if he had already suffered convulsions due to lack
> of oxygen.

When it came to tackling the cases specifically referred to in the parents' letter, the sad stories were relatively straightforward for Dr West. Of Michael Kelly, he wrote:

If Mr Kelly was treated as described and apparently resuscitated, it is possible that he has died as a result of hypoxic damage affecting his heart or as the result of some other form of respiratory obstruction. He appears not to have been placed in the recovery position and this may well be material. *There is nothing to indicate that this man was definitely dead by 3.15 pm; indeed the evidence available to me suggests otherwise.*

On Gary Church, he reported:

He had a dislocated right sternoclavicular joint. This type of injury is most likely to occur as a result of falling. It would require very severe crush injuries to dislocate the sternoclavicular joint and the postmortem findings do not appear to reflect severe local pressure on the chest or shoulder area. *It is possible that he received this injury as the result of falling over in an attempt to escape and has suffered pain and discomfort consequent upon this injury.*

So, like the parents of Kevin Williams, both the Kelly and the Church families appeared to have grounds for their actions. The other cases referred to him fell into one or other of the categories described in his preamble. His conclusions had to be noncommittal.

In relation to the individuals who have died of traumatic asphyxia; it is possible to say that, with sustained compression of the trunk, death could have occurred prior to 3.15 pm and that they were likely to have been quite rapidly rendered unconscious. There is no way, however, that one can state with any certainty that death occurred within that period. If the compression of the chest had been intermittent, they could well have survived well beyond 3.15 pm.

Of the individuals who have scanty signs or no signs of traumatic asphyxia, it is much more difficult to predict survival time. It is impossible to state purely from the medical point of view that a number of the young men could not have been alive at 3.15 pm. Those dying as the result of anoxic damage consequent to their chests being crushed could well have survived for a much longer period only to die subsequently from the effects of irreversible anoxia.

After his report had been submitted, Iain West received heart-rending letters of thanks from several of the families and finally, in April 1993, four years after the deaths, relatives of six of the victims were granted leave by the High Court to challenge the accidental death verdicts given by the inquest jury.

The hearing took place in November 1993 with Iain West's evidence, particularly on the likelihood of Kevin Williams' survival, getting widespread publicity. But, after a four-day sitting, the judges rejected the applications for a new inquest. The heartbroken families had failed.

The King's Cross fire

The London Underground is the oldest and biggest underground mass transportation system in the world. Every day the trains thunder through their holes in the ground in a rail network that would cover a country the size of Belgium. And from time to time, inevitably in a system which moves literally millions of people daily, there are fires. There used to be more fires than there are today. In 1980, for instance, there were 1,246 fires reported on the Underground. Some of them were relatively serious, causing hundreds of terrified passengers to be led to safety along smoke-filled tunnels. But, somehow, nothing much was done about the problem. Nothing, that is, until King's Cross.

King's Cross is one of the main termini at the pivotal hub of the system. Above ground is the mainline station serving the east coast of Scotland, including Aberdeen and Edinburgh, and the north-east of England. Underground, it is the place where six of London's eleven tube lines cross. Every day thousands of passengers from the Victoria, Northern, Hammersmith & City, Circle, Metropolitan and Piccadilly lines criss-cross constantly through a labyrinth of passages like so many ants scurrying about their business.

It was in the middle of this bustling scene that disaster struck with devastating speed at 7.33 pm on 18 November 1987. The first person to notice that anything was wrong was Philip Squire, a financial consultant on his way home to north-west London. He was travelling up the escalator from the Piccadilly line towards the central ticket office just below street level when he noticed what he thought was a smouldering cigarette-butt caught between the wooden treads of the moving stairway beneath his feet.

On closer inspection, Mr Squire realised that the smoke was coming from between the escalator steps. 'I looked through the gap and saw a ball of white sparks, like a child's sparkler,' he said. 'Smoke started to come out and pour down like dry ice. The sparks were intense, but there was no heat.'

He jumped over the smoke and ran up the escalator, where he reported the fire at the ticket office. An official there immediately raised the alarm by telephone.

According to evidence later published in the official report of the inquiry into the disaster, what followed in the next few chaotic minutes was a fatal catalogue of incompetence and confusion. There were no fire-fighting plans and no evacuation procedures. Hundreds of people continued to pour up and down the escalators. Trains stopped and disgorged their passengers. Many of them were directed to travel up the escalator beneath which the fire was taking hold.

The station's relief inspector, Chris Hayes, found the seat of the fire in the escalator chamber but, although he had a fire extinguisher in his hands, inexplicably he didn't use it. The area of flame was tiny and flickering at this stage, according to Mr Hayes, but he passed the water fog valves several times and did not turn them on, either because he had never seen them demonstrated or had never had any training in fire-fighting. When the local fire brigade arrived they had no layout plans for the station, as they were hidden away behind builders' panels. Firemen had no idea where the fire hydrants were, and they got very little sense out of the station staff.

By now the fire was beginning to take hold and trains were ordered to pass straight through the station without stopping. But still throngs of people were being directed through the passages close to the fire, using escalators and crowding the ticket hall. Many of the witnesses who gave such dramatic accounts at the later inquest and public inquiry were passing the foot of the no. 4 Piccadilly line up escalator and bending down out of curiosity to gaze upwards.

One woman described how she witnessed the final seconds in the life of Station Officer Colin Townsley, the only fireman to die in the tragedy. Mrs Sinder Parmar said, 'The fire was blazing. I could see orange flames about five to six feet in height. They seemed to be moving straight up. I looked to the top and saw a woman who seemed to be on fire. Her hair and coat were on fire and she was screaming. A fireman approached her to rescue her. I heard him shout reassuringly, "It's all right, love, it's all right."'

And then it happened. Suddenly a massive fireball, generating temperatures of 1,200°C and more than six megawatts of energy, exploded upwards consuming nearly four tonnes of material and incinerating thirty-one people in seconds.

'Everyone learned from mistakes at King's Cross,' said Dr West, 'and one mistake I learned from it was not going there on the night. But, by the time I heard about it, it was quite late in the evening and I didn't think I could contribute much by going there. In retrospect, that was probably a mistake.

'One aspect of the case which was interesting was why different individuals died in different ways and that relates to the type of fire we were dealing with and the way that it had spread. Some seemed to die primarily due to the effects of inhaling the usual products of combustion. Others showed evidence that they died rapidly following the flashover because, I suspect, they had been exposed to rather high concentrations of cyanide coming from the reactions with the paint and ceiling tiles which had been used there.'

Dr West was telephoned at home at midnight by the coroner's office. When he began his postmortems in the cramped, badly lit, surroundings of the outdated St Pancras mortuary, they were to last many hours. And because of the volume of bodies, just the most basic details were recorded on a standard form for the benefit of the coroner.

The first and most urgent job the police had for him was to look at the body of a young woman whom they thought might have been killed by a bomb. They were concerned that terrorists might have been responsible for the holocaust. Dr West was soon able to put their minds at rest on that score. She had been hit by a ball of molten débris that had destroyed one thigh – an injury which mimicked those sometimes seen in bomb victims, but not enough to fool such an experienced pathologist.

His next sad task was to examine the body of the hero of the fire, Colin Townsley, who lay there still dressed in his fireman's uniform with very little apparent fire damage visible on his impressive 6 feet 2 inches frame. 'Small partial thickness burning on the forehead, nose, right temple,' ran the report. 'Superficial burns on the neck and right arm. Partial thickness burns on the left thigh, left shin, both knees and both feet. Partial degloving of the left hand. There was a bruise on the undersurface of the right side of the forehead. No burns on larynx. Only a slight amount of soot in the air passages. Intense congestion of both lungs.'

Two years later Colin Townsley's widow launched an action for damages, and her lawyers approached Iain West for evidence to support a claim for 'pre-impact terror' – the fear of death he would have experienced. To do this they needed to know how long the fireman would have been conscious between the time of the flashover and the time of his death.

Dr West replied: 'Mr Townsley died from the inhalation of fire fumes, his significant burns being relatively minor. I would estimate that he would have survived for a period of several minutes once the flashover occurred, as it would appear that he had not suffered severe burns from the flash itself and therefore would not have lost consciousness from the shock related to severe flash burns. I would have expected him to have been capable of conscious actions for several minutes until the level of the fire fumes was sufficient to have overcome him. It is likely that he died within a very short period of being overcome, owing to the nature of the fumes inhaled.'

The other bodies he examined showed a mixture of injuries. Some were badly destroyed by burning and others, like Colin Townsley, seemed to have died from the poisonous nature of the fumes they had inhaled. One young man was known to be HIV-positive, so Dr West carried out the most limited internal examination as a personal safety precaution. Of another tall young man he was able to report: 'Mid to dark brown head hair with some lighter brown hair on both temples. Hair length approximately 2½ inches. Full moustache on upper lip. Eyebrows meet over the bridge of the nose.' Thus, a victim whose head had been untouched by the fire. By contrast, there was the body of a slim young woman wearing just the remains of some socks. In her case there was 'extensive charring of the whole of the head, face and neck with complete hair loss'.

In several cases the bodies had been virtually incinerated by the intense heat which detached limbs and cracked bones. One young woman found in the pugilistic attitude was described as having 'small areas of unburnt white skin and the remains of corduroy and black nylon on her legs. There was extensive charring with heat splitting of the scalp, face, neck, both hands, left arm and forearm, pelvis, both legs and thighs. The wrist joint on the left arm had been burnt through and the hand tightly contracted. The skin of the trunk had been burnt. There was no head hair. The air passages were filled with soot and mucus.'

Another man had suffered 'virtually complete skin loss with charring of underlying muscle on the back of the trunk, both upper limbs, the muscles of the thighs and both legs. The right foot was almost completely detached. The left foot was detached and examined separately. There were heat fractures in the legs and lower forearms. There was heat haematoma over the frontal aspects of the brain. The lungs contained a moderate amount of inhaled soot and mucus and were congested, showing changes due to heat.'

Almost a year after the disaster an intriguing mystery emerged: the case of the extra body. Three doctors – all experienced in dealing with major disasters – came forward to say that they had discovered a torso, a foot and part of a skull among the débris. But none of the remains belonged to any of the thirty-one people recorded as having died in the tragedy.

The doctors, Paul Davis, Peter Ernst and Robin Winch, all insisted that they had recovered a thirty-second body and should have been called to give evidence at the inquest. All three men made statements telling how they were being escorted through the tunnels at King's Cross at 3.30 am the morning after the fire. The fireman leading them stumbled over something, and Dr Winch – with twenty-two years' experience as an accident investigator – immediately called for a mobile light. In the eerie half-light the doctors saw a badly-charred human torso. The rib-cage, vertebrae and melted lungs could be clearly seen. A search of the immediate area revealed part of a skull and a foot welded to the ticket office by melted plastic.

Each item was separately bagged, tagged and removed by the police. But despite arguments to the contrary later, when the coroner ordered a fresh inquiry, those bags were never shown to Iain West. His postmortem reports showed that only one of the dead had a limb missing – a severed foot. But on the night of the disaster Fireman Flanagan of Clerkenwell Red Watch found a severed foot in the gutted station and handed it to a senior officer, at least four hours before the doctors' grim discovery.

Dr Ernst, the emergency consultant at Orsett Hospital in Essex, was appointed medical incident officer into the disaster. He said, 'I have no doubt at all that what I saw was a human torso. Otherwise I would not have called back my colleagues. Dr Winch and Dr Davis and another doctor all confirmed my view, and we were all in agreement that we should search the whole area.'

The other two doctors, fellow members of the North Eastern Metropolitan Accident Unit, were equally emphatic. 'All of us were quite certain that it was a human torso,' said Dr Winch. 'We could clearly recognise the ribs and the vertebrae and the gelatinised lungs. The base of the skull could also clearly be identified. There was no doubt at all about what we had found.' Dr Davis said: 'There is absolutely no doubt about it. I would not think it possible that we could be mistaken about this being a human torso.' Dr Ernst added: 'When a body is destroyed to that extent, it is easy to remove parts of it, particularly when you consider that high-pressure water hoses were being used.'

One of the first things Iain West had been asked to look at when he began his postmortems was a body-bag which apparently contained human remains. But he later testified: 'The bag contained no recognisable human remains either on a visual inspection or on inspection of the interior of the alleged remains. They were a mixture of inanimate débris from the scene. The main specimen that I was asked to examine resembled a roughly triangular-shaped piece of débris that I have subsequently recognised in a photograph of the booking hall.'

So could this have been the 'body' the three doctors found? They claimed that it could not have been, and insisted that Dr West examine photographs of their mysterious find. But to their intense disappointment he maintained his position.

Making a formal statement to the reconvened inquiry he said:

> I am satisfied from my examination of the bodies of the
> thirty-one victims of the fire that none of the victims
> could have been destroyed to this degree. The duration
> and intensity of the fire was insufficient to cause total
> thermal destruction of the limbs and head.
>
> The only explanation for the alleged fragment found as
> described by the doctors concerned would be disrupted
> injury caused by the detonation of high explosive. There
> is no evidence of the use of high explosive in the King's
> Cross fire. The only evidence of an explosion at the scene
> is that of the sudden flashover, and this could not
> produce any disruptive damage to the human body.

He went on dismissively:

> I have considerable experience of the destructive effects
> of both high explosive and fire, including cremation of
> human bodies, and based on this experience can
> absolutely discount the concept of the disintegration of a
> body as alleged by Doctors Davis, Ernst and Winch.
>
> The alleged torso described by Dr Winch which
> showed 'gelatinised lungs' cannot be correct. The lungs
> do not gelatinise but progressively decrease in size and
> solidify when exposed to prolonged heat until ultimately
> they are either burnt away or start to fragment.
>
> No human remains of any substance could have been
> destroyed by the effects of a high-pressure hose.

So that, effectively, was that. In any case, no one has ever
come forward to report a thirty-second victim missing. But if
there was an extra mystery body, perhaps it belonged to one

of the thousands of vagrants, homeless or missing persons who people the streets of London unloved, unwanted and not missed by anyone when they die.

Certainly one of the dead must still be assumed to fall into that category. He is known only as 'body 115', a very short man in his forties or fifties. The only possible method of identifying him was from his dentures, which were very well made using good quality materials. They bore the manufacturer's mark EH or FH but, despite an appeal in all dental journals, no clues came to light. The other significant thing Dr West noted about him at postmortem was evidence of recent brain surgery. 'There was a right frontal temporal osteoplastic flap, with a clip, in the skull which was not completely healed,' he reported. 'The dura was adhering to the osteoplastic flap. He was found in a pugilistic attitude, with almost total destruction of the skin and subcutaneous tissues with charring of the underlying muscles.' A scientist at Manchester University reconstructed the man's face from his bone structure, but despite widespread publicity for this face, the man has never been identified.

Although the cause of the fire is now agreed to have been a discarded cigarette or match falling between the escalator treads and igniting oily rags or paper detritus which had accumulated in the chamber below, no one has ever come up with a satisfactory explanation for the fireball. The piston-effect of the movement of Tube trains produces huge movements of air upwards through the tunnels, and anti-graffiti paint on the ceiling of the escalator shaft certainly played a crucial part in the spread of the flames.

When the report of the official inquiry into the fire chaired by Mr Desmond Fennell QC was published, it made 157 recommendations to improve safety on the London Underground. The bitingly critical report blamed management for failing to react to previous fires and being 'lulled into a false sense of security by the fact that no previous escalator fire had caused a death.'

Today the entire London Underground system is a no-smoking zone. All escalators are metal, surrounded by flame-retardant paint and covered by automatic sprinkler systems. Staff are rigorously trained in fire-fighting and evacuation procedures, and regular inspections are held to make sure that any flammable materials are cleared away.

Station Officer Colin Townsley was posthumously awarded the Queen's Gallantry Medal for Brave Conduct.

The Clapham rail crash

It was just after 8 o'clock on a bright, frosty, December morning that the lives of two trainloads of ordinary working people came into dreadful collision. The date was Monday, 12 December 1988. The 07.18 passenger train from Basingstoke to London Waterloo was stopped just outside Clapham Junction – the world's busiest railway junction – while the driver was out of his cab reporting, on the trackside telephone, a faulty signal he had just encountered. As usual at this time in the morning the train was packed with people on their way to work in London from their homes in the suburbs and southern counties' commuter belt.

Behind, on the same line and approaching fast, was the 06.25 express from Poole in Dorset to Waterloo, just five minutes away from its destination. This train was also packed. Every seat was taken, and the aisles and corridors were crowded with standing passengers.

The first train was obscured from the view of the driver, John Rolls, at the controls of the second train as he approached round a sharp bend at 60 mph. He had just passed through a green signal and had every right to expect the line in front of him to be clear. But, to his horror and too late, he found a stationary train in his way as he rounded the bend and ploughed into the back of it.

In a few chilling seconds, carriages from both trains were being tossed forty feet into the air like a toy train-set scattered by a petulant child. When they came crashing down to lie at crazy angles on the railway embankment and across the adjacent tracks, the resulting carnage left 35 people dead and 100 passengers horribly injured. An empty goods train coming the other way spotted the trouble, but couldn't pull up in time to avoid running into the wreckage.

A full-scale judicial inquiry under Sir Anthony Hidden QC took evidence which found that the crash had resulted from faulty signal wiring by an electrician, Brian Hemmingway, who had left a wire loose and had not been properly supervised. The inquiry made ninety-three recommendations to improve safety on the railways and awarded compensation to the victims.

For Iain West, a man all too familiar with death in all its forms, the memories of that tragic day remain horrifyingly vivid. 'Clapham led to a very concentrated two days' work,' he said. 'Probably the most exhausting period I have ever experienced. Certainly my team thought it was. We all felt quite drained afterwards. We thought we weren't going to be involved initially because the crash didn't happen in our area. But, because of the large number of bodies, it was decided to ask us to deal with it at Westminster mortuary which has plenty of room and better facilities.' The operation which Dr West and his team, including his deputy Dr Dick Shepherd and his wife Dr Vesna Djurovic, set up at Westminster proved to be the perfect model for handling the pathology in a major disaster of this kind.

During the period of several hours between the crash and the retrieval of the bodies, the pathologists planned a management scheme for the use of the mortuary. A database was set up and a computer terminal installed. A diagram showing the body flow through the mortuary, with different areas designated for different tasks, to avoid confusion and crowding, was produced. A set pattern was to be adopted for dealing with each body-bag as it was removed from the undertakers' vans. In the unloading bay each one was booked in, given a number, labelled and immediately refrigerated. Great care was taken to ensure that the numbers matched those on the outside of each fridge, and the body-bags were marked in indelible ink as an extra precaution. Each body then followed the same route, passing through different stages of processing until the identification process was completed. The contents of all the body-bags were first photographed and then put on trolleys and examined externally by a pathologist.

Four pathologists were working simultaneously at four work-stations, helped by mortuary technicians and the police officers who escorted each body. At this stage the external examination was limited to the description of clothing, jewellery, personal belongings and marks of identification, including major injuries such as loss of limbs. The findings were dictated to the police officers, who filled in the standard identification forms developed by Scotland Yard for such occasions. Then Polaroid photographs were taken of each body and all the remains, and numbered according to the existing system. The bodies were then fingerprinted, cleaned and re-photographed, and tissue and blood samples taken. All this took until the early hours of the following morning, and after a short break the pathologists were back in the mortuary to begin dental charting and full postmortem examinations of all the victims.

But the team were furious that they had not been called in early enough to have attended the scene of the crash before the bodies were actually moved, because taking photographs of the bodies *in situ* and observing their positions would have helped in the important task of reconstruction that was to follow.

Dr West commented: 'Clapham was typical of other major train crashes where there were serious problems in identifying victims and in assessing exactly how many victims there were. The most important aspect to a disaster like this is establishing how many people are there and who they are. In an aircraft disaster, you at least start by knowing how many people were on the plane and in most instances you will know their name – whether that is their real name or not is another matter. In a train disaster you have what is, in effect, an open disaster. In other words, you cannot know how many people were there in the first place. And obviously the most important aspect of the examination is establishing who they are.

'The nature of the injuries in that sort of disaster usually precludes visual identification in most instances. So identification has to be based on other factors such as dental records, fingerprints, clothing and personal belongings. But they, of course, can be misleading. We had one instance where there was the body of a young woman, and a handbag was with her. We searched the handbag and found some photographs, but they did not look like the deceased. In fact, that handbag turned out to come from one of the survivors. In another instance I was told we had a single body in one of the bags that had been brought up by the undertakers. It turned out to be parts of three different bodies, and there were some items of personal belongings in there, too. It had been assumed that the personal belongings came from the body in that bag. Actually they came from none of the individuals whose remains had been in that bag. They came from a jacket which had got into the bag and belonged to somebody else who had died.

'We decided not to work round the clock because that makes for mistakes, so we worked fairly intensively to get the identification done as quickly as possible. I think there were complaints from some relatives that they were not told for many hours, but in some cases it was a very difficult and long-winded process to make sure that we had the right person. We were not just accepting one method of identification, because in many cases none of the methods we were using gave an absolute result, so we had to keep cross-checking.'

The difficulty of the identification process at Clapham is graphically illustrated when one reads the distressing list of items to be matched with bodies which had been literally ripped apart. There were about sixty body-parts collected from the mangled wreckage, including a severed head, five feet, four arms, two legs, a jaw and a large number of pieces of brain, skull and internal organs such as kidneys, bowel and stomach.

But the work went ahead methodically and efficiently. On the computer a comprehensive tabulation of the details from each body was being entered. These data began with the name, if it was known, and the site in the carriage at the time of the crash, and the number of the body. The result of the identification, whether it was possible or not, followed along with details of the sex, height, weight, build, race, hair, face, eyes, nails, pigmentation, scars. and tattoos. Then a description of the clothing, jewellery, documents, dental records and the blood type was added.

Before making his report to the coroner and the subsequent inquiry, Dr West, in keeping with his reputation for thoroughness, first studied the plans indicating where the various victims were thought to have been positioned prior to the accident, then examined the wreckage of the three carriages involved, and arranged to be shown an identical driver's compartment. He also spent hours poring over colour photographs taken during the operation to retrieve the bodies.

Miraculously, the driver John Rolls had survived the impact, but died on the way to hospital. After his postmortem Dr West reported:

> Small linear abrasions on the right forehead. Compound fracture of the lower shinbones. It appears that he suffered from moderately severe narrowing of his left coronary artery, but I found nothing to indicate that this had contributed to death.
>
> The pattern of the injury clearly indicates that Mr Rolls was not standing or sitting squarely behind his controls at the time of impact. The injury to the lower leg region indicates that he was still within the cab and that his legs had been crushed by the drivers' footrest.
>
> The pattern of injury to the remainder of his body suggests that he was moving to his left, probably in an instinctive reaction to avoid the crash, at the time of the impact. If he had been behind the controls, the degree of destruction of the front part of the train was such that I would have expected extensive mutilating injuries to be present on the trunk of the deceased.

The postmortem reports on the rest of the dead catalogue a variety of horrendous injuries, all of which were carefully studied in order to discover what had caused them and the precise location of the victim at the time of the crash, so that efforts could be made to improve safety for the future.

The most devastating injuries had been suffered by a male passenger. Dr West recorded them as follows:

Traumatic amputation of the head and upper neck. Traumatic amputation of the right upper limb at shoulder level. Traumatic amputation of the left thigh above the pelvis with further traumatic amputation of the lower limb at knee level. Traumatic amputation of the right lower leg at knee level.

There were multiple lacerations on the scalp. Multiple areas of bruising abrasion on the face, the trachea and neck. Vessels protruding from the amputation ends appeared to be cleanly incised. There were extensive crush-type parchmented abrasions over the whole of the upper chest.

The deceased had suffered severe mutilation injuries as a result of being trapped within the deforming wreckage of the front of the first carriage. He could well have been standing and then subsequently suffered the extensive dismemberment after being struck by parts of the superstructure of the carriage. His other injuries were caused by his body being pulled under the wreckage by the force of the impact.

In another case he reported:

The pattern of injury shows severe crush injuries to the trunk, a violent impact to the head and injury to the lower limbs. This appears to be typical of the pattern seen in passengers who have been ejected from their seats following the collision, with the head impacting against a hard surface. The leg injuries appear to result from entrapment of the legs as the floor and seats deformed. The crush injuries to the chest are likely to be the result of propulsion of the body combined with subsequent crushing by débris.

In the case of a man who died from traumatic asphyxia, Dr West wrote:

The appearance indicated he had suffered severe compression of the chest and upper abdomen as a consequence of being crushed by débris. The relative absence of severe trauma suggests that he was compressed by relatively soft-surfaced objects, which probably means that he was seated at the time.'

An elderly woman was recorded as having wounds which indicated 'severe impact to the head occurring very shortly after the collision. There is severe destructive injury to the pelvis, indicating that the deceased was seated. The crush injuries to the chest occurred following ejection from the seat.'

Another man died from a 'severe compound fracture of the skull with fragmentation of the vault and base of skull and facial bones, particularly on the left side. Facial tissues and scalp tissues were extensively blackened, abraded and lacerated, and the extensive lacerations extended from the root of the nose across the left eye. The deceased has suffered an immediately lethal head injury which appears to be the result of a very substantial primary impact to the left side of his head. The pattern of injury of a crush nature affecting the chest and the pelvis strongly suggests that the deceased was seated and ejected from his seat after impact.'

A young woman 'died as the result of a crush injury to the neck causing an obstruction to the airway. She would appear to have been thrown forward at the time of the impact with her neck impacting against hard débris, possibly the edge of the seat.'

Having completed the harrowing task of identifying and examining all thirty-five victims of the crash, Dr West was determined that something positive should come out of the tragedy. So he set about preparing a report which might encourage others to do something about rail safety. The key findings of this report read:

Out of the seventy-one persons travelling in the first carriage of the Poole train, twenty-nine died. If the carriage is further broken up into zones, it transpires that the front nearside of this carriage was the most dangerous. No one escaped either death or serious injury in this area.

There were forty-three passengers in the second carriage of the Poole train which served as a buffet car. All six people who died in this coach were seated. Two were on the offside and four on the nearside of the rear part of this carriage, which suffered very severe damage. The relevance of the seating position lies in the influence of which seat orientation and position the victim had at the time of impact can have upon the intensity of injury sustained.

All but one of the victims are thought to have been seated at the time of the collision. Although this cannot be claimed with certainty, the medical evidence as deduced from the pattern of injuries supports this view.

It has been possible to place seventeen passengers in seats in the front compartment of the first carriage and, from the pattern of injuries suffered by many, it is possible that most of the twelve passengers who cannot be placed in seats were seated either at the very front of the carriage or in the nearside row of seats.

Injuries to victims who were placed in the front carriage showed two main patterns. Those seated at the front have suffered severe crushing injuries caused by destruction of the front of the carriage on impact – the further injuries caused by ejection from the seats at the time of impact. A small proportion of those seated at the front showed injuries primarily due to ejection.

Much of the mutilating injury suffered by the victims in this part of the train was due to postmortem damage caused by their bodies being drawn into the wreckage as the buffet car rolled over the front carriage.

The heavy toll among passengers seated at the rear nearside of the train appears to have resulted from forceful impact in that part of the carriage. They suffered severe primary impact, mainly to the side of the head and or trunk which was adjacent to the window. Many of these victims also showed severe injuries to the chest and abdomen caused by being crushed as they were ejected towards the offside of the carriage and by the subsequent collapse of the wreckage due to impaction under the second carriage.

Lower limb injuries, frequently of great severity, was also common among the passengers seated on the nearside of the carriage, due to their legs being trapped and crushed by the wreckage of the seats.

Traumatic or crush asphyxia was not a common cause of death among passengers killed in the first carriage. One victim who has been placed in seat seven suffered asphyixial damage caused by ejection from her seat and being thrown so that her neck struck a hard surface. A second victim who has been placed in seat fourteen suffered severe crush bruising, including an element of traumatic asphyxia. She had evidence of a primary impact to her head, although the most forceful impact appeared to have been to her chest and her stomach as she was ejected from her seat.

All of the six victims killed in the buffet car appeared to have been seated at tables. Two of these passengers died subsequently in hospital: one as a result of complications from injuries to his head, abdomen and legs, and the other as a result of primary impact to the neck caused by being hurled against a hard surface or being struck by a substantial piece of flying débris. A third victim in this carriage had suffered severe crush injuries to her chest and abdomen, but there was no element of traumatic asphyxia. The pattern suggests she was crushed against an unyielding surface with resultant skeletal damage. Being thrown against a table at which she was seated may have been responsible for some of the injury.

Of the three other victims seated in this carriage who died from traumatic asphyxia, two were seated in seats five and six respectively and appeared to have been asphyxiated by the table being forced back into the chest and abdomen. Marks on their bodies were consistent with pressure from the table-top. A third victim who died from traumatic asphyxia was seated in seat three, and the pattern of injury suggests that she had been thrown against her table and crushed against it by some of the débris.

The driver suffered injuries to the head and lower legs at the moment of primary impact. His head injuries occurred as protruding objects in his cab were driven backwards. Damage to his legs resulted from the edge of a steel footrest. He suffered crush injuries on ejection from the cab and further injuries on impact with the ground.

The British Rail employee who occupied the front offside cab has died as a result of being crushed while in the corridor behind the driver's cab.

Iain West's observations appear to have had the desired effect because, based on much of his data and material, Wing Commander I.R. Hill produced a survivability report on the Clapham rail crash in May 1989. His conclusions read:

While this was clearly a highly destructive accident, on the Poole train there were people who died from potentially remediable causes as a consequence of the collapse of the structure.

The appearance of the injuries shows that the severity of injury was enhanced because people were thrown from their seats. Some of them were thrown clear of the wreckage and appear to have been run over. The integrity of the seats is questionable.

There are many parts of the basic structure of the train's carriages which rendered them not crashworthy. That is, they are not cushioned so as to reduce the intensity of impacts or recessed so that the surfaces are smooth and free from protrusions. Nor are they frangible, thereby lessening the potential to cause injury.

Moreover, as occupants are not restrained, they are free to be thrown about in accidents.

This was a partially survivable accident in which some people died who ought not to have done so, and others sustained injuries which could have been prevented. Although some parts of the train were obviously lethal in that there was severe structural deformation leading to loss of occupant space, other areas were less severely damaged. Some of those who died did so from potentially remediable causes because the integrity of the occupant-containing area was not maintained.

Wing Commander Hill made ten recommendations:

1. Dynamic testing should be undertaken.
2. Potentially harmful features of carriages should be padded, recessed or made frangible so as to render them less dangerous.
3. Luggage racks which do not injure people and which restrain the luggage during a crash should be produced.
4. Seats should be anchored to the floor. They should be designed so that they will withstand impact forces tolerable to man.
5. Research should be undertaken into the practicality of incorporating energy-attenuation features into the structure.
6. Safety harnesses – seat belts for passengers and crew – should be fitted.
7. The structural strength of carriages should be reviewed in the light of current crashworthiness knowledge, paying particular attention to the tolerance of man to impact decelerations.
8, The behaviour of locks on train doors under impact loadings should be reviewed.
9. The practicability of having impact-absorbing structures in trains, especially at the front of driver units, should be examined.

10. Ways should be sought to prevent overriding of coaches during crashes.

The British travelling public is still waiting with interest to see if anything good will come out of the Clapham rail crash. With the Hill report having built on the sound pathological work of Dr West at the time, there seems little reason – apart from willingness and money – why real progress should not have been made towards greater safety on railways in Britain.

CHAPTER 6

'OLD BONES'

Pete Marsh

Lindow Moss is located a couple of miles west of Wilmslow, Cheshire, just outside the southern boundary of Greater Manchester. Its peat is extracted for use as a medium in growing mushrooms and other crops. Mechanical excavators slice off the exposed peat face to a depth of about a yard. The cut peat is stacked beside the face and left for six months to dry, then transported to a shredding mill. Two men are employed to search the peat before it is shredded in case it contains an object which might cause a blockage.

On 1 August 1984 one of these men, Andy Mould, picked out a human foot with a long strip of skin attached. The police were called, and so was the Cheshire county archaeologist. He took a careful look at the peat face opposite the stack in which the leg had been lodged and noticed a flap of dark skin hanging out. Over the next few days, with great care and effort, a large block of the peat from which the skin protruded was cut out and removed to the Macclesfield Hospital mortuary. As the peat was picked away, the top half of a human body was slowly exposed. Its depth in the bog, and the condition of the bone – its calcium long since devoured by the acids peat contains – indicated it was ancient.

The police began to lose interest, but the curiosity of archaeologists and scientists worldwide grew rapidly. An army of experts from many disciplines set to work to determine precise details of the ancient man's lifestyle.

It soon became clear that Lindow Man was the oldest body yet found in Britain. Quickly dubbed 'Pete Marsh' because of the location of the find, the body was discovered to be that of a young auburn-haired man who had died during the Iron Age – more than 2,500 years ago.

Only the torso and grotesquely lolling head were complete. His lower half had long since done duty as a mushroom bed. He had no eyes, and the upturned nose was damaged. One or two bones protruded from the skin and the face was distorted, sagging on the left side like that of a man who has suffered from a serious stroke. The close-cropped hair extended through trim sideburns to a short moustache and beard. The ear was shrivelled and cup-shaped and the brow was prominent.

He was passed into the care of the British Museum and taken to London, where some of the most advanced technology was deployed. Electron spin resonance spectroscopy determined the nature of his last meal. Terrestrial photogrammetry, a highly specialised technique never used for this purpose before, mapped the exact shape of his body. Endoscopy checked his surviving innards.

Radiocarbon-dating experiments at Harwell, Oxfordshire, and the British Museum pinned down the date of his death to some time between 300 BC and AD 400. His brain had turned into something akin to putty and most of his other inner organs had disintegrated. A detailed autopsy using xeroradiography and X-ray scanning techniques began to build up the picture of a healthy man in his late twenties with a fractured skull, broken ribs and massive dislocation of the neck.

It was at this point, some four months after the discovery, that the British Museum decided to call in Scotland Yard. In modern criminological terms they were looking at a 'suspicious death' and they needed special skills to determine how 'Pete Marsh' met his end. A team of forensic experts from the Yard Forensic Science Laboratory was called in along with Dr West, who was asked to carry out an examination of the apparent injuries. He recalls:

'They were looking for somebody to interpret the injuries and I was asked to make an examination. But it was a most unusual experience for me because I was not able to actually handle the body. It was in a very delicate state, being handled by the conservators prior to being freeze dried. But I was able to see the wounds and, with the aid of mirrors, magnifying equipment and strong lights I was able to look at the features of the external wounds. I was also able to look at the X-rays and make an assessment as to whether the wounds were likely to have been caused in life and about the nature of the wounds – in particular the relevance of the sinew thong around the neck with its very deeply indented ligature mark. There were two twists in the ligature, for instance, which some people have suggested were probably caused by roots growing through them. But if you look at the indentation on the neck, that sinew has been very tight around the neck and there's very little evidence that there has been a great deal of putrefactive distension of the neck. The tissues have shrunk away from the ligature, as opposed to closing and then shrinking.

'The wound on the side of the neck looks very clearly

incised and there is damage to the thyroid cartilage, which suggests a cutting or stabbing wound. The wound on the top of the head has a little bridge of skin, almost dividing it into two, suggesting that something pointed had been driven into the top of the head, pushing pieces of skull deep inside the brain. I didn't have any doubt that these three injuries looked like ante-mortem injuries.'

Iain West's report on the Lindow Man find makes fascinating reading, couched as it is in the clinical terms applied to the examination of the corpse from a modern murder, yet curiously applied to the body of a prehistoric victim. Let his written words tell the full story:

The two important forensic aspects of the examination of 'Pete Marsh' centred on, first, the injuries and possible injuries on the deceased, and second, on the varying state of preservation which his body exhibited.

The head was well preserved, although there was severe discoloration of the skin and some discoloration of the hair, beard, moustache, sideburns and, to a lesser degree, the head hair. Some of the scalp showed decomposition of the superficial layers, with sloughing of the epidermis, loss of some of the hair-bearing areas, and exposure of the tanned dermis and deeper scalp tissue. There was quite considerable flattening of the features, with loss of skin over the bridge of the nose, although the nose itself did not appear fractured.

There was considerable angulation of the neck, which was flexed and pressed against the right shoulder. Further injuries were thought to be present over the trunk, including a possible stab wound on the right upper chest. A posterior rib fracture was subsequently demonstrated by xeroradiography.

Turning to the head and neck injuries, Dr West's report begins to tackle the wounds one by one.

> The scalp laceration was roughly 'V'-shaped, about 35mm in length, and appeared to be formed by two lacerations, almost completely separated by a narrow triangular bridge of hair-bearing skin.
> Examination of the wound margins, using a stereoscopic dissecting microscope, revealed the typical features of a laceration with irregular split wound edges, displacement of hair follicles into the wound, small tissue bridges, and splits on the margins.
> It also indicated some persistent swelling of the wound margins, and this feature indicated that the wound was entirely consistent with an ante-mortem injury and that survival after the wound had been inflicted was of sufficient duration to allow swelling and, presumably, bruising of the surrounding tissues, although this bruising could no longer be seen.

So far, so good from the scientific point of view, but now the detective begins to show through.

> The presence of the bridge of skin passing across the majority of the long axis of the wound indicates that the injury could not have been received by one blow from a blunt weapon – assuming that the weapon had a single striking surface. The presence of bone fragments deeply embedded within the remains of the brain would indicate that the laceration was of a penetrating type, and that it would be consistent with use of a narrow-bladed, relatively blunt-edged weapon such as a small axe. Again the skin bridge indicates that, if such a weapon was used,

two blows must have been struck. The presence of two
contiguous injuries of this nature is not uncommonly
seen in current forensic pathological practice. If one blow
had caused the injury, then the weapon would be
required to have two projecting striking surfaces, both of
which were capable of penetrating through the crown of
the head.

Now Dr West begins to apply his considerable experience
and skills as a scientific detective in order to pinpoint precisely how 'Pete Marsh' died:

The position of the wound on the crown of the head
would suggest that it was caused while the deceased was
in a standing or kneeling position. It is an uncommon site
for an injury caused when somebody is lying on the
ground, but would be quite consistent with an injury
produced by a person striking the deceased from behind
with a weapon, with one blow rapidly being followed by a
second.

This injury would certainly have been fatal, but would
not necessarily have been immediately fatal. The injury
would have caused immediate loss of consciousness, but
survival for a period of hours.

But Dr West also found tell-tale signs of another possible
wound to the scalp, of which he reports:

The possible laceration over the occipital region could
not be confirmed as a definite wound, owing to
considerable scalp decomposition in the area. There are,
however, fracture lines in the skull in that area. If,
however, a blow had been delivered to the back of the

Press magnate Robert
Maxwell a couple of years
before his death
(Popperfoto)

Robert Maxwell on board
the *Lady Ghislaine* during
a stopover in Funchal
harbour on 2 November
1991 before leaving for
the Canary Islands
(Popperfoto)

The *Lady Ghislaine*
(Popperfoto)

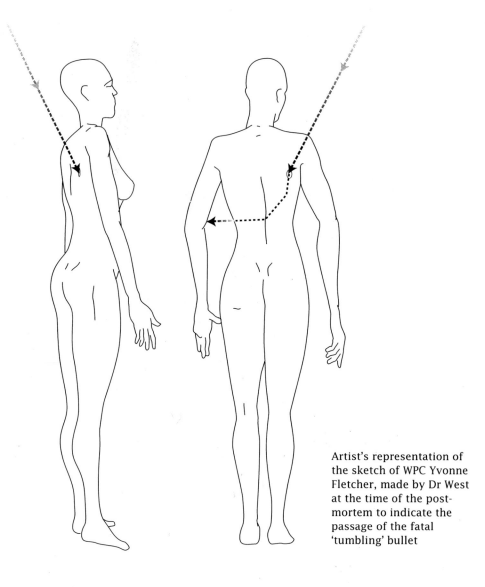

Artist's representation of the sketch of WPC Yvonne Fletcher, made by Dr West at the time of the post-mortem to indicate the passage of the fatal 'tumbling' bullet

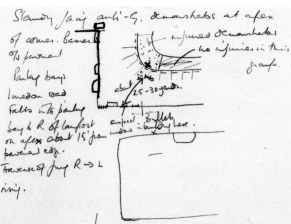

Dr West's original sketch from which he was able to calculate the angle and direction of the shot which killed Yvonne Fletcher

The shattered remains of a luxury suite in the Grand Hotel, Brighton after the IRA bomb blast in October 1984 (Sussex Police)

Anti-Terrorist Squad detectives sift through the debris at the foot of a section of bedrooms brought down by the bomb. The device exploded in a bathroom on the sixth floor and the whole section collapsed like a pack of cards (Sussex Police)

Bomb damage in a bathroom adjacent to the blast (Sussex Police)

Chart from which Dr West worked, showing the positions of the dead horses and soldiers in the troop relative to the seat of the explosion in the Hyde Park Bombing

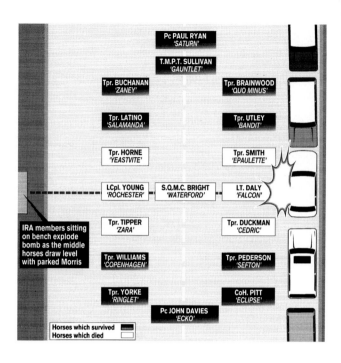

Pc PAUL RYAN
'SATURN'

T.M.P.T. SULLIVAN
'GAUNTLET'

Tpr. BUCHANAN
'ZANEY'

Tpr. BRAINWOOD
'QUO MINUS'

Tpr. LATINO
'SALAMANDA'

Tpr. UTLEY
'BANDIT'

Tpr. HORNE
'YEASTVITE'

Tpr. SMITH
'EPAULETTE'

LCpl. YOUNG
'ROCHESTER'

S.Q.M.C. BRIGHT
'WATERFORD'

LT. DALY
'FALCON'

IRA members sitting on bench explode bomb as the middle horses draw level with parked Morris

Tpr. TIPPER
'ZARA'

Tpr. DUCKMAN
'CEDRIC'

Tpr. WILLIAMS
'COPENHAGEN'

Tpr. PEDERSON
'SEFTON'

Tpr. YORKE
'RINGLET'

CoH. PITT
'ECLIPSE'

Pc JOHN DAVIES
'ECKO'

Horses which survived
Horses which died

Dr Iain West at work
(Mail on Sunday)

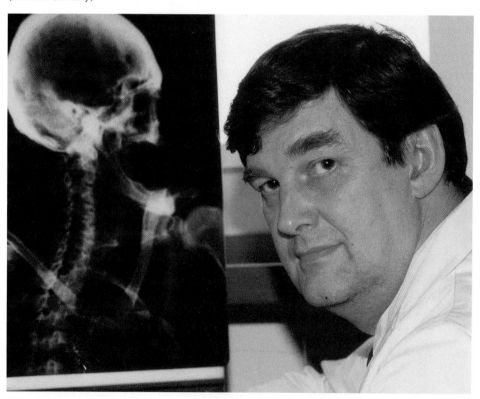

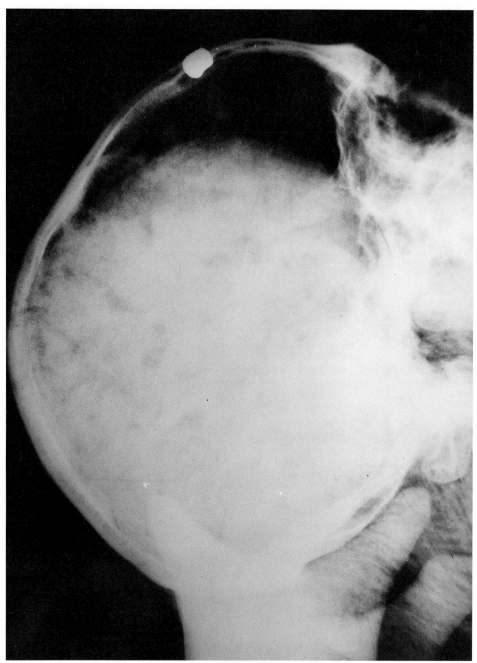

X-ray of Ali Giahour's
skull showing the bullet
entry wound

Dr West and Detective Superintendent John Troon are
flown by military helicopter from Nairobi to the scene
of Dr Robert Ouko's death

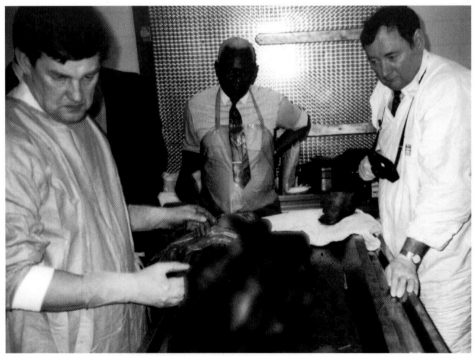

Dr West, Dr Jason Kaviti and Detective Superintendent
John Troon during the postmortem examination of
Dr Ouko's remains

Paper cut-out showing the position of Robert Ouko's body on the ground

String was used to calculate the line of fire from the body to the nick made by a bullet in the branch of a nearby tree

NG OF

←— 10 FT —→ ←— 7 FT —→

2ND TREE   1ST TREE

Composite showing the direction of the bullet from the body to the tree

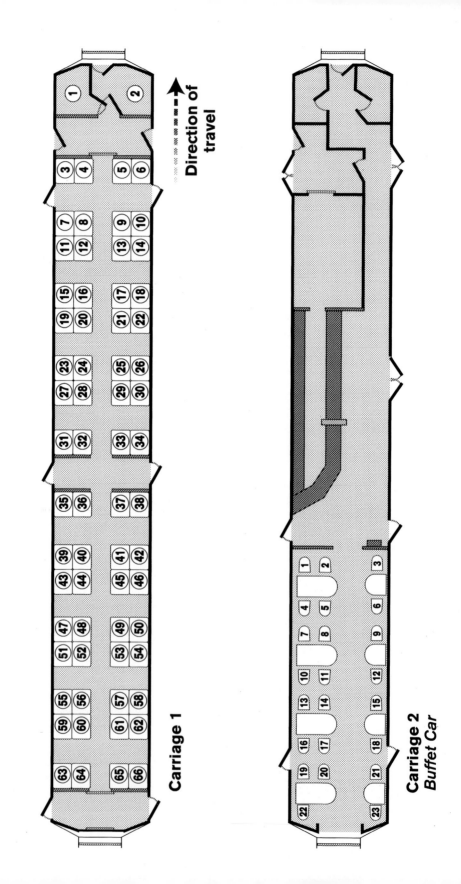

Direction of travel

Carriage 1

Carriage 2
Buffet Car

'Casa Ruby' – the holiday villa at Mojacar, Spain, where
John Baksh murdered his first wife (Press Association)

Dr Baksh with his
first wife, Ruby
(Press Association)

Chart of the seating
positions in the front
two carriages of the
Waterloo–Poole train
which helped Dr West
to determine the cause
of the fatal injuries in
the Clapham rail crash

Dr Baksh and his second wife, Madhu, on
their wedding day (Press Association)

Andrew Alder is led away in handcuffs after his arrest at
the home of Olympic swimmer Duncan Goodhew
(Press Association)

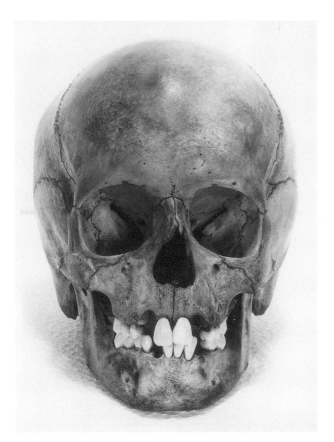

Skull showing the distinct tooth overlap from which Vishal Mehrotra was identified

Vishal Mehrotra

Dr Iain West bends down to examine the skull after its chance discovery by hunters in a Sussex copse

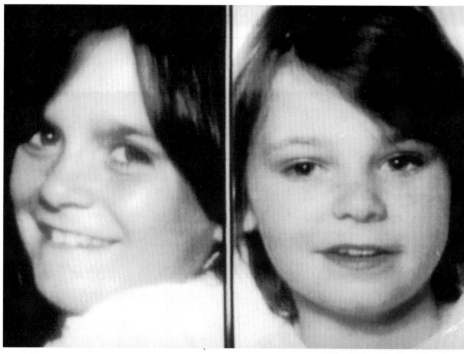

The Babes in the Wood,
Nicola Fellowes (left) &
Karen Haddaway (right)
(Press Association)

Farmer Graham
Backhouse's face displays
the giveaway knife wounds
(Press Association)

The block of flats from which John McCarthy fell; the blood-stained bath with the knife he was supposed to have used to commit suicide; and his bedroom, with the frying pan that led Iain West to believe he was murdered

John Fordham
(Press Association)

Aerial Scotland Yard picture shows the location (1) where the fatal stabbing took place in the bushes and the spot (2) where the fatally wounded policeman collapsed and died as he tried to crawl to safety (Metropolitan Police)

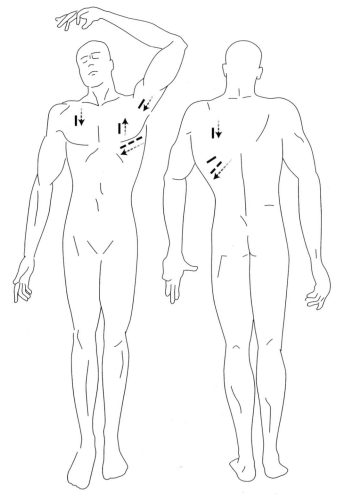

Artist's representation of the sketch of John Fordham, made by Dr West at the time of the postmortem to indicate the position and direction of the ten stab wounds

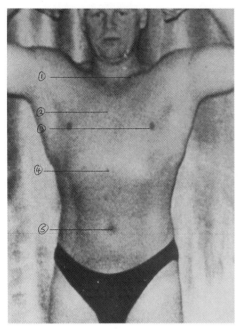 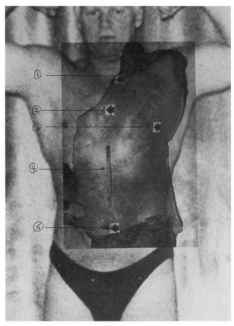

Stephen Davison strikes
the body-building pose
from which Dr West
was able to identify his
dead body

The torso overlay from
which the identification
was made

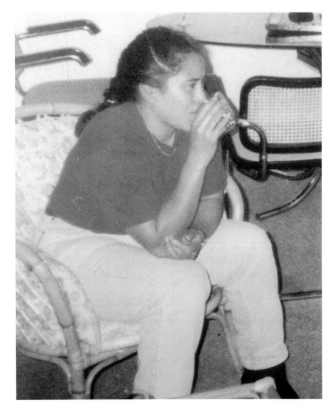

Graham Woodhatch's
assassin, Te Rangimaria
Ngarimu, caught in
a relaxing moment
(Photonews Old Bailey)

Gentle giant Kevin Gately towers head and shoulders above the crowd seconds before collapsing during the demonstration in Red Lion Square
(Press Association)

Picture taken by a hidden camera in a police observation point before the arrival of the gang who were attempting to seize a Securicor van which contained £800,000
(Surrey Police)

Police scenes of crime photograph showing pick-up van in situ with exhibits marked and pool of blood on the ground where Kenny Baker fell
(Surrey Police)

head with a heavy implement, such as an axe, then a full-thickness laceration would have occurred. A more blunt weapon – such as a cudgel – of course would not necessarily cause a full-thickness laceration, particularly if the striking area was relatively flat and broad.

So was 'Pete Marsh' struck with an axe on the top of the head twice from behind while he was standing or kneeling and then, though fatally wounded, beaten over the head with a cudgel, just for good measure? But whoever the killer was, they did not want to take any chances. They were certainly not prepared to leave the stricken man to die slowly over a period of hours, for around his neck the pathologist found the remains of a sinew loop and a visible ligature mark on the front and sides of the neck. 'There are a number of possible interpretations for the sinew loop present around the neck', said Dr West. 'Was this an ornament which he wore, or was it deliberately placed there – perhaps after he had been hit on the head and been rendered immobile?' Then, in his post-mortem report, he gets to the crux of the matter:

The use of a thin ligature of the diameter found here (1.5mm) as a means of strangulation, in the traditional sense, would be highly improbable – unless, of course, the sinew had been longer and had been broken off, or cut off, at knot level. The presence of two twists in the ligature at the back of the neck would, in my view, be highly significant if the sinew loop was used as a garrotte, rather than as a ligature which was tightened using the strength of an assailant's hands.

The twists in the sinew at the back of the neck would be quite typical of changes which might be left if a stout stick, or short piece of straight metal, had been inserted into the loop and then twisted until the neck had broken, and/or closure of the airway occurred. It would be perfectly feasible to break the neck in this fashion, and would account for the injuries seen at the level of the third and fourth cervical vertebrae on the deceased.

The presence of a well-defined ligature mark on the front and sides of the neck, but not at the back of the neck, again would be quite in keeping with the use of the sinew loop as a garrotte. The ligature mark was deeply indented and showed quite well-marked pressure abrasion of its surface, in keeping with a ligature compression of the neck occurring during life.

By now it is clear that Dr West favours the garrotting theory, but he turns his attention to the idea that the sinew might have been part of a necklace:

The circumference of the ligature indicates that it would have been extremely tight on the deceased's neck even allowing for some shrinkage of the sinew, if it had been worn as an ornament. The presence of this sinew loop is similar to the findings of a number of other bog bodies and the knotting is not dissimilar to that seen in the rope on Borre Fen Man, and suggests, perhaps, that this was placed around 'Pete Marsh's' neck as part of a ritual sacrifice.

Now we are beginning to get the picture. A ritual sacrifice in which the victim is cudgelled, axed and garrotted. But there's more – a wound on the side of the neck.

The wound on the right side of the neck initially looked as though it were an artefact produced by a combination of decomposition and the position in which the body was lying. At a subsequent examination, however, where the wound could be explored more fully, it was clearly apparent that the margins of this injury and the underlying soft tissues were cleanly incised. The superior border of the right lamina of the thyroid cartilage had been cut.

The appearance of this wound indicated an incisional injury with a sharp-edged weapon, and the position of the wound would be entirely in keeping with a wound caused with the intention of severing the jugular vein.

The haemorrhage from this wound would, of course, be accentuated if pressure on the neck was being applied by a garrotte, as the venous bleeding which would occur when the jugular vein is cut would be caused by blood coming back from the head, not blood going to the head. Twisting of the garrotte below the incision would, provided the carotid arteries had not been closed, still allow blood to pass into the head via the arteries, and would accentuate the bleeding from a cut jugular vein, causing all the blood to run via the cut vein.

A pretty gruesome scenario which, although expressed in clinical language, speaks volumes of the savagery of those times.

There were two other possible injuries Dr West discovered on the body of the unfortunate 'Pete Marsh':

The posterior rib fracture subsequently detected appeared to have been caused near to the time of death, and would be consistent with the effects of a heavy blow to the back of the chest. The possible stab wound on the right upper chest could not be confirmed, as there was considerable decomposition to the skin in this area, and this defect could result purely from the effects of decay.

Finally, the West report on 'Pete Marsh' turns to the variable state of preservation of the body:

Remarkable was the state of preservation of the skin of the face, where the hair-bearing areas were well preserved with no evidence of previous skin slippage, which would undoubtedly have been present if putrefactive decomposition had occurred following burial.

Loss of some head hair could well result from the effects of pressure of the peat overlying the body, but the fact that the deceased lay face downwards would tend to protect the hair-bearing areas of the face.

Similarly, the presence of the ligature mark caused by the sinew could not be explained in terms of putrefactive decomposition. The ligature mark did not have the appearance one commonly sees when a necklet or necklace is pressed deeply into the skin of the neck by the swelling induced by putrefactive decomposition. If the neck had been distended by decomposition, then the beard area would show some sign of that process.

It is likely that the deceased was buried in the bog when the weather was cold, and that burial took place within a very few hours of death, before the processes of putrefaction had commenced. Subsequent to burial, the deceased's body would have had no exposure to warmth or air and this would inhibit the process of decomposition.

From a forensic point of view, the injuries on 'Pete Marsh' would be in keeping with the patterns commonly found in the bog bodies unearthed in north-west Europe.

They suggest that he was killed as part of some ritual
sacrifice, with a possible sequence of wounding being two
blows to the head followed by the garrotting and then the
incision of the neck – although this was possibly
performed before the garrotte was tightened sufficiently
to break the neck.

Armed with this precise account of the way in which 'Pete
Marsh' died, other scientists began to piece together a picture
of his lifestyle at the time of his death. Dozens of further tests
on cell structure, body tissues, pollen, parasites and related
matters yielded further clues.

The facts were incontrovertible, transforming the misshapen remains of the crouching corpse into the shadowy
figure of a young Iron Age Briton. Apart from an armband of
fox fur, he was naked when they killed him.

But it was the analysis of his stomach contents – the
remains of a burnt bannock or flat cake of unleavened bar-
ley – which most interested the archaeologists. They soon
established the thesis that his last supper and possibly ritual
murder pins down his death to a precise date – May Day –
celebrated by the Celts as the feast of Beltane.

'Pete Marsh', they believe, was a Druid prince called
Lovernios who was sacrificed to placate the gods after the disastrous spring of AD 60 in which the Celts had suffered the
loss of their most hallowed Druidic stronghold on Anglesey
and the crushing of Boudicca's rebellion.

Some years after his unusual postmortem examination, Dr
West was invited back to the museum where he had examined
'Pete Marsh'. He recalls: 'They had found more parts from
other bog bodies including, we think, part of "Pete Marsh"
which wasn't found originally because it was damaged by the
peat-digging machinery. But there was certainly skin and

bone from other bog bodies which were not part of the original body – quite interesting – so one presumes that there are other bodies in that area preserved in the peat. There was nothing on the remains of the other bodies, which were badly mutilated, to suggest how they could have died.'

The body in Chichester harbour

'Pete Marsh' was not the only victim of violence in a bygone era whose mysterious death was investigated by Iain West. Some years earlier, in the late 1970s, a surgeon walking his dog along the beach in the estuary of Chichester harbour in Sussex made an interesting discovery.

He spotted something glistening in the mud, and when he looked closer he noticed that it was a skull vault. With his medical knowledge, he decided it was the skull of a young woman, and he got the impression that it was a recent death.

Police went along and excavated the remains, which were at a very shallow level. They were down no more than eighteen inches at the deepest, and almost a complete skeleton apart from some of the minor bones. There were no traces of soft tissue. It was covered in a thick, rather dank, mud. This is known to be a good preservative of skeletal remains

Dr West said: 'Some of the skull features were almost feminine – one of those skulls which is a little ambivalent – which is not uncommon. In a small proportion of skulls it may be difficult to determine the sex absolutely accurately, and this was a rather more delicate skull than normal. But when I looked from the lower jaw downwards, there was no doubt that the skeleton was that of a short, strong, muscularly-built male. The pelvic characteristics were undoubtedly those of a male.

'One of the first things I had to determine was the age and, interestingly, there was a shoe on the left foot which was clearly not of modern design – just a simple leather shoe with a built-up sole. Not only that, but when I looked in the mouth I found that the teeth displayed the character-istics of eating stoneground flour – the molars and premolars were worn flat – which dates the body as proba-bly coming from some time in the last century. Bones can exist for hundreds of years, of course, but it is likely that it was a body from the last century or the very early part of this century.

'The other significant feature of the examination was the discovery of a skull fracture. And it didn't look to me as though it was simply a separation of the skull caused by attri-tion from the sea or attrition caused by the passage of time. It looked as though there had been a direct impact by a small object against the temple, which had driven a piece of bone inwards, causing a depressed fracture.

'So, are we dealing with a seaman who's been accidentally hit by a swinging sail-boom and fallen over the side, or are we dealing with somebody who's been deliberately hit over the head and thrown overboard?

'I drilled into the skull. Normally when you do this, if it's an old bone, you get nothing back in the way of moisture – the marrow is dry and it smokes a little. But in this case when I took a section out of the skull, it looked red as though there was marrow in the interior. But the red coloration hadn't come from bone marrow – there was none present – but from algae. The matrix of the bone was filled with algae which had left a misleading red colour.

'Possibly a homicide; but if it was, it is way beyond living memory. I made my report to Sussex police, and the file was closed.'

The Abingdon skull

One Mayday in the spring of 1986 a man digging in the garden of a house he had recently bought in Abingdon, Oxfordshire, was horrified to come across a human skull. There was hair and flesh attached and it looked as though the person had not been dead for long. When detectives from the Thames Valley police force were called in, they, not unnaturally, concluded that they were dealing with a murder inquiry.

But when Iain West examined the find at the Abingdon mortuary later that day, he made two startling discoveries: the skull came from the last century and the lower jawbone came from another body. The clues were in the teeth, and, having had the skull X-rayed at Guy's Hospital, he took it to Bernie Simms, the leading forensic odontologist at the London Hospital Medical College, for confirmation of what he had found in the dentition.

'It was covered in mud and didn't look that old,' said Dr West, 'but when we cleaned the mud away from the mouth, it was fairly obvious that it was not recent because the molar teeth were ground flat. So it belonged to an individual who'd been used to eating bread made with stoneground flour. The grit had flattened the teeth, and this obviously put it back many years.

'There was the vault of the skull, base of the skull and facial structures, together with the mandible and a number of cervical vertebrae. Part of the right zygoma was missing. There was considerable scalp soft tissue remaining . . . and two plaits were adherent to the skull, partly secured by a tortoiseshell comb. The right-hand plait was detached. The left plait was intact and adherent to the head. The hair was light-coloured on washing.

'Subsequent examination of the hair at Guy's Hospital

revealed a considerable mixture of lightly pigmented hair with some darker hair, with no central pigmentation in a considerable number of the hairs.'

There were sutures in the scalp, but these did not help Dr West to determine the age of the deceased person. But the upper jaw, in which there was a total absence of teeth, was an important clue. 'There were no teeth present in the upper jaw, and the margins of the jaw had resorbed, leaving a relatively sharp profile to the maxillary margin – indicating that the teeth had been removed a considerable number of years prior to death,' he wrote.

'In the mandible there were a number of teeth present, the molars and premolars showing flattening of the crown, consistent with prolonged grinding during mastication.' And he added, significantly: 'I am not satisfied that the mandible is from the same body as the remainder of the skull, as one cannot get good articulation between the mandibles and the joints on the base of the skull, and the fit between the upper and lower jaw does not appear anatomically correct.'

In his conclusions, Dr West declared that the skull was that of an older woman. Microscopical examination of the hair indicated that she would have been grey-haired. 'The state of the lower dentition would be consistent with a person who has been eating stoneground flour and is in keeping with some skulls that one sees from persons interred in the last century,' he stated.

There were no injuries or indications of murder or violent death, so where had the skull come from and how long had it been there?

Again, Dr West was able to give the police vital clues. 'The skull was in an excellent state of preservation, as were the scalp soft tissues, indicating interment in wet conditions. It is impossible to age the duration of interment with any accuracy from a visual examination of the scalp; but radiological examination does reveal demineralisation consistent with prolonged interment and is entirely consistent with interment during the latter part of the last century.'

So now the police knew that they were dealing with the body of an elderly woman who had lived, died and been buried during Victorian times. But what was she doing in an Oxfordshire garden? The body was too well preserved to have lain there for long. Iain West's report provides the final clue: 'The remains would be consistent with those removed from a burial vault, but it is likely that parts of two heads have been removed.' So could the bizarre find be the work of body-snatchers?

While the pathologist was undertaking his scientific assessment, the detectives were hard at work. All they had to go on was the plastic bag in which the head had been wrapped. It bore the logo of an Oxford shop, so not much help. They set about tracing the previous owners of the house where the skull had been found.

They quickly traced a Mr and Mrs Frank Senogles living with their daughter in retirement in a picturesque West Country village. Under questioning, the couple readily admitted burying the skull in the back garden of their Abingdon home before they moved away from the area some six years previously.

They had found it in a plastic bag hidden on top of a cupboard in the bedroom of their son David, who had left home and with whom they had fallen out. Not knowing how to dispose of the gruesome object, they had simply buried it hoping it would never be discovered.

When the police began to look for David Senogles, he could not be found anywhere. Eventually they traced him to a flat in Bayswater, west London, but they were in for a shock. He was no longer a man.

Vivienne Rebecca West was a blonde nightclub hostess. David Senogles had undergone a sex-change operation and taken her new name from the *Gone with the Wind* star, Vivien Leigh. The story she had to tell was weird in the extreme, but she co-operated with the police, making full statements and giving the whole bizarre story in evidence at a subsequent court hearing.

Years earlier she had become fascinated by the occult and had joined a Satanist cult. In her desperation to become a woman, she had become convinced that going through a series of rituals using the skull of a woman would magically effect the transformation. So she broke into a century-old family crypt at Abney Park cemetery, Stoke Newington in north London, in the dead of night and attacked the grave of Mary Wood-Wilson, ripping the skull from the body with her bare hands.

In a lengthy statement to the police, the twenty-six-year-old said: 'I wanted to live out a horror movie to scare myself and prove I could do it. Before my operation, I used the skull in magic rituals at an old vicarage which I thought would make me a woman – but they had no effect.'

When Iain West insisted that, in his opinion, the lower jaw came from another body, the police went back to Vivienne West and challenged her on the details of her theft. She maintained that the head was complete and denied that she had taken parts of any other bodies. 'It was complete, it had skin on and everything,' she said. 'It was like a mummy. It was dry. It had blue mould on it. It gave me the impression that it had been dry in the coffin. But since the coffin had been opened, mould had begun to form on it.'

According to her version, she had slipped into the crypt through a hole and had found the lid of one coffin pulled down so that the upper half of a body dressed in a white shroud could be seen. She thought the hair had been reddish or blonde. 'It gave me the impression of being quite young, because of the hair,' she said. 'But I was surprised to discover when I looked on the tombstone to see that she was quite old.'

The mystery of the inconsistent lower jaw remained, however. Iain West was sure that it came from another body, and made a statement to the court in which he said: 'There were two major features of dissimilarity between the mandible or lower jaw and the remainder of the skull. The maxillar or upper jaw had no teeth present, and the bony margins of the gum were well healed and partially resorbed. There were, however, a considerable number of teeth present in the lower jaw which showed evidence of prolonged grinding of the biting surfaces during mastication. It is unlikely that that appearance would develop in the absence of teeth in the upper jaw. There was also poor fit between the upper and lower jaws at their points of articulation.'

In February 1987 Vivienne West was given a six-month suspended jail sentence at Snaresbrook Crown Court.

To this day nobody knows if Dr West was right in his assertion that the Abingdon skull came from two separate bodies.

CHAPTER 7

MURDER – DOMESTIC

The majority of murderers are known to their victims and most of them are members of the same family. The killings are very often spontaneous crimes of passion, but occasionally an ingenious premeditated plan will be employed and a cunning alibi will be prepared to aid the murderer's escape from justice. In such situations the police must frequently rely on the scantiest of clues, and it is often the body of the victim which will yield the most revealing information. But only the most skilled pathologists like Iain West are able to spot the tell-tale signs.

Dr John Baksh

Madhu Baksh owes her life to a bizarre combination of circumstances – a freezing cold night and a naturalist's passion for toads.

It was during one of the coldest nights on record on 4 January 1986 that Dr Keith Corbett set out for Keston Ponds, a well-known beauty spot on Hayes Common in suburban Kent to the south-east of London. His expedition took place in the early hours of the morning, when the absence of people would give him the best chance of finding the rare species of toad which was his speciality. But as he hunted through the undergrowth with a torch, the startled biologist made a discovery altogether more gruesome than he had been expecting. Following the gentle sound of wheezing and hissing in the bushes, he stumbled across what he thought was a woman's body with her throat slashed from ear to ear. When he checked her pulse, he discovered that, miraculously, she was still just alive. Another thirty minutes and she would have bled to death, but the freezing temperature had congealed her blood and slowed the flow.

The victim, Dr Madhu Baksh, was in general practice locally in partnership with her husband, Dr John Baksh. Through the night, surgeons battled to save her life, making the best job they could of repairing her gaping wound.

Her husband had reported her missing hours earlier, saying she had been hustled away by two strange men during a shopping trip to Bromley. When he heard of his wife's discovery and her desperate condition, he rushed to her bedside. Three times he kissed her on the forehead, and each time she winced. To the policemen and nurses watching, it looked like an emotional reunion.

Madhu tried to speak, but her vocal cords had been severed and the words would not form. Tenderly John leaned forward. Putting his fingers to his lips he whispered, 'Shhh . . . you can't speak. Your throat.' Then, muttering something in Hindi that the others in the room could not understand, he kissed his wife and left.

Madhu let out a sigh of relief. Turning to a policewoman, she pointed to a blackboard that had been brought into the ward so that she could communicate with detectives investigating the case. Painfully she began to write: 'My husband is a killer. Tell the judge he killed his first wife.'

It was an astonishing statement, which began an extraordinary investigation. As Madhu Baksh slowly began to recover, detectives were able to piece together the story of her near-fatal attraction to the Svengali figure of her husband. The couple had met almost four years earlier when Madhu Kumar joined the family practice in Bromley as a junior partner. Stuck in a lacklustre twenty-year marriage, John Baksh's sexual chemistry was immediately stimulated by the inaccessibility of the slim and pretty doctor who was ten years his junior. He began a relentless pursuit of her, but Madhu, brought up in a strict God-fearing Hindu family, would not respond. She had been divorced after an arranged marriage and told the amorous doctor, with whom she was slowly falling in love, that he must divorce his wife Ruby before she would consent to his sexual advances.

Within months Ruby was dead – struck down, at a remarkably young age, by a heart attack while on a New Year holiday in Spain with her husband and children. Back in England, a £90,000 life insurance payout on his wife's death eased the pain of bereavement for Dr Baksh and helped to wipe out his debts.

Taking advantage of the emotion of the moment, he arranged a Hindu marriage with Madhu and took her to Paris for a romantic weekend. On their last morning in the French capital as they lay in bed together, he was suddenly overwhelmed with remorse.

Leaning across to his new bride with tears streaming down his cheeks, he confessed, 'I sacrificed Ruby for you. I did it for you. That's why she died.' And slowly, to the horrified sobs of his young lover, he outlined the story of his first wife's murder.

How he had taken her a cup of hot milk laced with sleeping tablets and, when she was asleep, injected her with a massive dose of morphine which induced a heart attack from which she died in her sleep. The next morning he sent for an elderly Spanish doctor he had befriended, who was easily convinced that Ruby had simply suffered a fatal heart attack. Within a week, after a hastily arranged Spanish funeral, Mrs Baksh was buried in a graveyard not far from the family villa, Casa Ruby, and Baksh was back in England free to claim Madhu.

Confident in her love for him, Dr Baksh was now sure that Madhu would keep his dreadful secret, and for three years she did. But the pressure was getting to her and one day, during a furious row, she foolishly threatened to tell the police. It was a move which nearly sealed her fate. For Baksh, grappling with serious debts, had taken out a £250,000 life insurance policy on his wife, and was now convinced that she was on the verge of giving him away.

On the night of 4 January 1986 he cracked open a bottle of champagne and gave his wife a glass laced, once again, with sleeping tablets. As she slept, he injected her with morphine but decided not to make it a fatal dose. Putting her limp body in the family car, he drove to Keston Ponds where he expertly used a six-inch kitchen knife. Pushing the blade just beneath his wife's right ear and through the underside of her chin, he left a wound which he thought would cause her to die slowly enough to give him time to get home and establish a suitable alibi.

Instead, Madhu survived and was telling her story to the police. But it was her word against his, so the detectives turned to Iain West to help them prove their case.

With two of the south London officers assigned to the inquiry, West flew to Almeria in southern Spain and an unexpectedly inhospitable welcome. 'It was pouring with torrential rain, so I asked how often it rained in Almeria,' he said with a rueful grin. 'They said: "Twice a year, and this is one of them."'

The following day the Scotland Yard party took the long drive through the mountains to the provincial capital of Turre. The Baksh holiday home had been at the picturesque Moorish village of Mojacar nearby – a place much loved by British tourists.

It was early June, the start of the holiday season, and exactly six months since the attempted murder of Madhu. Despite the fact that the proper paperwork had been provided, the Spanish authorities took some persuading before they would agree to an exhumation. But, late on a Friday afternoon with more stormclouds gathering and the local officials anxious to get away for the weekend, a bizarre party assembled at the hillside cemetery.

The two British policemen, a detective superintendent and his sergeant, accompanied Dr West while a local doctor, who was to act as the pathologist, and Judge Antonio Ferrer, who had authorised the exhumation, looked on. The judge's secretary was also present, along with a gaggle of inquisitive Spanish policemen.

The men from London soon discovered that they had arrived not a moment too soon. 'In Spain they bury above ground in concrete mausoleums and people rent out the space for a particular period,' explained Dr West. 'John Baksh had rented the space for only about three years, so if we hadn't done the job when we did, the remains would have been moved, within weeks, to a communal grave and the exhumation would have been impossible.'

The body was in the top vault of a three-tier concrete mausoleum with the name of Ruby Baksh engraved on the end stone. A stonemason swiftly broke it open to reveal a black-painted chipboard coffin which was beginning to disintegrate.

Gingerly a team of workmen moved the coffin to a small stone-built mortuary on the outer edge of the cemetery. There was no glass in the windows through which those local officials who could not cram themselves inside gazed intently, murmuring advice in Spanish, accompanied by a cacophony of excited chatter from a large crowd of local people who had gathered out of curiosity in the grounds of the graveyard. There was no identification plate on the coffin, but the local undertaker was called and confirmed that it was the coffin he had supplied for the burial of Mrs Baksh three years earlier. Iain West had brought her dental records with him from England and was soon able to make a positive identification by matching these with the teeth in the skeleton.

Her funeral and burial had clearly been hurried and devoid of ceremony. She was oddly dressed in a woollen nightdress over which she wore a maroon blouse, a red and blue check skirt and green and beige shoes. Fortunately for Dr West, the body had been wrapped in a transparent plastic sheet, which had gone some way towards preserving the remains. But, nonetheless, it was going to test all his skills to determine a cause of death and prove murder from a body in such an advanced state of decomposition. 'We opened the coffin, and I had every expectation that we would be left with bone,' he said. 'I feared that the samples we needed so badly for toxicological examination would not be there and we would have to rely on bone. In fact the plastic covering had retained a lot of the moisture in the body – it hadn't evaporated – and although the upper part of her body which was slightly elevated was partially skeletonised, we were able to find many of the internal thoracic and abdominal organs.' Her straight black head hair remained but some of the organs were mummified. All the skin had disintegrated and much of the soft tissue had been reduced to adipocere, a long-lasting fatty tissue.

As a professional pathologist, Iain West was determined to carry out a full and thorough postmortem, but he began with two things uppermost in his mind – Baksh claimed his wife had died of a heart attack and Madhu said she had been killed by a morphine overdose. If Ruby had been murdered, it was important for Dr West to determine how. He could not simply accept Madhu's version. After all Baksh might not have given her the whole story or she might have been lying to get him into trouble.

In the gloom of the poorly-equipped mortuary, the Spanish pathologist worked quickly through the body from head to toe, observed by Iain West. The brain, which might have yielded vital clues, had long since rotted away but the skull, ribs, long bones and pelvis were undamaged. She had not been the victim of any kind of violent beating, at least not of the kind violent enough to have fractured any bones. The hyoid bone, hyoid processes and laryngeal skeleton were intact. She had not been strangled.

'Within the chest cavity I could identify both lungs and the heart,' Dr West wrote later in his official report. 'I was able to identify the liver, part of the intestine, some faecal masses, the diaphragm, remains of the kidney and the vagina. The tongue, oesophagus and upper trachea could not be recognised. The stomach, spleen and bladder also could not be recognised. A hysterectomy had been performed on the deceased.'

Here was further identification, if any were now needed, for Dr West, who also had with him nineteen pages of Ruby Baksh's medical records going back to the early 1970s – records which showed that, despite the hysterectomy and other minor surgical problems, she had been considered fit enough for her husband to take out an insurance policy on her life just two years before her death. The heart and the lungs were partially mummified and had shrunk, but everything was intact and capable of revealing whether or not she had died from a heart attack.

'Death had initially been ascribed to coronary thrombosis,' recalls Dr West. 'And at this stage the Spanish doctor shrugged and said: "There you are, there are the organs, we can't find anything." So I asked the judge if he minded if I had a look, and he didn't, so I took over.

'The coronary arteries were identified and opened and I found no evidence of significant atheroma and no evidence of thrombosis or stenosis. The pulmonary arteries showed no evidence of pulmonary embolism. The air passages and the lungs appeared dry. There was no sign in the peritoneal cavity of any inflammation.

'Then we were faced with the lower limbs, which were partially converted to a substance known as adipocere – produced when the body fats undergo a change in the presence of moisture and certain types of bacteria. Adipocere can be very protective because it takes quite a long time to form, but once it has formed it may remain for hundreds of years. It has more resemblance to wax than to normal body fat. I remember incising into the leg and finding pink muscle tissue protected by the adipocere. So I took samples from both legs.'

The sight of pink tissue was encouraging, because it meant that the muscle was not completely degraded and had been preserved from the effects of decomposition. 'It was a little surprising, but I've seen it many times before and since,' said Dr West. 'I recently did an exhumation for the purposes of paternity testing, for example. He had been dead for more than three years and there was pink muscle tissue visible, despite there having been an initial postmortem examination when you would expect decomposition to have been more rapid and extensive.'

As he worked, Dr West was expertly removing samples of tissue, bones and hair and adding samples from the coffin, shrouds and clothing. He was also about to enter the world of international diplomacy.

Over his shoulder he could hear a heated discussion going on between the British detective superintendent, Dave Stockford, and the judge. The Spanish were insisting that they keep all the samples. Permission had been granted only for the body to be exhumed and examined, they said; nothing was to leave Spain. But, mindful of the scientific methods sometimes adopted in Spain, Iain West was determined to take his own samples back to England. Eventually the judge relented and agreed that samples could be shared between the local authorities and the British contingent.

When it came to the share-out Dr West had an advantage over his Spanish counterpart, for what the local doctor did not know was that Madhu Baksh had been injected with morphine in her right thigh. Using his knowledge of the criminal mind and banking on the fact that John Baksh would always use the same *modus operandi*, Iain West took a gamble. Paying little attention to the samples the Spaniard was taking, he made sure that he took samples from the muscle tissue of the right thigh for himself. If morphine traces were to be found, it was these samples which were most likely to contain them.

With that little crisis overcome, the team stepped out into the eerie dusk of the now deserted cemetery and an unforgettable experience. 'The hills stood out against a black sky with a spectacular thunderstorm going on all around us,' said Iain West. 'The cemetery wall looked almost like the footlights in the foreground of a stage lit up by flashes of lightning. It was a scene infinitely more dramatic than anything Hammer Horror could ever have produced.'

Back in London, Dr West could turn his attention to the suggestion that the cause of death was a heart attack. He wrote:

> My preliminary conclusions are that, despite the duration of burial, I was able to recognise and examine a number of the body organs with the major exception of the brain. In particular I was able to examine the heart and major blood vessels and able to state categorically that there was no evidence of coronary artery disease or a pulmonary embolism. The heart valves appeared normal. The myocardium was too autolysed to comment upon. The heart did not appear to have been enlarged.

So it was all going to depend on the toxicological examination of the samples he had removed from Ruby's body. The tests were carried out by forensic scientists at Scotland Yard's Forensic Science Laboratory in Lambeth, south London, and six weeks later the results were known. There was morphine in four of the tissue samples, and in the dead woman's liver the level was 5.4 µg/g. Dr West wrote:

> The presence of morphine here is consistent with the administration of morphine or heroin to the deceased prior to her death. The level of morphine found in the liver is consistent with an overdose of morphine or heroin. Heroin breaks down to morphine within the body.
>
> The findings would be consistent with the administration of an intramuscular or intravenous

injection of morphine into the deceased. I give as a cause
of death: Opiate overdosage.

Interestingly, the samples also showed a combination of the
sleeping tablet Temazepam and morphine – exactly the same
as had been given to Madhu.

As the police murder squad began to build up a case
against John Baksh they again turned to the expertise of Iain
West, who was going to be a key prosecution witness. There
were strong suggestions that the defence were going to claim
that Ruby had committed suicide and that Madhu had
attempted also to take her own life.

'It is very unlikely that anybody other than a diabetic is
going to inject themselves with morphine into a muscle. They
would be much more likely to inject into a vein,' said West. 'A
doctor, and Ruby was a doctor herself, would almost certainly inject the drug into a vein in the elbow or hand – much
easier and more convenient than a vein in the lower limb.'

As for the injuries to Madhu's neck, he wrote in a sworn
statement: 'The photographs indicate irregularities on the
upper left-hand margin of the wound, which suggest at least
five movements of the knife were responsible for causing the
neck injury. The knife would have been used in a hacking or
sawing fashion. The cutting could be done from either side,
i.e. from Madhu Baksh's left to right if the knife was held in
the forehand or from right to left if held in the backhand. The
wound in the neck has none of the characteristics of a self-
inflicted or accidental incised wound. I have never seen an
injury, of this nature, on this part of the neck, except where it
has been caused deliberately by a third party.'

On 18 December 1986 at the Old Bailey, John Baksh was
found guilty of murdering his first wife and of the attempted
murder of his second. He was sentenced to twenty years and

fourteen years concurrently for the two offences respectively.

Madhu Baksh made a remarkable recovery, though her speech will remain impaired for life. She returned to live in the family home with her children and continued to practice from the Bromley surgery where she met her evil husband.

During his trial, new revelations about Dr Baksh began to emerge. Detectives questioned him about the deaths of two elderly partners – he benefited from both – and made extensive inquiries at nursing homes where patients in his care had died.

His own mother, Martha, died in a Bromley nursing home shortly after a visit from her son, who was footing the £250-a-month bill. Staff told police she had been in perfect health but was suddenly taken ill after his visit. She recovered, but two days later, after a second visit from the doctor, she died within hours of a heart attack. Dr Baksh ordered her to be cremated and no conclusive evidence remained. No criticism was ever made of him for his care of her and it was never suggested that he had been involved in her death.

The astounding postscript to John Baksh's story is his third marriage to a childhood sweetheart, the fifty-seven-year-old widow Tara Tewarson. She wed the wicked doctor in a prison ceremony attended by the son and daughter his first wife Ruby bore him. She moved into his Kent house with his son Sanjay, who always maintained respect for his father.

Andrew Alder

In the summer of 1981 the picturesque Sussex village of Oving near Chichester was rocked by a brutal double murder. A gardener making his weekly call at the secluded cottage of Oving Lodge found a broken lounge window and a pile of silverware on the floor. Unable to raise the owners, Gil and Ann Alder, he entered the house to find them both dead, apparently gunned down during the course of an aborted burglary attempt.

The Alders were a well-liked and much respected couple locally. Commander Alder had been a Fleet Air Arm pilot during World War II, later serving with Naval Intelligence in the Far East. Now retired in his fifties, he spent much time cruising on his 33-foot yacht. His wife was a pillar of the local parish church and a keen WRVS worker who took meals to the elderly. They had two children, Andrew, aged twenty-one, studying biology at Hatfield Polytechnic and nineteen-year-old Elizabeth, an English student at Durham University.

Iain West arrived at the cottage late on the Sunday evening and, with a police video crew following his every move and a large team of detectives in attendance, set off to survey the scene. The sight that met his eyes in the first-floor bedroom was gruesome in the extreme. But with his punctilious eye for detail, he recorded it faithfully in his report:

> The body of Ann Alder was lying in a double bed, with her trunk, limbs and part of her head covered by bedclothes. It was clear that part of her face and most of the top of her head had been blown open as the result of a gunshot wound.
>
> Pieces of brain, blood and pieces of dirt covered much of the pink velvet headboard above and behind her head, with numerous bloodstains and tissue stains on the wall to the right of the bed. Many were directed upwards with some downward-directed marks on the wall below the level of the mattress.

On the white ceiling above the body were bloodstains and pieces of adherent tissue resembling brain tissue. Blood and tissue stains were present on a bedside table and chair to the right of the body and on the articles which rested thereon. Part of a cerebral hemisphere lay on the carpet under the bedside table.

Turning to the death-bed itself, Dr West continued in his matter-of-fact style:

There was heavy bloodstaining on the pillow and sheets adjacent to the deceased's head. Fragments of brain and skull bone lay on the bedcover and a piece of skull bone lay on the carpet adjacent to the foot of the bed.

The bedclothing on the left-hand side of the bed had been partially rolled down and a piece of brain, spots of blood and tiny distorted fragments of grey metal lay on the bottom sheet in this area. A round piece of lead shot lay on the carpet by the right-hand side of the bed.

Gingerly the pathologist moved forward and peeled back, first the white bedcover, then a pink blanket, then a blue electric overblanket and finally the top sheet. The dead woman was lying on her back, turned slightly towards her left, with her knees slightly bent and her hands over her chest as if for protection.

The scene where her husband lay on the floor in a back bedroom was scarcely more attractive. He lay where he had fallen on his right side with his left arm outstretched and concealing his face. 'On lifting this arm, I could see a gaping, gutter-like, gunshot wound on the left side of his face and neck,' reported Dr West. 'There was a pool of blood under the head and fragments of bone and tooth lay near the body.'

The purpose of this visit to the scene of the crime was to help establish precisely what had happened and how. When a suspect was detained, the police would rely on the pathologist's evidence to check the killer's account of events and to match the murder weapon to the injuries.

To this end Dr West was at pains to describe the location where Commander Alder's body was found: 'The door to the room was fully open and traces of blood and tissue were present on the lower half of its surface. Traces of blood were also present on a cupboard door on the right-hand wall near the deceased's head. High on the left-hand wall of the room there were numerous blood and tissue stains, the majority just to the left of the window.'

Then comes an observation which could prove crucial later on. 'Stains on the pelmet above the window showed directional characteristics indicating that they had come from the direction of the door. Bloodstains were also present on the ceiling just to the left of the window.'

Two hours later, both bodies were in the mortuary of the local hospital and X-rays showed up dozens of lead shot pellets in them both.

Describing the external appearance of Mrs Alder, Dr West reported that she was wearing a hairnet and four blue plastic rollers in her hair. Such a mundane detail only serves to add greater poignancy to the awful bloodiness of the situation. With the skilled assistance of the mortuary assistant, the pathologist then carefully reconstructed Mrs Alder's forehead and scalp.

It was apparent that a single shotgun entry wound measuring about ¾ inch was present on the outer half of her right eyebrow. The margins of the wound were fissured, split and swollen and visibly contused over the outer part. I could see no smoke blackening, burning, or singeing of hair on the surface of the head or in the track of the wound.

He described in detail the destruction of the skull and brain, the recovery of shot and propellant residues, and the discovery of the plastic shotgun cartridge in the brain. There were no grip marks on the arms or defensive injuries on the hands and fore-arms. The report included the apparently irrelevant observation that 'the fingernails were lacquered but undamaged' – an indi-cation, however, that she had not scratched her attacker.

Turning to Commander Alder, Dr West observed that he was dressed in red and white patterned pyjamas with a hand-kerchief in the pocket and was wearing a Rolex watch – surely an oversight on the part of the murderer if he were indeed a professional thief. The first thing which struck him as odd was the fact that all the loose lead shot on the surface of the body appeared to be much smaller than those retrieved during the postmortem on Mrs Alder, an observation confirmed when he retrieved a shotgun wad from the neck that was of a dif-ferent design from that found in the dead woman. Dr West wrote:

There was a gaping, guttered shotgun wound on the left side of the face and neck. It extended from the left corner of the mouth to a point on the neck below and behind the left ear. The entry point of the wound lay at the left corner of the mouth, and by approximating the edges of the wound, the entry appears to have been oblique with the vertical diameter at the entry point of about ¾ inch to 1 inch. There was crushing and abrasion of the front end of the wound consistent with impact from a wing of an expanded plastic cartridge wad.

The bone of the upper and lower jaw on the left side was fragmented, the wound track had cut through and extensively lacerated the lining of the left side of the mouth and throat, the left side of the tongue and the muscles on the left side of the neck.

So what did all this scientific analysis tell him about the way in which the Alders died?

Of Commander Alder, Dr West concluded: 'The wound has been caused by the discharge of a shotgun which was being held about a yard or so away from his face. The appearances at the scene and at the postmortem suggest that he was shot by an assailant holding the gun near waist level with the deceased slightly bent forward and looking down at the weapon.'

On Mrs Alder, he added: 'The injury has been caused by the discharge of a shotgun while it was being held close to the right side of her head. The appearances at the scene are entirely consistent with her having been shot whilst lying in bed in the position in which she was found.'

Soon the investigating police had a stroke of luck which was eventually to lead them to the killer. As detectives made house-to-house inquiries in the village, a farm labourer told them of a white van parked in a deserted lane near the £100,000 murder house. The van had no connection with the deaths, but the tip led police to comb the ground nearby. They found freshly dug earth, and beneath it was the stock of a shotgun. The serial number of the weapon showed that it was part of a gun that had recently been reported stolen from a house in London Colney, Hertfordshire. The gun belonged to a student, Maxfield Follis, the best friend of the Alders' son Andrew, who lived nearby.

In the aftermath of the tragedy, Andrew and his sister were

being comforted at the home of the Olympic swimming gold medallist Duncan Goodhew, a close family friend. It was here that the police arrested him and soon discovered the horrifying truth.

Andrew had been convinced that he would fail exams he was due to sit the day after the murders and terrified of his father's displeasure when he did. Stealing his friend's shotgun, he sawed off the barrel and drove his motorcycle to the village, where he hid it in a hedgerow. He then broke a pane of glass and taped another to make it look like a professional burglary. Piling the silverware on the lounge floor to give the appearance of a burglar preparing to make off with his haul, he threw a vase at the family dog to wake his parents. When his pyjamaed father approached, calling his name, he blasted him once in the face. Then he ran to his parents' bedroom and shot his mother where she lay in bed. Returning to his motorcyle, he buried the gun in a nearby field before riding home and maintaining a pretence of shock and distress with family and friends until his discovery.

'I am so sorry. I am so sorry. I didn't want to kill them. I just didn't want to fail my exams, because Daddy was so cross the last time I failed. I never did anything right for him,' he said in a statement to police.

Details from that statement, given at his murder trial, described the way his parents had been shot – details which uncannily confirmed the conclusions Iain West had come to. Telling of the moment when he was discovered, Andrew said: 'Daddy must have heard me. I heard him yelling and coming down the stairs. I just froze in the dining-room. Daddy went into the drawing-room and that's when I ran upstairs into my room. He came upstairs. He came into the bedroom and put the light on. I was standing on the bed round the corner. I was shaking so much I nearly fell off. He saw me and called my name several times. I fired the gun and he fell down, and Mummy started to shout my name. I ran to her and she looked at me and buried her head. I shot her.'

Andrew Alder was jailed for life at Lewes Crown Court and excluded from the £219,000 inheritance it was thought he committed the murders to gain. His sister Elizabeth, who inherited the whole estate, later forgave him and began legal moves to share the money with her brother.

Iain West recalled:

It was one of those memorable cases. The mother shot in bed, the father shot on the landing and the whole place made to look as though there had been an aggravated burglary.

I remember coming back to the police station after the postmortem and hearing the police officers saying: 'This poor chap has just come down from Hertfordshire. His parents have been killed.'

It became apparent a few days later that he was the man responsible for setting up the killings with one of the most ridiculous motives I've ever come across – he did not want to sit an exam.

Barbara Gaul

Barbara Gaul was the fourth wife of the millionaire property developer John Gaul. Some twenty years younger than her husband, the raven-haired beauty, who had been a top fashion model before her marriage, fitted easily into the glamorous world of parties and high-profile charity events which became her life during the 1970s.

But nothing was ever straightforward for long in the life of

John Gaul. A silver-haired, compact man who dressed impeccably and spoke in the clipped tones of a post-war movie star, he made his fortune in the 1960s when he bought a string of rundown properties in Soho and rented rooms to prostitutes at inflated rents. In 1962 he was accused of living off the immoral earnings of prostitutes. He became the squire of Buchanan Park, a 264-acre estate in Sussex, where he entertained such international celebrities as Prince Rainier of Monaco.

Somehow John Gaul managed to flit between the demi-monde of callgirl London and the glitter of high society with ease. He surrounded himself with beautiful women, and, on the one hand seemed to revel in the sleaze and corruption associated with the world of vice, while on the other appeared to take a highly moralistic view about the behaviour of the women closest to him. But his opulent lifestyle was to change for ever one tragic night in 1976, the night that Barbara was shot.

As she stepped from her car in the car park of the Black Lion Hotel at Patcham, just north of Brighton, on 12 January, a man armed with a sawn-off shotgun ran up and blasted her in the chest at close range. Just to make sure, he gave her the second barrel full in the face. She was thirty-four.

Barbara Gaul died eleven weeks later, but not before she had whispered to detectives her belief that her husband was behind the shooting. It was an accusation which would lead to one of the most lurid and highly publicised manhunts in recent British criminal history.

The postmortem, at the Royal Sussex County Hospital in Brighton, was conducted by Hugh Johnson, then consultant pathologist and reader in forensic medicine at St Thomas's Hospital Medical School. Iain West was his deputy at the time, and assisted in the examination which was attended by a number of detectives and senior medical personnel.

The situation was unusual. The victim of the attack had survived for a considerable period and had undergone extensive surgery in a vain bid to save her life. It was now up to the pathologists not only to determine the cause of death but also to uncover sufficient evidence – if it was there – to convince a jury that she had been murdered.

Before they began, West and Johnson studied a series of X-rays which had been taken immediately after the shooting and in the weeks that followed. These showed large clusters of shot, particularly in the upper abdomen and around the left elbow joint. They began with this left arm and reported a 'superficially infected ununited compound fracture of the lower third of the left humerus with a healed surgical wound running down the outer side of the left upper arm from its middle over the outer side of the elbow to the upper end of the left forearm.' Professor Johnson went on: 'The whole of the middle of the arm was grossly deformed and infected with multiple adhesions to the bones around the elbow joint with healing fracture of the left radius below the joint.' There were portions of shot around the elbow joint. Three pieces were removed and handed to the police as exhibits.

When it came to the internal examination, more portions of shot were removed from the soft tissues of the left breast, chest and abdominal walls. These too were preserved as evidence. Much of the damage appeared to have been done in the chest, lung and heart region. Dr Johnson wrote:

There were multiple adhesions in the lower part of the left chest wall with scarring of the ribs and diaphragm and bony defects in the left seventh and eighth ribs.

The left side of the chest contained turbid orange fluid and the lower lobe of the left lung was partially collapsed. The whole of the left lung was covered with pleural exudate but there was no obvious consolidation of the lung itself. There was a little yellow fluid in the right side of the chest. The right lung appeared well expanded. The air passages contained frothy fluid. No sign of pulmonary embolism.

Mrs Gaul's heart appeared to be of normal size, but the pathologists found 'acute pericarditis with infected turbid fluid filling the pericardial sac under tension'.

But there was worse damage in the stomach area and to the internal organs. Johnson reported, 'A portion of the stomach had been removed surgically and the upper and lower parts of the stomach anastomosed together without leakage. Behind the stomach and beneath the left lobe of the liver was an enclosed abscess cavity with fat necrosis in the underlying pancreas, the tail of which had been removed surgically, together with the spleen. All the intestines were matted together, but there was no obstruction of the bowel and no generalised peritonitis.'

Dealing with the liver, he reported the removal of numerous portions of shot embedded in both lobes and the discovery of a piece of shot in the wall of the common bile duct. There was a laceration to the left kidney and a piece of shot was found in the left adrenal gland. Having removed the shot and portions of tissue for microscopic examination, it was time for the pathologists to come to their conclusions.

Professor Johnson was succinct and to the point:

Mrs Gaul appeared to have been a healthy woman prior

to the injuries which she received on the 12th January 1976. She died of the complications of a shotgun injury to the left upper abdomen and lower chest.

In addition, she had received a shotgun injury causing extensive damage to the left arm.

The original shotgun injury to the trunk appeared to have caused extensive destruction of the ribcage on the left side, the diaphragm, the stomach, the spleen and the tail of the pancreas, necessitating surgical removal of part of the stomach, the spleen and part of the pancreas.

All this surgery appeared to have been skilfully performed, but leakage of the stomach contents into the abdominal cavity following the original stomach injury led to the establishment of a chronic abscess cavity in the left upper quadrant of the abdomen beneath the liver, which persisted despite treatment and eventually led to the spread of infection to involve the liver and pericardial sac, causing her death.

And then, perhaps in a bid to prevent any clever defence lawyer attempting to blame her death on medical negligence, he added: 'All the surgery, both to the trunk and arm, and the associated treatment appeared to have been properly performed. It is surprising that she made an initial recovery, considering the extent and severity of her injuries.'

Dr West recalled: 'That was one of the first shooting homicides I'd seen. She had survived quite a long time in hospital, which makes the assessment obviously much more complicated.

'My most striking memory was the way in which shot had entered one of her blood vessels and was lying like a column along a vein in the chest and had cathodised within the chest.

'The other memory was how difficult it was to find shot. A month or two before, I had seen my first shotgun murder – again a man who had survived for about a week. You could see, on the X-ray, a mass of pellets, just as we could see pellets in Barbara Gaul. But it was so difficult to find them in reality because they become encased in inflamed tissue. I can't remember exactly how many we found, but it was certainly quite a number.'

So how did the killing of Mrs Gaul compare with other shotgun murders? 'Fairly typical,' said Dr West. 'If you are going to be shot at close range, the shot enters the body as a complete mass and then disperses quite widely. It is how it disperses that determines which organs are damaged and what complications there are. At very close range, the shot enters as a mass of solid lead but is expanding outwards, even at that stage. You effectively get a relatively small hole and the shot disperses as it enters, often causing quite severe damage to the organs. A handgun bullet, however, will be more destructive along the line that it travels.

'I remember a woman who was shot by her husband with a 4.10 shotgun at a range of about a yard. Just before he pulled the trigger, she managed to pull her knee up so that the mass of shots struck the surface of the knee and cut a furrow in the skin and underlying tissue on the inside of the knee. Because it had struck the skin, it spread and, instead of receiving a solid mass or column of shot through the front of the chest which would undoubtedly have killed her from that range, it spread a distance of about sixteen inches. Individual pellets penetrated the chest and she became seriously ill with a collapsed lung. But she survived.'

At the time of the shooting, Gaul and Barbara were living apart and divorce proceedings had started. Just hours before Sussex police issued a warrant for his arrest in connection with the murder, John Gaul fled the country taking with him twenty-one-year-old Angela Pilch, the family's nanny. The pair seemed to vanish from the face of the earth and, despite numerous apparent sightings and a massive worldwide police manhunt, it was more than two years before anything was heard of John Gaul.

In the meantime two east London brothers, Roy and Keith Edgeler, were jailed for life for the murder. They said they had been offered £5,000 for the contract by a man in a pub. On the day, they said, they had trailed the hapless Barbara Gaul for more than 300 miles until the opportunity arose to shoot her. The two brothers always refused to name the man in the pub.

In 1978 John Gaul suddenly surfaced in Malta. He had married Angela, they had a son, Xavier, and were living on board Gaul's £80,000 yacht *Lotus Eater* in Valletta harbour. For the next six years the British police tried unsuccessfully to have Gaul extradited to face murder charges in England, but his investments in Malta were considerable. Not only did he have a £40,000 hilltop villa, complete with swimming pool, at Madliena, five miles from Valletta, but he had built a 240-room holiday hotel which he leased to a local operator. In the end the Maltese managed to veto every extradition request.

The case against John Gaul collapsed dramatically in 1984 when the Crown's star witness, the businessman Rory Keegan, suddenly changed his evidence after eight years. Keegan, a childhood friend of Gaul's son Simon, had made a seven-page statement shortly after the murder, in which he claimed that Gaul broke down and confessed to him, when they met at a Rio hotel, that he had arranged the killing. For years Keegan lived in fear of reprisals if he repeated his allegations in court, and eventually he signed an affidavit changing his statement substantially.

Gaul immediately applied to be allowed back in to Britain without facing arrest so that he could be treated for a heart condition. The Director of Public Prosecutions ordered the arrest warrant to be withdrawn, and dropped the case on the grounds that witnesses could not be relied upon to remember accurately events that had happened eight years before.

John Gaul was free to return to Britain safe in the knowledge that a jury would never hear the incriminating evidence against him. No court would hear, for instance, that Gaul had tried to kill Barbara once before by throwing her off a yacht; that his second wife Anne warned Barbara he intended to harm her; that the Soho club-owner Vince Chercuti claimed he was offered £12,000 to do the shooting – by a man who looked like Gaul.

After that, Gaul lived a quiet life travelling between his homes in Switzerland and Malta. But even when he died five years later, there was a bizarre twist.

He was flying from Zurich to Malta when he had a heart attack. The plane diverted to Milan, where he was rushed to hospital in a critical state and died a few hours later. Nobody knew who he was and, despite attempts to contact next of kin, his body lay in the mortuary unclaimed. When he did not show up in Malta he was posted as a missing person, and it was more than three days before his family tracked him down. John Gaul was seventy-six, and had got away with murder.

The case of Barbara Gaul has other memories for Iain West. 'It was part of my apprenticeship.' he said. 'In those days one went out with a more senior man for two or three years. To begin with, on every case – murder was not that common then – you went on the murders and the unusual cases. Then, after a few months, I started doing murders and suspected murders by myself.

'It was an easy apprenticeship. I was not given anything difficult to do. Apart from the really straightforward cases, one would ring up for advice before giving the police advice. The only lottery came when Hugh was away. You never knew what you were going to pick up. In those days, if I had come across anything unduly complicated I would probably have passed it on to another pathologist. There were plenty on hand to give me assistance if need be from other hospitals.

'As time went on, I would go to Hugh's interesting cases to look and learn, and he would come to some of mine that were interesting. In those days, the number of cases was relatively small so one had a fairly easy introduction to the business.

'Things have changed now. There are a lot more cases. We tend to carry out techniques of dissection now which were not done then. There is much more intensive postmortem analysis than was the standard in those days. It has gradually developed from the late 1970s onwards. While people still serve apprenticeships, it is much more likely that they would have to do more at an earlier stage than ever I did.'

CHAPTER 8

MURDER

Murder excites the public imagination like no other crime and encourages the amateur sleuth in all of us. But for the detectives whose job it is to probe such killings the problems often begin with determining precisely who the victim is. When they finally face their suspect across an interview table they need to know as much about the way the murder was committed as he does. That is where the pathologist comes in, and Iain West has been involved in helping to solve some particularly high-profile murders

Vishal Mehrotra

Wednesday 29 July 1981 was a day of happiness and national celebration for millions of people. It was Royal Wedding Day, when crowds of flag-waving spectators thronged the streets of London to watch the heir to the throne, Prince Charles, marry Lady Diana Spencer at St Paul's Cathedral.

But for the police of south London it would also be remembered as the day that an eight-year-old Indian boy,

Vishal Mehrotra, disappeared. Like most other small boys that day, Vishal was enthralled by the spectacle of the pageantry – the horses, the soldiers, the bands, the bunting. He watched the procession from his father's office overlooking the route in Fleet Street. In the afternoon he went with his younger sister and their nanny on a shopping trip to buy sweets in the area of Putney where the family lived. Being tired after the exertions of the day, he asked his nanny if he could run on ahead when the party set off for home. Vishal was never seen again.

Despite a major police inquiry involving a reconstruction of his final walk, and massive international publicity, nothing more was heard of little Vishal Mehrotra for fully nine months. Then on the afternoon of Sunday 21 February 1982 two brothers, Basil and Roy Collins, made a disturbing discovery while out pigeon-shooting in Sussex. As they passed through Alder Copse, a wooded area of marshy ground near Rogate on the Sussex/Hampshire border, they stumbled across what looked like a human skull and a pile of bones. The skull was partially covered by leaves, but there was a sizeable tuft of black hair visible beneath it.

'I was fully aware of the Vishal Mehrotra case at the time,' recalled Iain West, 'because I had been doing another murder in the Tooting area when he went missing and the local detective superintendent, Mike Smith, was running both investigations. Mike and I talked about the missing boy case quite a few times. So when I got a call some months later from Sussex police to go down and look at some bones, I had an inkling of what it might be about. The detectives also had a fair idea when they looked at the skull and found that it was so small. The possibility of its being Vishal's body was well on the cards.'

★

On the Monday afternoon Dr West travelled to the copse at Rogate with a bevy of senior detectives in tow. He describes the scene in his report:

> The copse lay in the centre of a field encircled by a wire fence. The trees were bare of leaves and the ground within the copse was of variable consistency, being extremely marshy near to the place where the child's skeleton was found. The ground consisted largely of peat in this area and a stream ran through the copse a few yards away. At the base of a tree trunk I could see the skull, some ribs, several thoracic and cervical vertebrae and the bones of the left upper limb.

As the police looked on, Dr West himself began a search of the copse. It was winter, so the skull and other bones had been covered in fallen leaves and leaf mould and the immediate area was partially obscured by the broken branch of a tree. Nonetheless, a few yards away on some marshy ground, he spotted a tiny lower jaw which obviously came from the skull. On firmer ground some thirty-five feet away from the skull he came across a mat of very dark hair. By now darkness was closing in and there was nothing more to be done that day, so the bones and the hair were sealed in plastic bags, carefully labelled, and given to Dr West to take back to his laboratory at St Thomas's Hospital in London.

Now the police were determined to find the rest of the body, and a major search operation was mounted. Scores of policemen were drafted in from all over Sussex and, dressed in overalls and wellington boots, they began a fingertip search of the copse. The area immediately beneath where the body was found was dug to the depth at which the matted tree roots would have made it impossible for a body to have been buried, by either a human or an animal. The boggy nature of the ground was hampering the search, however, so over the ensuing fortnight the mud was shovelled into bins and carried across the adjacent field to a spot close to the road where a battery of empty bins fitted with sieves was installed. The mud was then tipped into the sieves and water washed through it until the slurry disappeared and only the vegetation remained for close scrutiny. The work was arduous and painfully slow, but gradually, as the dig moved outwards from the place where the skull had been found towards the points at which the lower jaw and the hair had been discovered, the officers were rewarded with fingernails, teeth and a few smaller bones. Eventually, after the excavation of nearby fox earths and several days of fruitless sieving – in which no more bones were found but 8,000 gallons of water were used – the search operation was called off and the real forensic work began.

In common with most parents facing such a traumatic experience, Vishal's anxious father, still hoping against hope that he would be found alive, had kept his son's bedroom exactly as the child had left it on the morning of Royal Wedding Day. Now, on a visit to the room, a skilled scenes of crime officer was able to find and remove several black hairs from the pillow. These were sent to the Home Office Forensic Science Laboratory at Aldermaston to be scientifically compared to the hair found in Alder Copse. These were the days before the technique of DNA genetic fingerprinting had been perfected, so the comparison involved lengthy microscopical examination and was never wholly conclusive.

At this stage there was still no convincing proof that the body was that of Vishal Mehrotra. So Dr West sought the assistance of the well-known forensic odontologist, Bernard Sims. 'The skull was obviously that of a young individual,' said Dr West, 'but too small, it seemed, for an eight-year-old.

The teeth were also too young for his age. They were first dentition and should have gone by then. But in fact, when we got his dental records, we found that he had kept his baby teeth.' The dental chart certainly proved that those teeth remaining in the jaw and skull, and the loose teeth which had been recovered from the bog, matched those of the missing boy.

It was the teeth which were to clinch the identification through a rather cunning piece of detection. Dr West said: 'The body matched all the parameters including the stature, age and so on, yet we still could not be one hundred per cent sure. But we had gone deep down into the peat to get the teeth out, and we got most of them, including all the front teeth. That was very fortunate, because we found that we had got a very distinctive overlap on the right front jaw – one tooth overlapping the other.

'When we looked at a family photograph, taken by relatives, of Vishal smiling, there was the overlap showing in the smile. So Bernard and I arranged to enlarge the photograph. Then we took a photograph of the skull in transparency form and enlarged that to precisely the same size. Then we overlaid the two, matching the various prominent landmarks on the head to make sure it was centred properly. The teeth superimposed perfectly – including the overlap – so we were then satisfied that it was him and nobody else.'

Dr West added, 'We never found the lower half of his body, only the upper half – the head, neck, chest, upper spine and upper limbs. There were signs of damage to the bones consistent with disturbance by animals, but I could find no signs of injury which could have occurred while he was still alive. We assume he had not been dismembered – there were certainly no indications of that. And I imagine that his body had simply been left on the surface, as there was no evidence of any attempt at burial. It had been intact, but the bones had probably been spread by a fox or wild mink. I've seen wild mink do some fairly destructive things to a body.'

With the identity of the skeleton established, the police turned their attention to finding the killer. Once again they launched a massive publicity drive to find witnesses and piece together the final hours of Vishal's young life. Detectives visited the winter quarters of a fair camped on land near the spot where the body was found. Members of that community had been running a fair in Putney on Royal Wedding Day. Videotaped appeals were made to racegoers at the Glorious Goodwood race meeting nearby, a meeting which had been on during the Royal Wedding celebrations the year before.

The nearest the murder squad ever came to finding a useful clue was a reported sighting, on the afternoon of Royal Wedding day, of a six-foot man dressed in army-style combat jacket and matching cap accompanied by a young Asian boy. The pair were seen strolling hand-in-hand along the South Downs at Beacon Hill not far from Rogate.

Detectives knew that Vishal had disappeared at 2 pm that day quite close to the A3 London to Portsmouth Road. The mystery couple were spotted at 3.30 pm, not half a mile from the A3. A motorist came forward to say that he had spotted a car parked at an odd angle as he drove past Alder Copse. He jotted down the number on a cigarette packet but later threw it away. Police even used a hypnotist to try and help him remember the number, but to no avail.

With thoughts of the Royal Wedding procession still in his mind, could little Vishal have been lured into the car of a paedophile killer dressed like a soldier, and driven the one-hour journey from Putney down the A3 to the Downs? No one has ever been able to answer that question.

There were insufficient remains for Iain West to determine a cause of death. No murder weapon was ever found, neither were Vishal's clothes. An inquest into his death returned an open verdict.

A year after the discovery of his skull, Vishal's remains were cremated, flown to India, and his ashes scattered on the sacred River Ganges in accordance with Hindu tradition.

The Babes in the Wood

The Sussex seaside town of Brighton was gripped by a terrible fear in the autumn of 1986. A sex killer was on the loose, and parents of small children were petrified that their little ones might fall victim to him.

It all began with a double killing that became known as the 'Babes in the Wood' murders. Two nine-year-old playmates, Nicola Fellows and Karen Hadaway, vanished on 9 October after leaving their homes on the Moulscomb council estate to go to their favourite fish and chip shop. It was early evening and darkness was falling as the pair were last seen near the entrance to Wild Park, a few hundred yards from their homes and a favourite play area for local children.

It was not until twenty-two hours later that they were found. Hundreds of friends and neighbours turned out to search for the missing schoolgirls and one of them, an unemployed teenager, Matthew Marchant, made the grim discovery. He spotted a piece of clothing protruding from behind bushes, and in a cave of dense undergrowth he found the bodies of the two little girls. They were lying with their arms around each other as if for protection. Their eyes were open in mute supplication. They had been strangled and sexually assaulted, although they were fully clothed.

It is a bizarre facet of murder investigations that frequently totally innocent people, for a variety of reasons, will suddenly feel a compulsion to come forward and claim to be the killer. Sometimes, too, a suspect under questioning will quite irrationally admit to the crime even though he or she is not the murderer. In these circumstances it is vitally important for the detectives to be able to sort fact from fiction in the accounts they are being told. And in any murder, of course, there are one or two features of the killing that only the real murderer will know. If the police are also aware of these secrets, it will make it much easier to eliminate the innocent and ultimately trap the true killer.

Obviously the expert may be the best person to highlight some of these clues, so most murder scenes are preserved intact until the pathologist has carried out an examination of the body *in situ* and has supervised the photography of the corpse and the area immediately surrounding it. Wounds later discovered during the postmortem may make much more sense when married up with the position of the body and will often help to give a more accurate picture of the actions of the killer and his victim in their final moments together.

In the case of the Babes in the Wood, Iain West's statement is, as ever, matter-of-fact and precise.

He arrived in Wild Park at 6.30 on the evening of Friday 10 October 1986, some three hours after the gruesome find. Describing the pathetic scene, he writes:

> Nicola Fellows was lying on her back at the opening to the clearing near to an elder tree. Her left arm lay by her side. Her right arm flexed across her chest. She appeared to be fully clothed. By her left hand lay articles of clothing, including a pair of pants.
>
> Karen Hadaway lay face down and at right angles to Nicola Fellows and towards the farthest end of the

clearing. Her right arm was extended over Nicola's body and her head rested on her own right arm and on Nicola's abdomen. The left arm was extended at right angles to her body. She was not wearing pants, but appeared to be otherwise fully clothed.

There were visible bruises around both necks.

Sadly, these were not the first child murder victims whose bodies Iain West had seen, nor were they to be the last. Despite his lengthy experience and ruthless professionalism, as a father himself he could not escape a twinge of emotion on seeing the two tiny bodies lying before him. He said: 'You never get used to that sort of thing. It is always a jolt to the system, but after that initial shock you put it to one side in your mind and just get on with assessing the case. You become rather detached from the human side of it because you've got to make sure that everything that should be done is done. You make a decision as to where you do it: whether you do it at the scene or whether to wait and do it in the mortuary. The constraints at the scene will usually dictate that.

'In this case I got to the scene in the early evening and obviously we were limited by the failing daylight. It was an awkward scene to get to and to remove the bodies from. Given different circumstances I might have decided to take all the fibre evidence and the swabs at the scene, but I decided that we were limited by available daylight and the majority of the tests – including taking the body temperature – would have to be taken at the mortuary.'

It was a decision which would later be criticised in court by defence lawyers building up an alibi and desperate to challenge the precise time of death – something often best determined by reference to the body temperature.

'The mortuary was just around the corner, so there was no

delay and it didn't make any difference whether I took the temperature there or at the scene,' said Dr West. 'As it happened, their bodies were at what we call environmental temperature and they had been dead long enough for there to have been substantial fluctuations in the ambient temperature.

'Environmental temperature is not as useful an indicator as some people think. It is fine for a body which has been discovered indoors, assuming that the temperature in the house remains constant, but for the outdoors scene, temperature measurements are notoriously unreliable because environmental conditions vary so much. The wind changes, and you may get rain. And a body will cool much more dramatically when it is wet or when there is a high wind. So it becomes a much more difficult scientific assessment. As it happened, they had been dead long enough for temperatures to reach environmental level.'

In this case, the difficulty of access to the scene of the murder dictated a change in the normal routine which the pathologist would go through. 'It is a principle that one looks at a scene to decide what is appropriate and then has a discussion with the police about the best action to take.' said Dr West. 'Usually one would carefully take what was on the surface of the body, anything that one could see, and then move carefully one body – in this case lying partially across the other body – on to a body-sheet and then have done the tapings, swabs and other sampling that one may need to do. I may even go to the extent of removing clothing to reduce the possibility of contamination or to reduce the possibility of losing evidence from the surface of the clothing, because the body will go into a plastic bag, and these bags often develop a static electric charge so that fibres may move from the surface of the clothing on to the surface of the body-sheet which may be heavily contaminated, for instance, with blood.'

There are a number of ways to take the body temperature at the scene of a murder.

'If you are going to use the back passage, for instance, you would have to take the swabs first,' said Dr West. 'Another method is to take the liver temperature, which is close to the core of the body. That is easily enough done if you've got a naked body and it is lying face up. If the body is clothed, as in this case, you have to look at the merits and demerits of removing the clothing at the scene, which is not necessarily an ideal place to examine the body, or carrying it out in the mortuary. I've done this at a number of other scenes – taken the clothes off, simply made an incision into the abdomen and measured the temperature in the liver. But when I first looked at these two, it was obvious that they had been dead for quite a number of hours, so I felt that it would be better to try and preserve any contact trace evidence than worry about taking a scene body temperature which might damage evidence.'

So, two hours after his arrival at the murder scene, Dr West began the postmortem at Brighton mortuary. He dealt with Karen's body first. Her clothing was heavily soiled with dirt and vegetation. There was a hair lying in the centre of her blue T-shirt. He lifted this and other samples from her arm, lower abdomen, thighs and buttocks with an adhesive tape so that they could be forensically examined in the laboratory. As he moved painstakingly over the child's body, the pathologist carefully noted every, mostly tiny, bruise, scratch and abrasion – fifty-eight in all. When dealing in clinical detail with the little girl's neck, the postmortem reads:

There was a band of bruising, grazing and intradermal haemorrhage on the front of the neck extending symmetrically . . . with oval grazes on either side of the

232

voicebox. Linear grazes and two linear intradermal bruises running obliquely down right to left below the voicebox . . . multiple small bruises on the right side of the front of the neck, a fingertip bruise below the left angle of the jaw . . . bruise on the left side of lower jaw . . . bruise under left side of chin . . . bruise under and on right side of chin with three fine scratches.

In other words, someone had strangled her with his bare hands.

The same process was gone through with Nicola and a very similar pattern discovered, except that her pants were worn inside out, as though they had been replaced hurriedly. There were two blue splash-marks on her leg – perhaps the result of a childish accident with a pen. Dr West reported:

There were two faint specks of what I took to be blood, three hairs and one piece of fibre around the genitals.

Nicola appeared to have been more brutally treated. There was a bruise on her right arm, showing that she had been tightly gripped there. Her cheek was bruised. There were bruises and grazes inside her mouth. Her tongue had been bitten and her genitals had been injured.

After taking swabs and other samples, Dr West wrote his conclusions. Of Karen's death, he said:

The appearances are consistent with manual compression of the neck causing obstruction of airway and blood supply to the brain. Loss of consciousness could have been rapid, but death would not be instantaneous.

Of Nicola he also wrote:

The appearances are entirely consistent with manual compression of the neck leading primarily to compression of the airway. Unconsciousness was caused by compression of the neck and generally would take longer to effect than in the case of Karen Hadaway. The bruising of the left cheek is consistent with a blow to the face such as from a punch.

One of the most active participants in the search for the little girls had been a close neighbour of theirs, twenty-one-year-old father-of-two, Russell Bishop. The unemployed man was one of the last people to see the pair alive, and he borrowed Nicola's anorak from her mother so that he could try to track the child with his dog Misty.

Bishop was well known locally as a Walter Mitty character, and very soon he was telling lurid stories about how he had found the girls' bodies and checked their pulses to see if they were still alive. It was a lie, but it hardened detectives' suspicions.

Three weeks after the killings, they questioned Bishop for fifty-one hours before releasing him.

Feelings were running high on the Moulscomb estate. The crime had shocked the nation, and rumours about Bishop's drug-taking and weird sexual practices soon began to circulate. He and his family were marked out for abuse and hatred. It wasn't long before the police returned to charge him with the murders. He was remanded in custody for his own protection. Throughout the interrogation, Bishop protested his innocence but changed his story several times about what he was doing at the time of the murders. He was unable to account for an hour at around the time the girls were murdered, and detectives could find no one who saw him at that time.

His defence lawyers set about trying to muddy the waters. Did the children actually die during the time when Bishop could not account for his movements? Were they killed elsewhere and dumped in the wood? Were they really sexually assaulted, and was there any scientific evidence linking their client to sexual activity with the girls?

Patiently Dr West did his best to deal with these queries. He could not give an accurate time of death since the bodies were found so much later, but his findings indicated that death had occurred some time on the Thursday evening. 'In my opinion, death had taken place within the small copse where they were found,' he wrote. 'I found nothing to suggest that they had been dragged there from another site.' The bodies might have been turned over or the limbs moved immediately after they were killed and before rigor mortis set in, but that was the only possibility of movement he could detect.

On the subject of sexual interference, he replied: 'I can only restate . . . in the case of Karen the graze on the vaginal opening is consistent with a roughened surface. It could have been caused by a fingernail.' In Nicola's case, an attempt had been made to insert a smooth, blunt object – a finger or a penis – into her anus. No semen had been found on any of the swabs Dr West took during the postmortem.

Almost a year later the case, by now sensational, came to trial at Lewes Crown Court.

During the month-long proceedings the prosecution relied heavily on forensic evidence, alleging that a blue sweatshirt discarded on a grass verge a mile from the murder scene belonged to Bishop. Fibres on the sweatshirt matched the fibres Dr West had lifted from the girls' clothing and paint-flakes on the shirt were identical to paint samples from a Cortina and a Mini that Bishop had resprayed. Turtle-wax residues embedded in the fibre could be married to a tin of wax kept at Bishop's home. But because both the wax and the paint were mass produced, the evidence was deemed to be inconclusive.

There was never any doubt that the shirt belonged to the killer. Both the sweatshirt and the girls' clothing were covered in minute hairs from a rare ivy plant that matched the leaves from the ivy-covered den where they were killed.

But the prosecution case was flawed. Bishop's common-law wife Jenny Johnson had originally told the police that the sweatshirt belonged to him. But, in evidence, she was allowed to get away with a denial and gave him an alibi for the night of the killings. Other witnesses who knew the sweatshirt belonged to him were not called to give evidence, and the court did not hear a damning scientific report commissioned by Bishop's own lawyer which said: 'There is extremely strong evidence that at some time the Pinto sweatshirt has been in contact with all these items: Hadaway's sweatshirt, T-shirt and skirt, Fellows' sweatshirt, Bishop's trousers. This logically proves . . . Bishop knows who owned or used the Pinto sweatshirt. Bishop's denial of ownership may conceivably be true. But his denial of knowledge of the garment is without doubt a complete lie.'

The jury took just two hours to acquit him, to the astonishment and fury of the dead children's families and friends.

It was a trial which still lives in Iain West's memory because of the heavy cross-examination he faced in the witness box – a cross-examination based, to his intense irritation, not on information from another pathologist but on the ideas of a junior forensic scientist who had no practical experience of homicide

'A number of things were put forward by the defence which I remember,' he said. 'First of all there was this assumption made by the defence team that the taking of a body temperature at the scene would have solved everything in terms of determining the time of death, which is absolute nonsense. Criticism was also levelled at me for not measuring the distance between individual bruises on the neck – almost relating them in a three-dimensional sense – so that one could map the hand that was responsible.' Rocking back in his chair and flexing his fingers in the air, he went on: 'If one looks at the adult, or for that matter the juvenile, hand it is a highly mobile structure, so measuring the distance between bruises is largely irrelevant. All bruises may not be produced by a single positioning of the hand; the hand may move away and be re-positioned and produce a further set of bruises. There are occasions when the arrangement of bruises around the neck may be of relevance and that's where the open hand has spanned the neck and it is clear that the hand must have been fully extended. I can remember cases where it is obvious that the hand has left a series of gouge scratch-marks at the back of the neck with a thumb mark opposing them. But we did not have that in the case of these children, so it wasn't relevant.'

Dr West was also quizzed about why the killer's fingerprints had not been lifted from his tiny victims' skin. 'We have tried over the last ten or eleven years, using ultraviolet light and lasers, to remove fingerprints from skin. So far, none of these experiments has been successful,' he said.

The end of the Babes in the Wood trial was not the last the world was to hear of Russell Bishop, however. Three years later a couple out walking on the Sussex Downs at Devil's Dyke near Brighton were startled by the sight of a small girl stumbling out of a bramble thicket.

The child, a seven-year-old, was in a dreadful state. Her

clothing was in shreds. Her back was covered in scratches. Her feet and legs had been pierced by thorns. Her eyes were surrounded by red specks of blood from broken blood vessels. There were the unmistakable marks of a man's hands around her neck. She had been sexually assaulted and strangled. But somehow, miraculously, she had survived.

As soon as she had been treated for her injuries and shock, the brave little girl told detectives how she had been snatched by a man as she roller-skated on the pavement near her Brighton home. She had been bundled into the boot of a car and threatened with death by her abductor if she screamed. She was driven to the Devil's Dyke area – four miles from Wild Park where the Babes in the Wood had been killed – and sexually assaulted before the man suffocated her and left her for dead. When she came to, she was alone.

Before the child had finished her story, the detectives already had a suspect in mind. The description she gave of her assailant matched Russell Bishop, but when she described the car, police could not believe their luck. It was the same make and colour as Bishop's. Forensic tests on the boot of Bishop's car soon confirmed that the terrified schoolgirl had been held inside it.

He was arrested, charged, and this time convicted. The judge at Lewes Crown Court gave him a life sentence to protect other children from his evil clutches.

'I gave advice on that case in terms of what was likely to have happened to her,' said Iain West. 'But the star witness was the child herself, who was extremely able. Her recollection was clear. She was quick thinking – noted what was in the boot, left marks in the boot. She was very lucky to be left alive.'

But that was not the end of the story as far as he was concerned. To his utter astonishment, late in 1993 he began to receive letters addressed to his office at Guy's Hospital from Whitemoor Prison in Cambridgeshire. Russell Bishop was suing the Chief Constable of Sussex for malicious prosecution, unlawful arrest and false imprisonment, claiming his reputation had been damaged over the Babes in the Wood case. He was calling Dr West to give evidence on his behalf.

Once again the issue of time of death was going to be the main plank of Bishop's extraordinary court action. In a typed letter from his prison cell, Bishop revealed his illiteracy and lack of learning when he wrote:

> Mr West it would be of a help to me and you if you could make a further statement in this matter with regards to the times of death of the two girls on the 9th October 1986, I no that you say in your statements that you can not give an accurate time of death, but you did give a time of at the trial in 1987, when it was pout to you that the two girls were seen by 7 witness on the 9th October 1986 two of them saying that they see the two girls eating chips at 6.30pm, Dr Peabody made an examination of the contents of the girls stomachs and noted the girls had been eating chips the night the girls went missing, theirfore we no that the girls were not kiled before 6.30pm on the 9th October 1986, it would save a lot of your time in court and the courts time if you could make a statement with regards to comeing to a time of death by looking at the time it takes for food to digest other death.

He added, considerately: 'If you could be of help I would be more than willing to pay for the statement as well as for your time in court and your costs. If I can be of any more help to you then please write back.'

On another occasion Bishop wrote: 'If you are worried

about being named in this court case or being named in any newspaper then please write to me here or give a note to an officer of the court as soon as you attend court.' Generously he added: 'Please have a note made of what the day at court has cost you so you can be refunded,' finishing off reassuringly: 'If you have any worries then please write to: Russell Bishop, HMP Whitemoor, Longhill Road, March, Cambs, PE15 0PR.'

In February 1994 Bishop's action against the Sussex Chief Constable was to be heard in the High Court with the convicted man presenting his own case from behind the bars of a heavily guarded dock. But with two weeks of court time set aside for the hearing, Bishop changed his mind at the end of the first day of the hearing as he was being subjected to tenacious cross-examination by Michael Gale QC. He dropped the action, leaving the ratepayers of Sussex with a bill for £75,000, charges the Sussex police had incurred in preparing their defence against the outrageous action.

Rachel McLean

Auburn-haired Rachel McLean set her heart on getting to Oxford and worked hard to leave her native Blackpool and gain a place at St Hilda's College.

When she got to the city of the dreaming spires, she threw herself into university life with abandon. She joined the Oxford Union, the Industrial Society and the university rock society, attending rock concerts regularly. Often dressed in black, her outfits reflected her passion for heavy metal groups such as Guns 'n' Roses. But she also enjoyed classical music, ate vegetarian food and became a keen environmentalist. A committed Christian, Rachel worked as a volunteer for the

Samaritans, fasted for Christian Aid and gained a Duke of Edinburgh bronze award.

By the time she reached her second year, the nineteen-year-old was sharing a student house in Cowley with four other girls but did not spend weekends there, for Rachel McLean was in love. During the previous summer holidays she had met a handsome New Zealander, John Tanner, who was working in a Blackpool nightclub. Tanner was three years older, and a student of classical civilisation at Nottingham University. The pair became inseparable, telephoning each other daily, writing constantly and spending every weekend in each other's company.

Tanner's love for Rachel was possessive and all-consuming. Rachel was a romantic who felt love with a passion, but was frightened of a lasting relationship and of growing up. During the Easter holidays in 1991 the couple spent the weekend together in Rachel's house. The other girls were away, and Rachel was glad of the peace and quiet to complete revision for her forthcoming summer exams. John arrived on the Saturday and returned to Nottingham on the Monday morning. When he got back he telephoned Rachel, as was his habit, but got no reply. He had written her a letter as he waited on Oxford station for his train. In it he said how worried he was about her being in the house on her own.

The letter arrived a few days later, but Rachel was not there to receive it. She had simply disappeared and was now the subject of a major missing persons inquiry. The police searched the house, where she was last seen, very thoroughly. Nothing was found, but the detectives did have one clue, given to them by Rachel's distraught boyfriend, to go on.

According to John Tanner, Rachel had accompanied him to Oxford station to see him off. While they were on the station, a young man whom Rachel appeared to know well came up and joined them. Rachel seemed so much at ease in this man's company that Tanner felt reassured that he would see his girlfriend home safely. Having kissed her goodbye, the last time John had seen Rachel she was going off happily with this young stranger, while he himself sat down to write her a letter.

The investigation into Rachel's disappearance was being led by Detective Superintendent John Bound, and this slightly bizarre account of the last sighting of her gave him an idea. By now he had interviewed all Rachel's friends and had read her diary. It was clear that Tanner's possessiveness and jealousy was becoming too much for her. He would interrogate her vigorously if she was not home when he telephoned, and always wanted to know where she had been and with whom. Yet here he was happily allowing her to go off with a man he did not know and writing to her about her good luck in meeting a man she knew to take her home. The whole thing did not ring true.

John Bound, however, decided to give Tanner the impression that he believed his story. 'By this stage I was not optimistic about Rachel being found alive, and I obviously had my suspicions about Tanner. It was not possible to progress with a case against Tanner, and had we simply arrested him he would have had a right to remain silent. We needed Tanner to help us, and we decided to go along with his story and not put any pressure on him.'

In front of television cameras and newspaper reporters the police staged a very public reconstruction of Tanner's version of the couple's final moments together. But instead of witnesses coming forward to identify the mystery man, two people came forward who had seen John Tanner – alone. One had been a passenger on the bus he caught to the station who described the long-haired student with the ripped jeans getting on alone. The other remembered seeing him alone in the station writing his letter.

Now the police renewed their search of Rachel's house and found her body under the floorboards. Eighteen days had passed since she went missing.

'I had been aware of the fact that Rachel was missing through press reports,' Iain West recalled, 'and I know I was not alone in believing that there was something fishy about the case. Then one afternoon a colleague and I were coming back from dealing with another case in Oxford. I was just on the city boundary heading for London when the mobile phone went to say that the body had been found in the house.'

At the scene, Iain West joined the police inquiry team. 'They had searched the house before, and when they searched it again it was only because a police officer got on his hands and knees in a cupboard under the stairs and peered into the crawl-space under the floorboards that he actually saw the body – concealed in a space a few inches high,' he said. 'You couldn't smell it although it had obviously been there for some time. She was partially mummified, but was well preserved because an airbrick nearby allowed a flow of dry air from the conservatory to pass through. Access to her body was initially gained through this cupboard leading from the kitchen. I could see part of one of her legs lying on the earthen subfloor.'

Most of Rachel's body was under the hall of the house, with her head and shoulders under her own bedroom. She had been clumsily covered with a carpet. 'On raising some of the floorboards, her head hair and part of her face could be seen and it was clear that she was lying on her left side in a foetal position,' Dr West reported. She was wearing a black T-shirt, black tights and turquoise pants. There was a piece of string across her left shoulder, an elasticated bangle on her right wrist and a gold stud in her right ear.

'Our biggest problem was getting access to where she had been lying,' he remembered. 'Obviously I didn't want to create any more disturbance than necessary and certainly not lose any potential evidence which might have been on the body surface. So we had to devise a means of cutting through the floorboards and joists so that we could extract her with the minimum of disturbance.' This operation took many hours, and it was after midnight before anyone could leave for home – a familiar experience for a busy pathologist. The postmortem was arranged for the next morning.

'I was part-way to Oxford when I got a call to say that we could not start the postmortem that morning, as arranged, because we could not get access to a mortuary,' he recalled. 'It was 2 o'clock in the afternoon before we could get started, which was very annoying, to say the least. It was a very important case and the delay in the investigation could have been very significant, given other circumstances.'

When it did get started, the postmortem took place at the John Radcliffe Hospital in Oxford. Dr West immediately noted a number of minor superficial injuries, most of which had been caused after Rachel's death when her killer was manoeuvring her lifeless body into position beneath the floorboards. The most obvious indication of how she had died was a dark brown mark running round the front and sides of her neck. She had been strangled with a ligature.

Dr West's experience told him a lot when he examined the ligature mark more closely. 'There was clear evidence of strangulation by an assailant applying a thin smooth ligature from behind and to the deceased's left. The appearances are consistent with strangulation effected while she was lying face downwards with her assailant crouching over her back.'

Other marks on Rachel's neck told the pathologist that an attempt had been made at manual strangulation. The discovery threw up the age-old question, so beloved of mystery writers, as to how much can be told about a strangler from the marks he leaves on his victim's neck. Can you tell if he is right- or left-handed, for instance? Dr West said: 'It is not possible in most of these cases to tell whether the person is right- or left-handed. The clues are simply in the way the pressure is applied, and that will depend on a number of factors – whether one or two hands are used, the orientation of the neck at the time, the relationship between the two bodies, whether they are facing or whether it is being carried out to the side or from behind. If you get clear finger and thumb marks in a single-grip pattern, you can usually say "right, left or two". But one is more often in the position where you can see marks left by one hand but you can't exclude the possibility of the other hand being employed. One may however be able, in some cases, to indicate the handedness of the assailant. But even that may be a problem because all you can say is that somebody is using one hand or the other. Most right-handers would use their right hand, but left-handers might use either, certainly if they are truly ambidextrous. For fine work, an individual will use his predominant hand. For more crude or violent usage of the hands, you may use the hand nearest to the victim. There is nothing to stop a right-hander from strangling with his left hand if, for instance, he is using his right hand to restrain his victim in a situation where he needs more force to restrain than he does to strangle. It may sound great in detective fiction, but it is not an area where things are as clear cut as they might appear to be.'

Rachel's shoulder-length auburn hair was to feature later in a minor mystery. During the postmortem, Iain West recovered a cluster of about thirty hairs clasped tightly in her right hand. They were sent away to the Forensic Science Laboratory at Aldermaston for analysis, and found to have been freshly plucked from the dead girl's own scalp. The police and lawyers were baffled as to what this could mean, and turned to Dr West for help.

He added a fresh statement: 'The number of hairs suggests that she may well have pulled hair from the surface of her scalp, the hair becoming adherent to, and being retained within, the hand. I have seen this occur in other cases where an individual is being strangled by a ligature. In an attempt to relieve the pressure of the ligature the victim may inadvertently catch a tuft of hair and pull it free with their hand, or hands, during desperate attempts to remove the ligature.'

With the postmortem complete, the police were ready to move. John Tanner was immediately arrested and the next night confessed to murdering his girlfriend. At his subsequent trial he told how his passion for Rachel had spoiled their relationship and caused him to live in a world of unreality. He had simply killed her in a rage when she refused his offer of an engagement. He was jailed for life.

The American and the rent boys

Death comes in many forms, and is sometimes not at all what it seems. Homicide, for instance, can be committed in a variety of ways which can occasionally be mistaken for something else. Even the most experienced practitioner – doctor, detective or even pathologist – may misinterpret the signs or miss vital clues and attribute a cause of death to suicide or natural causes when the victim has actually been murdered.

Iain West vividly recalls one such case when a hunch saved him from embarrassment, and the eventual discovery of an

246

otherwise easily overlooked detail helped the police to trap a killer.

He told the story in his own words.

A man had come over from San Francisco – a retired dentist – to borrow a friend's flat in London. He hadn't been seen for a few days and his body was found, lying naked, face down on top of the bed with his head over the edge, although we didn't get that detail until later on.

He was known to have a history of heart disease and he was brought into the mortuary for postmortem. Obviously no death certificate had been issued, and he was quite decomposed, certainly from the knees upwards.

At postmortem I found quite significant heart disease, certainly sufficient to kill someone. But I was a bit unhappy about the pattern of hypostasis [the way in which blood drains and settles in a body after death]. He had an awful lot of hypostasis in the upper body – the shoulders and the head – so I decided that although there was considerable heart disease, I was not going to give a cause of death at that stage.

I told the coroner's officer, and a couple of days later he called me early in the morning to ask for a second examination. In the meantime the owner of the flat had returned and discovered several thousand pounds-worth of silverware and other valuables missing. The apartment had been burgled and the CID were now involved.

I went through the postmortem again, and found nothing new until I turned the body over and opened up the back of the trunk – a practice which is commonplace now but was rare in those days unless there was strong indication of suspicious death. I didn't find anything to begin with, and then I looked between the layers of the lower chest muscles and found two bruises which extended over the surface of the ribs. Examining them closely, I could see that the shape of the bruises fitted the pattern of a pair of hands pressing on the lower ribs and the back of the chest.

By that stage we had discovered that he was homosexual, but I could see no injury in his anus because of the degree of decomposition. I just wondered aloud whether he might have died during the course of buggery, without any proof other than the hand-marks. It looked to me as though he had been face down, was being buggered, whilst someone was pressing their hands against the back of his chest and he had suffocated during the process.

A few days later a rather bright police constable picked up a couple of youths using some credit cards that turned out to have belonged to the dead man. When they were interviewed, they said he had picked them up and taken them back to the flat where they had suggested they give him the latest aphrodisiac – some Scotch and barbiturates – traces of which were found in his body.

One of them admitted to having sex with him. They were thieves, and their method had been to give their victims this 'aphrodisiac', which has a strong sedative, have anal intercourse until the victim fell asleep and then rob him. Only this chap did not just simply fall asleep. He died. His heart condition, plus the pressure on his back restricting his breathing, caused his fatal collapse.

CHAPTER 9

SERIAL KILLERS

There can be nothing more damaging to public morale than the chilling realisation that a serial killer is on the loose. When killing follows killing and the police seem powerless to stem the murderous tide, a feeling of mass panic is never far beneath the surface in the local community. But some serial killings may have one characteristic which makes them easier to detect – a common pattern linking all the deaths. If that pattern can be picked out early enough, the chances of trapping the murderer are enormously enhanced. Piecing together the linking clues left behind on the bodies is one of the abilities that many pathologists acquire. It is one of Dr West's greatest skills.

Michael Lupo

By day, Michael Lupo was a successful fashion consultant noted for his wit, charm and wide circle of friends among the rich and famous. But when night fell the handsome Italian, whose name means 'Wolf', became 'Rudi', a notorious homosexual prostitute boasting of 400 lovers, stalking gay clubs and selling sex for £100 a time.

Then, to his horror, Lupo discovered that he had Aids and embarked on an orgy of revenge against the twilight world where he had caught the disease. In a terrifying fifty-five-day crusade of killing, the thirty-four-year-old sado-masochist strangled three homosexuals he had picked up, and choked to death a tramp who asked him for a cigarette. Two other men Lupo lured away for sex escaped his clutches, and one became a human 'bait' to help police trap the so far unknown serial killer. When he was finally caught, Lupo was sentenced to life imprisonment four times over for the killings and a total of fourteen years for the two attempted murders.

The first hint that a perverted killer was at large came in April 1986 when the body of twenty-six-year-old Anthony Connelly was found on a railway embankment in Brixton, south London. He was a regular drinker at the Prince of Wales, a local bar frequented by gay men, but the homosexual community closed ranks, and detectives had little information to help their hunt for the killer.

Then, in an inspired move, the murder squad were advised to watch Al Pacino's hit movie *Cruising*, in which a perverted killer stalks his homosexual prey. From the film they picked up valuable tips about the secret codes used by the gay community.

A month later the breakthrough came when thirty-year-old David Cole, who had narrowly escaped being strangled by Lupo, agreed to help track down the killer. So it was to the Prince of Wales that Cole led the undercover detectives who watched as he lured Lupo into a trap.

Once detained, Lupo, a former choirboy, began to confess to his murders. But his confessions would have been useless in law unless backed up by independent evidence that the killings were committed by the same man and in a way the public did not yet know about.

In his confession, Lupo told detectives that his first victim had been thirty-six-year-old James Burns, whom he had picked up and strangled in a basement as they had sex. Connelly was the second. His next victim was a sixty-year-old tramp whose true identity was discovered only years later. The poor old man had merely asked him for a light as he shuffled across the Hungerford Bridge in central London. The following night twenty-one-year-old Mark Leyland narrowly escaped death when Lupo beat him about the head with an iron bar. The fourth and final victim was an Irishman, Damien McClusky, who was picked up in Kensington. Special Branch detectives believed he had links with the IRA. McClusky's body was found after Lupo had admitted to his killing.

As luck would have it, Iain West had been called to the scene of two of the murders – Burns and McClusky – and had carried out a postmortem examination on the vagrant. There had been no apparent connection between the death of Burns and the vagrant.

The postmortem on Connelly had been conducted by Dr Hugh Johnson of St Thomas's Hospital, who had been forced to tackle the job in two parts because the dead man was known to have consorted with an Aids carrier. In those days it was considered not safe to carry out an internal examination until tests proved that the body was not infected with the virus.

After Lupo had made his confession, the police called Dr West in to back up the killer's claims and show as much evidence as possible to prove that the same person was responsible for the murders. The task would not be easy, since some of the bodies had not been discovered immediately and were in early stages of decay. Borrowing the Connelly file from

Hugh Johnson and re-examining his own papers on the other three, Iain West set about looking for clues.

Scanning the scenes of crime photographs, he was soon able to recall the examination of James Burns' body lying in the semi-derelict basement of a house under renovation in Warwick Road in west London, exactly as Lupo had said. Reading his own report, Dr West remembered a particularly bizarre and unusual feature of this murder. 'The front of the trunk was smeared with blood and faeces from collarbone level to the groin, with the smearing extending on to the upper thighs. The smearing was characteristic of the patterning which might be made by hands.' The face had also been smeared with blood.

The first and most obvious common factor was that Burns' motorcyle leggings and underpants had been pulled down, leaving his genitalia exposed. Looking at his report on the murder of Damien McClusky, Dr West saw that he had noted at the time: 'The jeans had been pulled down to mid-thigh level and the fly was open. The crotch of the pants had been pulled down around the genitals to expose the penis and scrotum.' Similarly Dr Johnson had written of Anthony Connelly: 'The blue jeans, long johns and jockstrap were pulled down, exposing the lower abdomen, genitalia and the upper part of both legs.' He had gone on to report 'dirt soiling of the buttocks and backs of the arms'. This too began to show a link with the other killings. In the cases of Burns and McClusky, Dr West had noted soiling on the backs, indicating that both bodies had been dragged. 'That was one common factor', he said. 'All the victims were dragged. Burns' body had been moved, and McClusky had been dragged and hidden in a cubbyhole in the basement area of a disused house. He obviously hadn't been killed there. But dragging is not enough to be a signature because it is so common in crimes of that type.'

There were a number of mutilative wounds in each case, though Burns, perhaps because he was the first to be killed after Lupo learned that he had Aids, had suffered the most brutal treatment. His body was covered in bite-marks, his tongue had been bitten off and faeces had been stuffed into his mouth. 'There has been mutilation of the body and, in my opinion, the tongue has been bitten off by an assailant, not by the deceased,' Dr West wrote. 'There were no dentures or teeth in the deceased's upper jaw and therefore he would have been incapable of biting through his own tongue.'

Dr West said, 'It is not common to see mutilation of this kind, but I have seen it from time to time in cases of this type. However, it wasn't a linking feature signature in this series because he didn't inflict it on all of his victims.'

Surely the pathologist, who is after all a human being, must find such mutilation distasteful?

'Depending on the circumstances, violent killing can be distasteful,' said Iain West, 'but that is something which flits through your mind and out again; when you start working you have other thoughts to occupy yourself with. The people who might be most affected are those who are standing around with no function in the postmortem, and they may develop a somewhat voyeuristic attitude.'

McClusky also had a bite-mark on his tongue and, in common with Connolly and the vagrant, had died with his tongue clenched between his teeth. But, perhaps not surprisingly, the pathologists noted that all three homosexual victims showed no real sign of putting up a fight in self-defence, although Connolly showed 'superficial external injuries in keeping with a struggle'. They clearly had been willing and unsuspecting partners in the sexual activity which was to be the precursor to their deaths.

When it came to the method of killing, there was no doubt.

All four men had been strangled with a ligature. In at least two cases the killer had also used his bare hands. Perhaps significantly, the pattern of the neck injuries showed a distinct tendency towards the right side.

'Around the neck was a red Paisley-type scarf tightly wound round with one full turn and two half turns, the ends not tied,' Dr Johnson wrote of Connelly. 'Above this ligature there was cyanosis of the features with abundant petechial haemorrhages in the skin of the face and in the eyes' – the giveaway signs of a strangling.

He went on: 'After photography, I removed the scarf, revealing grooving of the neck beneath the ligature and indistinct linear abrasions.' He noted four further wounds on the right side of the neck.

In the case of McClusky, Dr West had written: 'There was a visible ligature mark seen on the front and sides of the neck . . . blue and red discoloration over the right sternomastoid muscle on the right side of the jaw . . . and apparent bruising over the right side of the chin. There was a bruise behind the right ear-lobe.'

Of Burns, he noted a 'well-defined ligature mark on the front and right side of the neck' and went on to point out a 'linear abrasion which extended from the right side of the larynx, horizontally around the right side and back of the neck to become less distinct behind the left ear'. This was a 'pressure abrasion', he wrote, noting other injuries to the right side of the neck. 'He had been strangled very violently and I think not very rapidly. It looked as though they were involved with sado-sexual games to start with.' His conclusion was that Burns had been killed by a 'violent compression of the neck, with a ligature mark partially encircling the neck. This mark could have been left by the use of clothing as a ligature – perhaps accentuated by pressure from a folded arm and forearm.'

That conclusion had a familiar ring to it when compared to the scarf ligature around the neck of Connelly. The killer had used not only a ligature. When examining McClusky's body, Iain West reported that the injuries were 'consistent with compression of the neck by a combination of manual pressure and a ligature. In this case he showed considerable skill in strangling with the hand. He got the pressure on the carotid artery at just the right points. He pushed the muscle that intervenes out of the way and pressed the fingers in underneath. It is certainly a technique I've heard of – going from behind and pushing fingers in to squeeze the artery from both sides. It is not a military technique, so I don't know where he might have learned it. The body was beginning to decompose, but you could still see three bruises on the surface of the carotid artery where the artery had been occluded on the left side.'

The combination of hand and ligature seemed also to have been the fate of the unfortunate down-and-out who met his death on Hungerford Bridge. In this case, Dr West wrote: 'Running across the voicebox 2 inches below the chin was a linear graze and bruise. It ran horizontally. Within this area and in the area formed by the reddening on the left side of the jaw were three small coalescing bruises and grazes. There was a small graze to the left of the pressure mark. From the right side of the neck there was a ligature mark which extended around the back of the neck to the left side.' In his conclusion, the pathologist gave the opinion that the appearance of the tramp's neck was 'consistent with death due to the use of a garrotte'.

In this case, too, the victim had been dragged. The marks of his heels could be clearly seen making parallel tracks for a short distance along the damp and dirty surface of Hungerford Bridge. 'Dragging the man on Hungerford Bridge simply kept him off balance so that he couldn't fight,' said Iain

West. 'The killer obviously just walked backwards, choking him until he felt the body go limp, held on a little longer and then just let him drop. The length of the trail shows just how rapidly somebody can die from this type of strangulation.'

So was this all just an invention of Lupo's fevered imagination or were the killings truly the work of a serial killer? 'There was a pattern which linked the four crimes without there being a clear signature in terms of this man leaving his mark on the bodies, as some serial killers may do,' said Dr West. 'To some extent the picture was confused by the vagrant who simply stopped, asked for a fag, and was killed. A truly opportunistic murder.'

But, despite this minor deviation, the pathological pattern and the links between the four crimes had been established. Dr West had given the police investigating team sufficient information so that they would know when Lupo was telling them something only the real killer could know – sufficient information to convince a court that they had the right man. Now all that was left was for the detectives to piece together a full picture of their prisoner's amazing lifestyle.

It soon became clear that Lupo had been living a double life – a man who mixed with some of the best-known names in the country but whose craving for perverted sex also took him into the heart of the rough trade. When they raided Lupo's £300,000 mews house in Chelsea, police discovered a set of coded diaries containing more than 700 names of society and showbusiness personalities. At least four names were so sensitive that Special Branch detectives were called in. The diaries also revealed that Lupo had links with the IRA and Libya's Colonel Gaddafi. The Fiat heir Prince Egon van Furstenberg, a cousin of Prince Rainier of Monaco, was included in the diaries, and the dress designer Bruce Oldfield, the royal photographer Norman Parkinson and the comedian Kenny Everett were all questioned by police.

At another flat in Earls Court, detectives found a torture chamber Lupo kept for sex sessions. But it was not until they came across an old notepad with the imprint of the name of a Harley Street Aids specialist that they discovered the real motivation behind his murder spree.

On 17 February 1995, almost nine years after his brief reign of terror, Michael Lupo died of an Aids-related illness in the hospital wing of the top-security Durham Prison. He was forty-two.

Colin Ireland

Peter Walker's naked body was found in Battersea, south London, on 10 March 1993. He was in his own flat, lying on the bed beneath a duvet. His hands had been tied with rope shortly before he died from asphyxiation. A former dancer, forty-five-year-old Mr Walker was director of choreography for the West End production of *City of Angels* and had many credits as a choreographer, including *Chess* and *The Pirates of Penzance*.

At first, police believed it was a brutal but isolated killing. Walker, who was gay and HIV-positive, was known to be promiscuous and interested in sado-masochistic practices. He had simply fallen victim to a moment of uncontrolled passion with a lover he had picked up in a gay bar, reasoned the detectives. His death made short-lived headlines.

Seven weeks later, on 30 May, a thirty-seven-year-old librarian, Christopher Dunn, was found dead at his home in Wealdstone, north-west London. He was wearing a harness and other sexual equipment and had been throttled with straps. He, too, was gay, and police believed the death was accidental.

Five days after the discovery of Mr Dunn, the body of a thirty-five-year-old American, not known to be gay, Perry Bradley III, was found in his Kensington, west London, flat. He was lying in bed and had been strangled. Five more days elapsed and in the East End of London another gay man, thirty-three-year-old Andrew Collier, was found in his flat at the sheltered housing centre in Dalston where he worked as a nurse. Nearby was a letter confirming that he, too, was HIV-positive.

After these four, apparently unconnected, deaths, the police began to receive a series of sinister anonymous telephone calls. Chillingly, the caller revealed tiny details about the state in which some of the bodies had been found to suggest that he was the killer and, to their horror, Scotland Yard began to realise that they had a serial killer on their hands.

'If you don't stop me, I will do one a week,' he taunted in a telephone call to Kensington police station. 'It started as an exercise to see if it could be done and I could get away with it.' Later that same day he rang Battersea police to say: 'I will keep going until I am caught. I will do another one. I have always dreamed of doing the perfect murder.' Hours later, he carried out his deadly threat.

A landlady spotted a fire in a bedsit at Catford, south-east London, where the forty-one-year-old Maltese chef Emmanuel Spiteri lived. The fire brigade got there quickly enough to put the fire out before it could destroy the flat, and inside they found the body of Mr Spiteri. He had been strangled during a sado-masochistic ritual.

The discovery set off a huge manhunt. Although each of the previous deaths had been investigated individually by a senior detective and bodies had been examined by different pathologists, the time had come to co-ordinate the investigation. A murder squad headquarters was set up at Kensington police station and Detective Chief Superintendent Ken John took overall charge. One of the first things he did was to call for Iain West, to put him in charge of reviewing each case and co-ordinating the pathological procedures.

Dr West had carried out the postmortem examination on the body of the first victim, Peter Walker, several months before, little thinking at the time that he would have to review his own work so soon or that he would be involved in a nationwide hunt for a serial killer. Now he set about his task in the manner of an old-time detective, poring over the scenes of crime photographs and carefully reading the statements of the police officers who had visited the murder sites, searching for clues. What Iain West discovered was going to be crucial to the success of Ken John and his team. Tiny clues about the methods used by the killer could prove vital in trapping him and might assume greater importance when it came to interviewing suspects. Was the same murderer responsible for all five deaths? If he was not and the police proceeded against him for the wrong killing, their case would be fatally flawed when it came to court and might perhaps lead to two killers being free to kill again.

Dr West began by going over the postmortem reports on all five murder victims and then conducting his own post-mortems on all but Christopher Dunn, whose body had already been cremated. In the case of the American Perry Bradley III, he examined the body with the original patholo-gist Dr Ian Hill, and reviewed the postmortem findings. Next he visited the scenes of the crimes personally, with the exception of Peter Walker's flat.

When he submitted his report to Ken John on 16 August 1993, it was a masterpiece. 'I have considered the pathologi-cal findings, together with the scene appearances in each case, and wish to make the following observations,' he wrote.

All five victims had indulged in sado-sexual activities with bondage being a common feature. There were marks on the bodies of Walker, Bradley, Dunn and Collier suggesting mild flagellation. Dr West stated: 'The pattern suggested that all victims had been willing participants in at least the initial stages of the sado-sexual activity and that they had allowed themselves to be restrained.'

He went on: 'Restraint had been effected using more than one type of instrument. A rope or cord appears to have been employed in the case of Walker and on the ankles of Dunn. The appearances suggest that handcuffs may have been used to restrain the other victims, and that in the cases of Collier, Walker and Dunn there have been determined attempts by the deceased to struggle against their bindings.' Each man had died from asphyxiation. He reported:

> In the case of Walker, death had resulted from suffoc-
> ation by obstruction of the mouth and nose and I cannot
> exclude the possibility of a plastic bag being employed.
>
> In the other four cases death had resulted from
> strangulation and the appearances suggest the use of a
> thin cord. A soft nylon cord between ⅛ and ¼ inch in
> diameter could have left the marks seen on the four
> bodies.
>
> Strangulation appears to have been effected from
> behind with all the deceased lying face downwards. The
> appearances suggest a relatively slow death from
> sustained application of the ligature which has
> constricted the deceased's airways and jugular veins.
>
> Ligature strangulation to the point of partial asphyxia
> is not uncommonly associated with sado-sexual activity,
> and it is possible that the victims could have been willing

participants at this stage and that they allowed the
ligatures to be placed around their necks in anticipation
of being subjected only to partial strangulation.

With the exception of Bradley, there were no marks on
the body to indicate that they had struggled violently
during the assault. This has probably been because of the
presence of the assailant's body on the various deceaseds'
backs, the body weight causing further restraint. There
was evidence from Spiteri and Walker to indicate pressure
on the back such as might be caused by kneeling or
leaning against the back of the chest.

In the case of Bradley, there were some minor injuries
which indicate that he had struggled against the assailant,
probably during strangulation.

Dr West then turned his attention to some of the more
unusual common factors, reporting:

In the cases of Walker and Collier there was evidence of
burns, possibly from cigarettes. A fire had been started at
the scene of Spiteri's death, although there was no direct
evidence of burns on his body. The way in which the
furnishings were piled up suggests that the motive for
initiating the fire was more likely to be an attempt to
cause early discovery of the body rather than to destroy
evidence of the body.

Next, Dr West pointed out a bizarre linking clue. 'A feature
common to both Walker and Collier was the use of condoms
which appeared to have been placed in the mouths of both
deceased. There was no evidence of the use of condoms in the
other cases. In the instance of Walker, a condom had also
been placed on his nose and, in respect of Collier, a condom

had been placed over the tail of a dead cat which lay along the front of the deceased's trunk.'

After death, when the heart is no longer pumping, gravity takes over and blood drains and congeals in the lower parts of the body, depending upon its position, leaving tell-tale patterns caused by the pressure of the weight of the body on the surfaces against which it rests. In these cases, having examined the way in which the bodies had been found and some of the postmortem marks on them, Dr West offers the opinion that they did not die in the position where they were found, but had been moved after death.

> The bodies of Walker and Collier had been deliberately arranged and in effect 'decorated'. It is likely that Bradley, Dunn and Spiteri were killed on the beds on which they were found, but in the case of the former two victims, they had been moved into different positions after death.
>
> The pattern of hypostasis on the bodies of Walker, Bradley and Collier indicated that their bodies had been moved a considerable time after death; in the case of Bradley it is likely not to have been less than an hour, in the case of Collier the evidence suggests that he had been lying in a different position for a period of some hours. The patterned blanching on the back of Collier shows that he had been lying on a firm surface which had a series of smooth parallel linear protrusions. Lying on his back on the bed in the position in which he was found would not leave this pattern within hypostasis.
>
> The appearances suggest that all of the bodies have been left in the positions in which they were found after the assailant had deliberated for some time over the way in which the victims' bodies were to be left at the scene.

There were other details that Iain West spotted.

> There were marks on the bodies of Walker, Collier and
> Spiteri indicating the use of a pointed object to puncture
> the skin. A pointed metallic or wooden object could be
> responsible. There were marks on the penis of Walker and
> on the back of Dunn's chest suggesting fresh suction bites.
> Harnesses of the type associated with 'bondage'
> activity were present on the bodies of Dunn and Spiteri.
> There are unexplained marks in the hypostasis on the
> front of the body of Bradley, indicating that a patterned
> object had been pressed into his abdomen. The marks
> were not typical of the type of harness used on Dunn and
> Spiteri, but suggest the use of some other apparatus
> which had subsequently been removed from the scene. I
> could identify nothing at the scene of Bradley's death
> which would have accounted for these marks.

Finally Dr West turned to an examination of the death scene
of Emmanuel Spiteri, made more difficult, as it was, by the
fire which damaged part of the room. 'The ligature marks on
the back of Spiteri's neck appeared pale and showed strikingly
against the partially decomposed and soot soiled surface of
the remainder of the body,' he wrote. For the benefit of the
unscientifically trained minds of the detectives, he went on to
explain:

> The blanching is due to compression of the underlying
> tissues so that they remained bloodless. Having reviewed
> the position of the body and the appearances of the bed
> after the body had been removed, I do not consider that
> the pallor of the ligature mark could be taken to indicate
> the absence of soot staining.

In my opinion the appearances of soot staining on the back of the body had been exaggerated by the presence of changes of decomposition. The photograph of the bed, taken after the body was moved, shows no soot staining in the underlying bedclothing and the imprint left indicates the body of Spiteri was not moved after soot had begun to be generated by the fire.

In fact, as Dr West was later to recall, the examination of Spiteri was not simply complicated by the loss of clues on the surface of the body due to soot contamination. The fire had produced another potentially more misleading effect.

'The biggest problem was the rapidly decomposing state of the body accelerated by the heat from the fire,' he said. 'The fire had extinguished itself by running out of oxygen, but it had generated enough heat to speed up the rate of decay.

'One of the problems you get with decay is that bruising becomes more difficult to detect, and if you are looking for small areas of bruising, they may become obscured by decomposition with great rapidity.

'I've seen people who, for instance, have been strangled and placed in a bath and not found until some two or three days later. In a hot humid environment, bruising may become totally obscured, although any fractures such as in the hyoid bone would still be detected.'

But to return to his report – was the same killer responsible?

The appearances both from the postmortem examinations and from the scene examinations indicate a high degree of probability that all five were killed by the same assailant. All had died of asphyxia, four from ligature strangulation with an identical type of ligature being employed in each case. The bodies had been 'arranged' after death, with the exception of Spiteri, where it is the artefacts in the room which have been arranged. The circumstances indicate that the assailant had spent a considerable period at the premises of most of the deceased after death had taken place.

Later, recalling some of the interesting aspects of the case and the lessons to be learned from them, Iain West said: 'There was a good signature there – the use of condoms; the use of fire; the use of the S & M gear, though that is not uncommon in homosexual killings; ligature strangulation with the same thin nylon cord, which turned out to be a tenting cord obtained from a camping supplier in Essex.'

So Iain West had done his job, confirming the suspicions of Ken John and his team. Now it was up to the detectives to bring their serial killer to book. The manhunt sent shockwaves through the gay community and generated a huge media response. The killer continued to taunt. Revelling in his notoriety, he called the Samaritans and the newspapers, admitting the killings and making ever more threatening claims.

One of the few non-forensic linking factors was the fact that the killer had stolen credit cards from most of his victims and had somehow found out their PIN numbers, thereby enabling him to draw cash from their accounts.

Desperately short of clues, Ken John was keen to seize on a security video taken at Charing Cross railway station on the night of the Spiteri murder. Although the picture quality was a little fuzzy, the hapless chef could clearly be identified beginning his final journey home in the company of a very tall man with short hair. The film was shown on television in a bid to jog the memories of potential witnesses. Although Spiteri's companion's face could not be seen, the TV exposure had an unsettling effect on the killer, who up until that

point had been cool and meticulous in his planning and execution.

To the astonishment of detectives, Colin Ireland, a thirty-
nine-year-old former soldier, walked into Southend police
station to say that he was the mystery man pictured in the
out-of-focus video film. He had invented a fancy story about
what he was doing walking along the platform alongside the
murdered man, but it did not convince Ken John.

Ireland was arrested. Witnesses began to pick him out on
identity parades, and a month later he admitted to all five
murders. Slowly he began to detail each killing to horrified
detectives. The more he talked, the more he confirmed Iain
West's uncannily accurate piece of scientific sleuthing.

He had suffocated his first victim, Peter Walker, by holding
a plastic bag over his face after tying him to a bed and whip-
ping him, exactly as Dr West had suspected all along. He
watched a sado-masochistic video with Christopher Dunn
before binding and gagging the mild-mannered librarian. He
then tortured the unfortunate man to get his bank card PIN
number before strangling him with a cord. Perry Bradley
allowed himself to be tied up, and Ireland put a noose around
his neck. After frightening the American into revealing his
PIN number and the whereabouts of £100 cash, he tightened
the noose until his victim was dead.

Andrew Collier was tied up and beaten, then quizzed
about his credit cards and PIN number. When the man who
worked so patiently with elderly patients became suspicious
and irate, Ireland tied a noose around his neck and strangled
him with it. 'I killed him quickly,' he told police. After going
through his victim's papers and discovering his medical condition, he burned parts of the body and killed the cat which
he knew his victim had been fond of. He laid the dead animal on Mr Collier's chest. 'I was reaching the point where it

was accelerating,' he told police. 'It was just speeding up and getting far worse. It wasn't just him making me angry, it was just like a roller-coaster effect.'

That roller-coaster effect led him inexorably to his fifth and final victim, Emmanuel Spiteri. Ireland told detectives that the little Maltese was very brave and refused to give him his PIN number, despite having a noose around his neck. 'I couldn't allow him to stick around and recognise me, so I killed him,' he said.

When he appeared at the Old Bailey five months later, the full horror of Ireland's reign of terror began to emerge. He chose his victims from customers at the Colehearne pub in London's Brompton Road, a well-known meeting place for homosexuals. His planning was extremely thorough. He took a different pair of gloves on each murder expedition so as not to leave fingerprints. He took cord to tie up his victims – a type so common that police would be unable to trace it. Ireland also took handcuffs to immobilise the men, having been careful to buy them at different shops. Before setting out to kill, he emptied his pockets of everything except money, so there was no risk of his leaving personal belongings at the murder scenes. After each killing, he wiped surfaces clean and packed up everything he had taken with him to secure his victims, plus cups and plates he had used and any food he had left uneaten.

As Dr West had correctly surmised in his report to Ken John, Ireland usually stayed in his victims' homes for some hours after killing them so that he could leave inconspicuously in the early morning by mingling with crowds of people going to work as he made his way home to Southend via Fenchurch Street station. He told detectives that he thought of targeting women, but chose homosexual men because he did not think people would have much sympathy for them.

Many people were daunted by his appearance – over 6 feet, 15 stone, and often dressed in combat-style clothing. When he began his killing spree, he was unemployed and living in a hostel in Southend, with two failed marriages and a prison record behind him.

Colin Ireland's motivation for the orgy of killing is difficult to determine. He wanted history to remember him as a serial killer, that is certain, and he had a clear idea of how many murders he had to commit to achieve that aim. In one of the many telephone calls to police before his arrest, he said he had read an American book which classified a serial killer as someone who had killed 'one over four'. He added, 'I know how many you have to do – you have to do one over four.' Although he is claiming from his prison cell to have killed several more gay men, those claims are being treated as bravado. Emmanuel Spiteri was Ireland's fifth and last victim, just enough to classify him as a serial killer.

Looking back on the most complicated investigation of his distinguished career as a detective, Ken John is warm in his praise for the contribution of Dr West, who had been his personal choice. He said:

'I had done several jobs with Iain West, and the previous experiences were instrumental in my decision to ask him to be the pathology co-ordinator for the whole of the case. In my view, he is the top in his field, nobody better, and I wanted him.

'It has been my experience of pathologists, over the years, that pathology, in many instances, is not an exact science. And whereas you get pathologists who may be very strong initially in telling you what you want to hear, when it comes to the point of giving evidence they equivocate, they produce other factors which could present other answers. But when Iain does an examination, you can guarantee that what he says on Day One will be what he sticks to throughout.'

There were other qualities which made Iain West stand out as the perfect choice for the tricky investigation. 'We had a co-ordinating scientist, a criminal psychologist and a team from the Crown Prosecution Service, and he was able through his experience and the esteem in which he was held to inter-relate with them all,' Mr John recalled. 'There were things being asked by all sorts of people that Iain could answer and relate to.'

It was an effective working relationship based on mutual respect between the two men. 'Iain has a highly developed sense of the theatrical,' Ken John chuckled. 'I will always remember, after our first case conference when we were still assessing whether or not we had a serial killer, he looked up at me from the table with all the photographs spread out on it, took a long drag on a huge cigar, and simply said: "We've got a problem." It was the last thing I wanted to hear but the "we" was reassuring. It meant that Iain now saw the two of us as a team.'

Once the skills of Iain West were available to the team, the detectives came up with a unique strategy. Mr John said, 'The day after he was appointed, Iain confirmed our worst fears that it was one man responsible for the killings. But there was still a lot of work to do because there had been threats of one murder a week and the scientific evidence was a little thin on the ground. We didn't want a sixth killing, but with Iain in place we knew that number six would probably have helped us in the forensic sense. So we decided that, if there was a sixth murder, the scene would be totally frozen – treated as a bomb scene, virtually. We would exclude people like coroners' officers and scenes of crime officers. We would have the serious crime examination unit on standby, but that scene would be frozen specifically for Iain's use. It was the first time in my service, in the context of forensic medicine, that I had come across a trade-off of this kind. We were prepared to trade-off certain things if we could find, at that scene, things we were lacking up until then.

'The thing was that Iain by his experience was giving us the one thing we needed in the inquiry, which was "similar fact" evidence.'

The value of Dr West's 'similar fact' evidence was proved when it came to interrogating Colin Ireland. Ken John said, 'Ireland had persuaded himself that there were calculated reasons for what he did, but even though he pleaded guilty, there was a damage limitation strategy on his part. We wanted to get into the man's mind as to what actually happened, and in the interviews we used Iain's "similar fact" material which was very powerful: the time taken to die, the movement of bodies, the ligatures, removal of ligatures, his change of clothing, the meals.

'Usually, when these sort of things are put to a suspect, if they're comfortable with them, they'll agree. This was one area where Ireland would not readily agree, he was uncomfortable with it, so this in itself became part of the "similar fact". We were beginning to know more in the negative way through Iain's pathology.'

Summing up Dr West's contribution, Mr John said: 'I thought Iain West's professionalism was unique in being so finite in what he was doing and what he was saying and what he would have said, had it come to trial.'

CHAPTER 10

SUICIDES

For a pathologist, investigating suicide may not always be straightforward. Some murders are skilfully made to look like suicide. Some suicides are mistaken for murder. Sometimes people fake their own suicides. Here, from Iain West's casebook, are examples of all three.

Graham Backhouse

There were strange goings-on in the Cotswold village of Horton during the spring of 1984. The place was so discreet and careful that it didn't even risk a pub, and its church was half a mile away. Nothing ever happened in Horton, and the outside world hadn't even heard its name. Then, one day, there was an explosion that rocked the community.

A farmer's wife, Margaret Backhouse, needed to fetch supplies from the vet, but her car wouldn't start, so she borrowed her husband's Volvo estate. As she turned the key in the ignition, a bomb exploded beneath the driver's seat causing serious injuries to the unfortunate woman's back and lower legs. Within days, a severed sheep's head was found impaled on the fence at Widden Hill farm where Mrs Backhouse, her husband Graham and two young children lived. There was a note with it which read: 'You Next'. And very soon Mr Backhouse began to receive threatening letters and phonecalls.

Police mounted an armed guard on the farm for a few days but withdrew when the threats ceased. Slowly a discernible pattern began to emerge, and details of a long-running feud between Mr Backhouse and his neighbour Colyn Bedale-Taylor started to leak out.

Three weeks after the bombing, while Mrs Bedale-Taylor was out chairing a meeting of the village hall committee, a man entered the secluded Widden Hill farmhouse. Graham Backhouse struggled with him, was stabbed in the chest and groin and slashed about the face. In a desperate bid to defend himself, he fired a shot from his shotgun and the intruder fell dead. Before collapsing, Mr Backhouse punched a panic alarm button that had been installed after the car bombing. When police arrived, he was lying sobbing in a pool of blood behind the body. The dead man was Colyn Bedale-Taylor. Clutched in his hand was a bloodstained Stanley knife. Mr Backhouse was raced to the Frenchay Hospital in Bristol, where his wife was recovering from two operations, and underwent emergency surgery himself.

Now the whole region was rife with rumour. It was no secret in Horton that Mr Bedale-Taylor had been acting strangely since losing his executive position as personnel officer with a Bristol firm three years earlier. There was said to be animosity between Mr Bedale-Taylor and Mr Backhouse over the death of Mr Bedale-Taylor's nineteen-year-old son in a car crash involving a tractor owned by Mr Backhouse. But the police could not work out why Mr Backhouse should have invited his enemy into his home, or why Mr Bedale-Taylor should have gone. They had a tricky investigation on their hands.

Who had planted the bomb which injured Mrs Backhouse? Was it Mr Bedale-Taylor, who intended to kill Graham Backhouse? Or was it Mr Backhouse, who intended to kill his wife and make it look like a murder plot by Mr Bedale-Taylor? And what of the shooting? Why was Mr Bedale-Taylor in Mr Backhouse's home alone with him? Had he gone there to attack Graham Backhouse or to confess to planting the bomb? Or had Backhouse set the whole thing up so that he could murder his neighbour and make it appear to be an act of self-defence?

As the detectives worked their way through the various options, they became more and more certain that Graham Backhouse had lured Colyn Bedale-Taylor into a murder trap. They theorised that the farmer had attempted to murder his wife in a car-bomb explosion and, when that had not worked, he had invented a hate campaign against his family to make it look as though Bedale-Taylor was the culprit. He then orchestrated a confrontation with his chosen scapegoat through which, apparently in self-defence, he could eliminate the only person who could disprove his story.

But for the police to convince a jury of their beliefs, they had to be able to reconstruct accurately the struggle between the two men and the moment of murder. If they were right, then Backhouse's appalling wounds had to have been self-inflicted. This was where the skills of Iain West came in.

'A senior police officer from the Avon & Somerset force come to see me one day,' said Dr West, 'with a request to look at one specific aspect of the case, and that was the wounds found on Mr Backhouse. His story was that he shot the old boy in self-defence as a result of being slashed with a Stanley knife. One injury was a huge wound, which went from one side of the chest to the other, plus he had slash injuries on the face.'

The story appeared convincing as the detective unfolded it to Dr West, but the pathologist insisted on reading the medical reports of treatment and demanded a full and detailed set of colour photographs of the injuries, taken from all angles, so that he could enlarge them and study them carefully before delivering his expert opinion.

'It was my view that these were self-inflicted injuries and not at all similar to the type of attack you get from a weapon such as a Stanley knife,' he declared. 'There was too much control, too much of an evenness in the depth of the wound. And I, certainly, have never seen somebody slashed with such a short weapon on the trunk – on the body – and producing such a long injury. The human body – even though you may not do it voluntarily – will reflexly withdraw if someone else is attacking and injuring you; you would get an entirely different pattern of injury – differing depths and varying lengths of cut, interrupted wounds and perhaps even stab-wounds. I had no doubt whatsoever that these could not be anything other than self-inflicted injuries.'

It was a conviction Iain West would later deliver with devastating clarity to a jury.

When he finally came to court, Graham Backhouse was charged with attempting to murder his wife and murdering Colyn Bedale-Taylor. The Crown alleged that he was desperately short of cash and wanted to kill his wife in order to collect a £100,000 life insurance pay-out. He had made Bedale-Taylor a scapegoat when his plot backfired, and chose to eliminate him.

After a sixteen-day trial, he was convicted and jailed for life.

A year later, his wife Margaret was granted a divorce on the grounds of unreasonable behaviour.

Vicky de Lambray

The mysterious death of the nightclub transvestite Vicky de Lambray sent shivers of apprehension through London's high society and sparked off a major security scare in Whitehall. For the thirty-seven-year-old male prostitute, whose real name was David Lloyd Gibbon, had been the central figure in a spy scandal and was poised to expose a senior member of the British aristocracy as a drugs baron.

It was just after 3.30 am on 8 August 1986 when the telephone rang on the night newsdesk of the Press Association in Fleet Street. A reporter, Julie Stretton, picked up the call to hear a distressed de Lambray sob, 'I have just been killed. I have been injected with a huge amount of heroin. I am desperate. There is nothing anyone can do to help me.' He went on to say that he was working with a Sunday newspaper journalist on an exposure story about drug-taking and the aristocracy.

Julie Stretton called the police immediately, but when they arrived at de Lambray's flat in Brixton, south London, they could get no reply. The following morning a neighbour found him dead in bed.

The internal police report at the time said, in rather matter-of-fact language: 'Nothing is known at this stage of the deceased's medical history. He was a well-known transvestite of public interest.' It went on to state, wrongly, that de Lambray claimed to have injected himself with heroin in his dramatic cry for help to the Press Association, continuing: 'The deceased was found in bed lying face down with his head on one side.

275

He was dressed in a jogging suit. Inspector Diddams attended the scene, but could find no trace of drug paraphernalia.'

The discovery of the body launched an immediate murder inquiry, for de Lambray, who claimed to be the illegitimate son of a viscount, lived in a twilight world on the edge of espionage and political intrigue. Among the lovers he claimed to have had were a Russian naval attaché, Anatoly Zotov, who was expelled from Britain for spying; Sir James Dunnett, former Permanent Under-Secretary at the Ministry of Defence; and Sir Maurice Oldfield, the head of MI6. [Sir Maurice's personal life had been the subject of a public admission in the House of Commons by the prime minister, Margaret Thatcher, amid fears that Britain's security was being put at risk.] His diaries were packed with the names of the rich and famous whom he met at glittering West End parties which he hosted. There were even cryptic references to the bank accounts of the missing earl, Lord Lucan.

And a few months before his death, police investigating the string of homosexual murders committed by serial killer Michael Lupo (see Chapter 9) had found his name among a catalogue of celebrities in the multiple murderer's own diaries.

So, with the Special Branch and security services hovering, police were keen to get to the bottom of de Lambray's desperate last cry for help. He had been seen at all his usual haunts the night before his death and seemed in excellent spirits. The taxi-driver who took him home at 2.30 am confirmed this. All his friends insisted that, although he was addicted to champagne, he did not take drugs. So, had he been murdered to shut him up before he could expose some terrible secret? Had he, as he claimed, been forcibly injected with a massive dose of heroin to make it look as though he was a junkie who had accidentally overdosed?

Professor Hugh Johnson was called in to carry out the postmortem, and immediately spotted the tell-tale signs of previous suicide attempts. He reported:

Fourteen parallel old linear scars on the front of the right wrist and forearm. Three similar scars on the front of the left wrist. The backs of the hands had been shaved. There were no old round scars, thrombosed veins or old or fresh needle-puncture marks recognisable on either arm.

De Lambray's friends had been right, therefore, to insist that he was not a junkie. But the real mystery was why he had claimed to have been injected with heroin when his body gave evidence that he clearly had not. Neither had he apparently been involved in any kind of struggle or fight, for Dr Johnson reported no defence wounds on the hands or arms and no facial injury. The rest of the postmortem report is unremarkable. There were no fractures, no bruising to speak of. No indications of strangulation. No obvious tablet remains in the stomach.

A wide range of samples were taken for analysis, and two days later, because of growing police and public concern over the continuing mystery, Professor Johnson re-examined the body. By this time a small abrasion had become apparent on the right side of the chin and one or two very tiny scratches, but still there was nothing obviously sinister to be found.

This was to be one of the last postmortem reports written by Hugh Johnson, because he died of a heart attack shortly afterwards while waiting to give evidence at the Old Bailey. Iain West's friend and mentor had left the de Lambray file incomplete because he could not commit himself to giving a cause of death until all the toxicology and forensic tests on the body samples had been completed.

When it came to tying up the loose ends of the case for the inquest, therefore, it was Dr West who submitted the report, writing:

> The postmortem report on the deceased indicates no evidence of recent injury but shows that the deceased had asphyxial changes without apparent cause at the time of the postmortem examination. There was no significant natural disease, but the liver showed fatty change consistent with previous alcohol abuse.

He went on to refer to a report from Scotland Yard's Forensic Science Laboratory which 'indicates the presence of amylobarbitone and alcohol in the deceased's blood at levels which can be associated with death from the combined effects of amylobarbitone and alcohol. Amylobarbitone is a Controlled Drug, and is a recognised drug of abuse,' he added, giving the cause of death as amylobarbitone and alcohol intoxication.

Dr West told the inquest that de Lambray had 280 milligrams of alcohol in his blood. The sodium amytal in his stomach could not have been there in that concentration if they had been taken by injection.

So Vicky de Lambray had failed in his last deception. He was a drug-abuser, but he had not been murdered with a heroin overdose. The coroner recorded an open verdict on a 'pathetic and lonely man' whose public face hid his real character.

John McCarthy

When the body of the wealthy British diamond-dealer John McCarthy was found early in 1988 on the forecourt of his block of flats in the Zairean capital, Kinshasa, the local police assumed that he had committed suicide by jumping from his fourth-floor balcony. Their theory was backed up by the discovery, in his apartment, of a suicide note written in the dead man's own hand. Their conviction was further confirmed by slash marks on his wrists and neck and a knife found in his bloodstained bathroom.

But McCarthy's employer was not so willing to accept the suicide story. The thirty-year-old man had been on a routine diamond-buying assignment to Zaire – something he had done many times before – and he was concerned that he might have been murdered.

Had he been killed by feuding rival diamond-dealers? Had he become embroiled in an affair with a woman, whose jealous boyfriend had sought revenge?

'I did an examination on behalf of his employers because they were rather concerned – obviously because of the nature of his work – as to whether there was anything sinister,' said Dr West. 'The story presented at that stage – and by this time even the Zairean police were having some doubts – appeared to be that this man had been depressed, decided to kill himself, cut his wrists and his throat, and then jumped out of the building. An investigator went over on behalf of his employers and sent me some photographs of the scene, from both inside and outside the flat. The first thing that I noticed was that the injuries found on the body were not consistent with a fall from his fourth-floor flat.'

A postmortem had already taken place in Africa, but within days of McCarthy's company becoming involved in the inquiry, his body was flown back to his home town of Gravesend in Kent, where the local coroner took an interest. A pathologist and colleague of Dr West, Dr Jerreat, performed a second postmortem under the watchful eye of Kent police and in the presence of Iain West, who submitted a six-page report to the company which had hired him. He concluded that John McCarthy had died 'as a result of blood loss due to cutting wounds to the wrist and neck'.

But in this case, such a conclusion did not automatically mean suicide. Dr West's report goes on to detail the full extent of the dead man's injuries:

> There was a scalp injury to the area behind the right ear with an associated skull fracture and brain damage. This injury did not appear at all consistent with the deceased falling from a height into the area in which he was found.

With a keen eye, Dr West had studied every detail in the photographs sent from Zaire before he entered the mortuary. In particular he had noted every household utensil which did not appear to be in its proper place. The positioning of a heavy metal frying-pan in the bedroom, for instance, puzzled him. Now he thought he had an explanation.

> The pattern of this injury indicates that the deceased struck, or was struck by, a flat surface, and it would be typical of the effect of a heavy blow from an object such as a frying-pan seen in the photographs. This injury would have rendered him unconscious. The severity of the bruising of the brain indicates the injury was received some minutes prior to death.

But what about the slashing of the wrists and the slitting of the throat? The body had more than a hundred such knife wounds. Could they have been self-inflicted? Dr West reported:

There were numerous deep and superficial cutting wounds on the forearms and neck, which superficially would be consistent with self-inflicted injuries. In my opinion, however, although these injuries were inflicted in life as far as the deep wounds are concerned, many of the superficial grazes appeared to have been caused after death. The number of wounds is far in excess of that seen in most cases of suicidal cutting. I have seen this number of wounds only in individuals who are suffering from a severe psychotic disturbance of the mind.

There were a number of marks on the body which looked as though they had been caused by falling on to the stony court-yard of the apartment block. The report next deals with the injuries which might have been sustained by jumping from the fourth-floor balcony. Dr West stated:

> The pattern of injury on the arms and parts of the legs would be consistent with a fall from a moderate height, but would not be consistent with a fall from a fourth-floor flat, particularly in view of the lack of skeletal injury and the lack of significant deep muscle bruising. I feel that the maximum height that he could have fallen from would have been one storey. The relative lack of bruising associated with these injuries indicate that he was dead when he fell into the area in which he was found.

Suicide? Not likely.

In summary, Dr West wrote:

> I feel the deceased did not kill himself and that the likely scenario is that he was struck on the back of his head, probably with the frying-pan, and thereby rendered

281

unconscious. He was then carried to the bath, where his neck and wrists were stabbed and cut resulting in severe haemorrhage. Further, the cutting injuries were inflicted in an attempt to mimic suicidal injuries and he was then removed from the bath and wrapped in some covering and thrown from a lower level in that block of flats.

It was this point which led him to his final and most damning conclusion. Dr West had noticed something else in the photographs that struck a jarring note in his mind. There had been a trail of blood on the tiled flooring leading from the bath to the balcony, but there was something wrong. Not enough blood. 'He would have bled heavily from the wounds on his body and would have left a distinct trail of heavy bloodstains if he had moved to the window under his own volition or had been carried without being wrapped in some covering.'

Talking about the case recently, Dr West recalled the give-away clues.

'He did have a large bruise, about six inches across, on the back of his scalp without there being any skull damage; simply not consistent with somebody jumping from that height. And what was immediately apparent from those cuts was that they did not look like self-inflicted injuries. The method of infliction was wrong, the direction of infliction was wrong, the position was wrong. They fanned sharply outwards, for instance, when they should have gone horizontally. Although the scene had been salted – there was blood in the bath, there was a bloodstained knife by the bath – everything about it was wrong. They were not in the position where somebody would elect to cut themselves.'

Long after his report had been submitted and he had been paid for his work, Iain West was given a version of what had really happened to John McCarthy. 'The investigation revealed that he had become involved in a domestic dispute,' he said. 'A group of individuals went to his flat, hit him on the back of the head with a cast-iron pan, knocked him out, placed him in the bath, cut his wrists while he was still alive, salted a trail of blood, wrapped him in a carpet and then took him downstairs to dump his body.

'I don't know whether the person responsible was ever brought to trial, but although this was originally thought to have been connected with the diamond trade, it turned out to be a domestic matter.'

Uncannily that scenario accords in every detail with the explanation originally put forward to McCarthy's employers by Iain West himself, including his hunches and theoretical suppositions based on his forensic findings.

But one nagging question remains. What kind of threat would force a man to write a false suicide note?

CHAPTER 11

FOREIGN INQUIRIES

Since Iain West has developed an international reputation for his remarkable detective ability, he has been increasingly in demand from foreign governments keen to make use of his talents as a pathologist. He has travelled the globe, probing death in all its forms, and occasionally accompanies Scotland Yard murder squad detectives on their more difficult overseas assignments.

The Zimbabwean hostages

Peace did not come immediately to Zimbabwe after the first free elections which brought Robert Mugabe to power. The vast armies of guerillas which had fought the lengthy bush war of independence were not easily disbanded. Delivering the prosperity which had been promised proved a slow process, and finding work to occupy these highly trained but undisciplined men was even more difficult for the new government. As a result, in the more remote parts of the country, law and order were virtually non-existent as bands of heavily armed brigands roamed the countryside, plundering and looting.

The situation was particularly grave in the bush country of Matabeleland to the west of the country, where the former ZIPRA guerillas loyal to the opposition leader Joshua Nkomo's ZAPU party held sway. It was through this dangerous bandit country that a party of tourists was travelling when disaster struck in July 1982.

The group had paid £1,425 each to travel overland from London to Johannesburg, and had been on the road for several weeks. They had been to visit the spectacular Victoria Falls and were making their way in a Bedford minibus towards the town of Bulawayo. They rounded a bend to find a tree blocking the road and others being felled in their path. As they slowed down, there were repeated bursts of machine-gun fire from the bushes on either side of the road, and within seconds a gang of heavily armed Ndebele tribesmen had them surrounded. The driver of a car following the bus had a lucky escape. He managed to brake just before a falling tree hit his car, and turning round under a hail of bullets drove off to raise the alarm.

Meanwhile the gang released three women from Australia, Austria and Holland and allowed the tour leader, the New Zealander Bruce Watkins, to go free with a ransom note addressed to President Mugabe, demanding the release of two former guerillas accused of treason. Ominously, the note added that if they were not freed, 'We will blast these kids.'

The six male hostages with which the gang made off into the bush were soon named as eighteen-year-old James Greenwell, an old Etonian from Wales; Martyn Hodgson, a thirty-five-year-old civil engineer from Peterborough; two Americans, Brett Baldwin and Kevin Ellis, and two Australians, Tony Bazjelz and William Butler.

The Zimbabwean government poured hundreds of troops into the region, and a three-man team from the British Special Air Services flew in secretly to help. Within days they had pinpointed a spot in the Tjolotjo tribal area where the party was said to be being held. Over the ensuing weeks, rumour and counter-rumour circulated as to whether the hostages were still alive. But as the weeks turned into months and then years, hopes for survival began to fade.

Eventually, after almost three years, two members of the terrorist gang were caught and led the security forces to a series of shallow graves near a remote village. There was not much left in the graves – just an assorted collection of bones – because the villagers had repeatedly reburied the bodies after scavenging attacks by wild dogs and hyenas.

The pathetic find might have ended the sad saga but for the fact that one of the Americans had been insured against kidnapping. His family now wanted to make a multi-million-dollar claim, and the insurers were contesting it. The true identity of each body and how each man died had to be established.

The relatives commissioned Iain West to undertake this difficult task. He arrived in Harare in a still tense political atmosphere and was given one of ex-premier Ian Smith's former police officers to escort him.

'A number of the bodies had been brought to the surface, or appeared to have been brought to the surface, by animal activity,' he remembered. 'There was only one grave site that had remained permanently undisturbed. One of the problems we faced was that it was very hot, very humid, and the burials were relatively shallow with a lot of surface insect activity in a loose, rather sandy, soil. The bones were deteriorating fairly rapidly, which caused problems in terms of interpreting injuries which were found on the skeletons.'

Before he began any kind of forensic work, Dr West insisted on seeing for himself the burial sites so that he could get an idea of how the bodies had been interred and how they had been exhumed. He recalled:

'We were supposed to have gone over by helicopter to the site, but we had problems with one of the Zimbabwean air force helicopters, which had crashed, so it was decided that it would be safer for us to go by land convoy. We flew to Bulawayo and then went out in armoured LandRovers to the part of Matabeleland where the bodies had been found.

'We faced a little bit of vehicle unreliability. One of our escort LandRovers was struggling to keep up with the rest of the party. Then we lost one of the vehicles carrying members of the party and his escort, which caused concern because we were in the middle of bandit country with the guerillas still quite active. But when we went back we discovered, to our great relief, that they had just suffered a puncture.

'I remember going to the burial site, looking at it, and thinking, "We're missing quite a lot of bones." The original pathologist was not with us, as he was suffering from a tropical disease he had caught when he first visited the scene. So it was up to me to make an assessment as to how much more digging would have to be done to make sure there were no other remains there. As the bodies had been disturbed, they might well have been scattered over quite an area.'

In fact he was later to issue a damning indictment in his final report by writing:

The exhumations had been performed in a random and illogical manner. The bodies had been recovered by direct digging down on to sites which were indicated by one of the captured terrorists. I indicated the necessity for a complete methodical exhumation of the whole grave-site and the surrounding area, plus excavation of a further site where a terrorist indicated two bodies may have been buried. I have also recommended that a far more extensive search of the surrounding bush should be undertaken for any remains which may have been moved by animals.

Apart from the threat of attack from bandits while he worked, the visit to the burial site placed Iain West in danger of another kind. 'We looked at the remains of the village, and I will always remember going towards the hut where the killings were supposed to have taken place. I had a Zimbabwean soldier with me. He was carrying a rifle, and he suddenly dropped the weapon in front of me, came to an abrupt halt and said: "We will go no further . . . mambas!" And there on the ground in front of us was a snake. He said: "The hut will be full of mambas," so I never got to see inside.'

Back at the main hospital in Harare the next day, Dr West found that much of the preliminary work had been done by the local pathologist, who had X-rayed the four intact skulls which had been found and had prepared plaster casts of the jaws. There was, of course, no soft tissue left on the bodies, so determining a precise cause of death was going to be impossible. But Dr West had brought with him dental charts of the six men to aid in identification. The bones had been gathered together in six collections and labelled in accordance with the six grave-sites in which they had been found.

Group one came from the only burial site which had not been disturbed. Iain West wrote in this report:

The bones had been recovered from a single grave approximately 18 inches deep near to the base of a tree, the tree having been marked by the locals. The remains were those of a single Caucasian male, and the skeleton is substantially intact except for the smaller bones of the hands and feet.

Measuring the leg-bones, he was able to estimate the dead man's height but could find no bullet-marks anywhere on the skeleton. Comparison of the dental charts with the post-mortem X-rays identified this man as the American, Kevin Ellis.

The same method was used to identify groups two and four as the remains of William Butler and James Greenwell respectively. The bodies had been found partially curled up and lying side by side. Much of Butler's skeleton was missing, but Greenwell seemed largely intact. Dr West wrote:

This skeleton was that of a Caucasian male, and the long-bone measurements indicated that the deceased had been between 5 feet 9 inches and 5 feet 11 inches in height, and that he was approximately nineteen years of age.

Adjacent to this body was found a clump of light to mid reddish-brown hair and a knotted pieced of material which apparently had been round the deceased's neck. There was damage to this material, in the form of tears, some associated with decay of the material during burial, but others were more regular and suggested cuts within the fabric.

Then came the first and only hint of how the hostages might have been killed. Still referring to the young Briton, Greenwell, Dr West reported:

Examination of the skeleton, which showed signs of

deterioration, revealed two stab-type injuries near the anterior end of the upper surface of the first rib. Both injuries were linear with clearly defined margins separated by a gap of ⅛ inch. One of the stab injuries had completely penetrated the bone. The injuries were consistent with wounds produced by a sharp-tipped and edged weapon, and could have been produced by a knife or a bayonet.

The bones comprising group three were identified as the other Briton, Martyn Hodgson, again through dental records. In this case, only the skull and lower jaw remained intact.

Of the other two groups of bones there was little to assist identification. Some had been bleached in the sun, and some were taken back to London for further anatomical analysis. Having measured them all, Iain West was of the opinion that they had probably come from either Butler or Hodgson, two of the incomplete bodies already identified.

Back in London, he gave the X-rays and dental charts to his old friend Bernie Sims, the forensic odontologist, as a double-check. The fillings in four upper molars and two lower molars confirmed the identity of Kevin Ellis. In the case of Butler, Professor Sims found sixteen points of correspondence between the postmortem X-rays and the dental chart prepared while he was alive. The most significant feature was a gold filling in the upper right incisor. A gold crown along with eight other points of correspondence clinched the identity of Martyn Hodgson, and six points of similarity confirmed James Greenwell's identity. Iain West's conclusions had been proved right.

At Scotland Yard's Forensic Science Laboratory, the scientist Roger Cook was given James Greenwell's neckerchief to examine. 'Two of its corners had been tightly knotted together,' he reported. 'The item was woven from polyester fibres and was extensively damaged. There were many small holes and a number of larger ones. I was unable to establish the cause of the damage, but, as the cloth is made from a synthetic material, it would not be caused by rotting. However, it has been known for insects to cut their way through this material. I found no categorical evidence of weapon damage.'

Further examination of the remaining unidentified bones proved inconclusive, but they appeared unlikely to have come from either of the other two hostages Brett Baldwin or Tony Bazjelz. 'I think it is likely that only four bodies have so far been found, and that there is a strong possibility that two graves remain to be discovered or that those graves were disturbed in the past and the remains moved by animal activity,' said Dr West.

When, in November 1985, it came to the inquest on the two Britons in London, a statement from President Mugabe was read to the court. He revealed that the six men had been made to walk for sixty miles through the bush, where razor-sharp thorns had cut their bare feet to ribbons. The blood-trail they left was too slight for security forces to follow, so helicopters were sent to comb the bush. After two days' march they were herded into a hut in a village and, as a helicopter flew overhead, they screamed for help. But the gunmen acted swiftly: Mr Hodgson was shot dead, another man was throttled as he tried to escape and the others were gunned down. All the victims were buried in shallow graves, and the gang ordered the villagers to walk cattle repeatedly over the spot to trample down the earth.

Of the original gang of twenty-two who had staged the abduction, most had been killed in clashes with the security forces. The gang leader who ordered the executions, Gilbert 'Sitchela' Ngwenya, had been captured and sentenced to death.

'It was an interesting trip,' said Dr West, looking back on his Matabeleland adventure. 'I thoroughly enjoyed Zimbabwe. The people were extremely pleasant and I'd like to go back one day. I remember flying back, then getting into a car, having flown overnight from Africa, and arriving at Lewes Crown Court to give evidence at 10.30 in the morning. So many foreign trips are like that. You have to get back in time for court, and you may have no time even to get your head down before you go into the witness box.'

The body in the Maltese Crusaders' well

The rocky isle of Malta has a history closely linked to the bitter religious conflicts that devastated the Mediterranean region during the Middle Ages. In particular, the island is known to have been the base for many a Crusader army going off to fight the infidel in Africa and the Middle East. Everywhere there are reminders of those times in the names of the places, the buildings and the artefacts.

One such landmark is the well at Il-Bosk on the edge of the Ghirghenti valley. For centuries, ever since the Crusaders first refreshed themselves from its sparkling waters, local people have relied on the well to sustain them against the arid climate. In modern times, as piped water has become available to much of the populace, the ancient watering hole has taken on a variety of domestic and leisure uses.

It was in pursuit of one such use that a local man made perhaps the most macabre find in the colourful history of the Crusaders' well. At midday on 10 November 1985 he went to the well to fill a pail to wash his car. On removing the iron cover, he spotted something floating on the surface of the water many feet below. Peering into the darkness, the man became convinced that he was looking at a lump of flesh and bone. Was it human or was it part of an animal carcass? He could not be sure.

When the police arrived, the first call they made was to a nearby farmhouse to inquire if any dead animals had been disposed of in the well recently. When they received a negative reply, the CID were summoned and the strange object was fished out of the well. It proved to a be a human torso, thought to be that of a woman.

The order was immediately given to pump the well dry – a lengthy process involving the fire brigade and several frogmen. When this operation had been completed, the director of Malta's Forensic Science Laboratory, Dr Abela Medici, and the local police chief were lowered to the bottom of the well. Beneath a pile of rocks and stones they quickly discovered a number of black plastic bags partially buried in the mud. With a police excavation team also lowered into the darkness, the men began the delicate task of removing the bags – a job made dangerous by the crumbling state of the well's sides.

By the time the operation was complete, five bags had been recovered – four containing parts of a dismembered human body and the fifth a large hammer. Some of the pieces were better preserved than others, as they had been sealed inside the bags.

The skull was also recovered with, according to eyewitnesses, a visible fracture to the side of the head. Obviously the body had been chopped up and the bags lowered into the well before heavy stones were dropped in to hold them down. The stones must eventually have shifted to allow the torso to float to the surface. The detectives soon declared that they were investigating a murder. They could not identify the victim, but the killing must have occurred within the past ten years because of the type of plastic bag used to dispose of the body.

This case illustrates the chaotic and busy work schedule which daily confronts Iain West. 'We were having a meeting of the British Association in Forensic Medicine at Guy's Hospital one Saturday morning, when I got a call from Scotland Yard asking if I would be interested in a case in Malta,' he said. 'I had to give evidence in a trial on the Monday, so I agreed to fly out that Monday evening.'

In any event, Dr West's packed programme would allow only a flying two-day visit to the island, and when he arrived he realised the reason for his sudden invitation. 'There had been problems in the medical profession in Malta, and a lot of the doctors had left because there had been an alteration in the terms and conditions of service,' he said. 'So there was no pathologist, as such, and the postmortem was going to be carried out by the professor of anatomy. We actually did it in the anatomy department of the university.'

After a visit to the well itself, the postmortem began and Dr West noted that, when pieced together, the body was complete apart from one or two of the smaller bones. 'It was a mixture of skeletonised remains with a large quantity of soft tissue left,' he said. 'I will always remember the buttocks because, although the full shape was there, they had obviously changed shape with decomposition. They looked like the buttocks of a female. When I looked at the photographs they showed me that evening, I said: "It looks like a woman from the shape of her buttocks."' But appearances can be deceptive, as Dr West's postmortem report reveals.

Estimation of sex from the pelvis, the diameters of the heads of long bones – particularly the femur and humerus – indicated that although there were equivocal features the skeleton was that of a male. The examination of the soft tissue remaining around the pelvis revealed . . . the shape of the base of the scrotal sac. I could see no evidence of female genital organs. On incision of the perineum, tubular structures could be seen in the position normally occupied by the lower ductus deferens and seminal vesicles. The appearance of the soft tissue confirms the sex as being male.

This was a diagnosis later backed up by histological examination of samples back in Guy's Hospital laboratory in London.

Most of the flesh and muscle tissue had converted into a fatty wax-like substance known as adipocere, and it was clear that the body had been cut up in a frantic, random, fashion by someone with no knowledge of anatomy or surgery.

The skeleton showed evidence of mechanical dismemberment, with cuts through segments of long bones and incomplete cuts in long bones, indicating the use of a handsaw, and other cuts in bone indicating the use of a powered saw consistent with a powered circular saw.

So ran the rather stilted language of the postmortem report.

'It was clear that they'd tried to dismember him without using a knife,' said Dr West. 'But the saw blade had not been deep enough to cut through the bone, so they had to complete it with a handsaw.'

An attempt was made to work out accurately the height of the dead man using calculations based on the length of the long bones – an exercise which threw up a fascinating insight into the things pathologists can determine simply from looking at skeletons. 'It would appear from the size of the bones that the deceased was right-handed,' observed Dr West.

When it came to determining the cause of death, you did not have to be a genius to work out what had happened

> The skull and face showed considerable fragmentation. The vault of the skull showed a large defect anteriorly, laterally and involving part of the base.

There were holes in the skull on both the right and the left, holes on the face and a broken jaw. There were fragments of bone embedded in what was left of the brain. The holes in the head were rectangular and the edges were bevelled. The margins of one of the holes were 'cleanly punched out and straight'.

The police now produced the hammer which had been found with the body in the well for Dr West to examine. 'It weighed 4.28kg and had a 6cm striking surface at one end with bevelled margins,' he reported. 'I was able to fit this hammer into the defect in the right temporal region, and am satisfied that there is an anatomical fit between this implement and the wound in the skull. The shape of the injury to the left side of the skull would be consistent with a further blow from a hammer.'

In summing up, he wrote:

> The deceased was an adult male with a height of between 5 feet 6 inches and 5 feet 8 inches, and approximately between thirty and forty years of age. Death had resulted from blunt injury to the head entirely in keeping with at least two blows in life to the sides of the skull and at least one further blow to the face – although whether this occurred in life is impossible to say.

So who was the man who had met such a violent end?

Armed with Dr West's analysis and the remains of the skull, a Maltese dentist set about reconstructing the face. When he had finished, the plaster head he had made bore a striking resemblance to a man named Paul Gauchi who had been missing for four years. No medical or dental records could be found for this man, but his age and height corresponded so closely to what Dr West had determined that the local authorities decided to tell his family that the mystery of his disappearance had been tragically solved.

'Interestingly enough, the machine-marks on the bags in which the body were found showed that they had been imported from Britain,' Dr West said, 'and the batch they came from had only been imported during the six-month period which coincided exactly with the time when Gauchi went missing. The investigation later discovered that he appeared to have been involved with an organised crime syndicate and may have double-crossed them. I presume they dumped him in the Crusaders' well thinking that was the last anybody would ever see of him.'

Victor Bruce

In October 1986, the Governor of the National Bank of Sierra Leone died in suspicious circumstances. He fell from the balcony of the Governor's house in a suburb of the capital, Freetown, and his houseboys were arrested on suspicion of complicity in his death. Murder was not ruled out.

The bank then searched abroad for a replacement and appointed a distinguished sixty-eight-year-old Trinidadian, Victor Bruce, as the new Governor. But soon he, too, was dead. And in the same house. The muscular six-footer was found lying face downwards across the toilet in the bathroom on the lower ground floor, just below a window. His dying posture was strange. His feet were off the ground, his head was in contact with the floor and his arms were folded beneath him. There was a pool of urine and traces of blood. The bathroom door and the window were closed.

The suspicious deaths of two successive bank Governors in the same house was too much of a coincidence. The Sierra Leone government ordered a full-scale murder inquiry and once again the houseboys were arrested.

The Trinidad government called in Iain West. 'The police met me and flew me by helicopter to the local mortuary, which was extremely primitive,' he said, 'and I did a post-mortem with half the neighbourhood looking on.' That assertion is supported by his report, which lists no less than twelve official observers at the autopsy including eight doctors and just one policeman.

To all intents and purposes the late Governor had been a healthy man. The postmortem revealed no disease or injury that could have accounted for his death. There were no marks on his body to suggest that he had been in a fight or had tried to defend himself. There were no bullet wounds, stab wounds or injection holes. There were no strangulation marks round his neck. There were no pills in his stomach. The only vaguely inexplicable marks were a bruise on the left leg, which the pathologist could tell had happened after death, and a large bruise on the right thigh, occasioned while Mr Bruce was alive. By now, Iain West was forming a possible scenario in his head. The next day he visited the Governor's house, which the local people now firmly believed to be cursed.

'I was shown a charcoal-burner which he used to heat the house,' he said, 'and told that it was found smouldering in the bathroom when the body was discovered. Then I knew exactly what had happened.

'He'd gone to have a bath and taken the coal-box into the bathroom with him, but hadn't opened any windows. With no ventilation, the coal-box was giving off carbon monoxide fumes. While he was having his bath he began to feel the effects of carbon monoxide poisoning and, realising what was happening, got out of the bath. By that stage he was in a state almost like drunkenness as a result of the effects of the carbon monoxide, so he fell and injured himself while he was trying to open the window. He then became unconscious and died. It looked as though something sinister had taken place, but it was pure accident.'

Back in London, the samples Dr West took confirmed his analysis. Gas chromatography tests showed that Victor Bruce had a 57 per cent saturation of carboxyhaemoglobin in his blood. This was well within the range at which inhalation of the odourless fumes would kill. His stomach contained only caffeine – no drugs, no alcohol. The bruise on his right leg had been sustained when he fell over the toilet, and the post-mortem bruise on his leg could have been caused on moving his body.

But if that was the last Iain West thought he would see of Sierra Leone, he was mistaken. The Freetown government insisted that he go back to give evidence at the inquest and he was persuaded reluctantly to return.

It was December, just days before Christmas. For the pathologist, it was to be a chastening experience of the way things work in the Third World. 'No one was there to meet me when I arrived,' he recalled. 'I had not checked my passport and my visa had expired, so I was thrown into a detention room with a guard outside. When the Chief Immigration Officer eventually came, I was recognised and allowed to go on my way. Until then, I would have been happy to take the next plane back.' On his first trip, he had been met by an official from the president's office and was expecting at least a representative from the foreign ministry. But slowly it began to dawn that he was on his own. 'There were masses of people milling about outside the airport and a choice of several taxis,' he said. 'I got in one and we got about half a mile down the road when we joined the queue for the road ferry across the estuary into the city. The taxi-driver said it would take about two hours to get across, but agreed to drive me to the foot ferry when I protested. He tried to charge me about twenty pounds for a couple of miles, but I bargained him down to about seven.

'The foot ferry was quite a pleasant little trip, and I got a bus the other side to the hotel, only to discover that they were not expecting me either. There was nobody to meet me at the hotel, so I was beginning to wonder if I'd come at the right time, to the right place, or even the right country.

'I walked into my room, dumped my bags and found a snake in the bath. There were hundreds of multi-legged creatures all over the floor. There were lizards on the wall. It was a nightmare. When, in desperation, I went to the bar for a beer, the local hooker came up and introduced herself. That was just the last straw.'

After a restless night, Dr West took a taxi to police headquarters and had to fight his way through a throng of people waiting to be dealt with for a variety of misdemeanours before finally meeting the apologetic officers who were deputed to look after him. He had been expected the previous day, but his arrival had been overlooked by everyone due to bureaucratic bungling.

'The inquest was held by one of the magistrates in the old court,' he recalls. 'It was a lovely old court building dating back to Victorian days. And it was the longest evidence I have ever given at an inquest. The jury asked questions for over an hour.'

The local people were so grateful that they invited their star witness to stay in Freetown for Christmas. But he declined. 'The difficulty was that there was only one flight going back before Christmas, and that was full,' he said. 'They laid on a second flight, but that turned out to be a cargo plane. Fortunately they managed to find me a first class seat, so I managed to get back home just in time for the festivities.'

Mrs Arah Hector

The romantically-named Jabberwock Beach on the beautiful Caribbean island of Antigua is a place of calm and tranquillity. Palm trees wave in the breeze and the azure sea laps gently against sparkling white sands. A holidaymaker's paradise.

But the peace of this delightful spot was shattered one late May day in 1989 by a horrific discovery. A hand bearing two rings, a bracelet and a gold watch was seen protruding from beneath the sand. Further excavation by the police, who were hurriedly summoned to the spot, revealed the naked and badly decomposed body of a woman. Her feet were tied together by a single loop of rope. Her hands were bound with a piece of rope fashioned in a figure of eight and crossing between the wrists. Around her neck was a pair of blue trousers tied at the front in a granny knot. The remains of a floral-patterned dress were bunched under her shoulders and neck.

This was the body of Mrs Arah Hector, the popular wife of Antigua's Marxist opposition leader. She had been missing from home for three days.

Since the victim was married to such a prominent opposition politician, the Antiguan government felt it wise to call in Scotland Yard to investigate, and a team of detectives were soon on their way. The local pathologist had conducted an initial postmortem, but the Yard murder squad were not confident that he would have the experience to spot those tiny details which might make the difference between success or failure in their quest to trap the murderer.

They were operating in another jurisdiction, however, and could not simply impose a British expert on the Antiguans. Diplomatic niceties also prevented them from removing the body from the island. So Detective Superintendent John Barker, who was leading the inquiry, devised a plan which would allow him to seek the advice and expertise of Iain West.

He sent his detective sergeant back to Britain with a video-tape taken on the beach, showing the discovery and removal of the body. The officer also took with him a full album of photographs taken at the postmortem depicting all the injuries and, most important of all, several key portions of the body. These were all frozen in plastic bags and included the vagina, cervix, uterus, anus and part of the rectum, together with parts of the skin and flesh from the neck, the hyoid bone, cervical vertebrae and the larynx.

At his laboratory in Guy's Hospital Iain West thawed these vital exhibits and examined them before placing them in formalin to preserve them. He also looked at various other items like the rope, the dress and a broom handle which had been sent back for forensic testing.

Armed with all this information and having read the report of the Antiguan pathologist, Dr West was ready to submit his own report. Mrs Hector had suffered two significant injuries. There was a gaping wound on the front of her neck, which had almost severed her head from her body, and there was a penetrating wound in her vagina which had been caused by a blunt object. Dr West's conclusions tell the whole ghastly story.

> The incised wounds to the neck had been made by three blows from a heavy-bladed weapon. A machete could have caused these injuries. Moderate force would have been required although I do not think that severe force was used, as a heavy-bladed weapon such as a machete might have been expected to have produced considerably more injury to the spine with the use of great force.
>
> In my opinion, the neck has been cut by a combination of both backhand and forehand passes of the weapon held in the assailant's right hand.
>
> Radiological examination of the hyoid bone reveals a tiny undisplaced fracture of the tip of the greater horn, but I do not think this was caused in an attempted strangulation. It could have resulted, after death had occurred, from attempts at manhandling the body.
>
> There were three defensive incised wounds on both hands. These wounds are typical of the effects of grasping the blade of a weapon in an attempt to prevent oneself being cut on the face or trunk. They are not typical of injuries caused by warding off a blow from a sharp-edged weapon, as such an action would be expected to result in deeper wounds. If the weapon used has a heavy blade, then warding off injuries tends to involve injury to the bones of the hands or forearms.
>
> There is injury to the deceased's vaginal vault. One is a penetrating wound which has been caused by the insertion of a smooth, round-ended, cylindrical object into the vagina employing a moderate degree of force.

The lack of visible bruising in relation to the injury suggests that it was caused after death.

A second vaginal injury in the form of a small red abrasion on the vaginal vault is consistent with an injury caused in life and is entirely consistent with the insertion of a firm or hard object into the vagina. Forceful intercourse could cause this latter injury. In my opinion, the abrasion was caused separately from the penetrating wound to the vaginal vault.

The deceased's hands and feet had been tied together. The appearances are typical of the type of bindings employed when a body is tied up after death in an attempt to make it more easily manhandled. In my opinion, these bindings were not placed on the deceased during life.

The deceased was in a well-established state of decomposition and no accurate time of death can be given. I note that there was no apparent insect infestation of her body. The appearances are consistent with death occurring on the day that she was last seen alive.

I give as cause of death: haemorrhage due to incised wounds to the neck.

The report is a classic example of Iain West's particular skills. That he can tell so much from looking at photographs and examining pieces of decomposed flesh flown to him from the other side of the world is quite remarkable.

So Arah Hector was probably raped and then attacked by a right-hander wielding a machete. She tried to grab the weapon, but he slashed her throat three times before sexually assaulting her lifeless body again, probably with a broom handle. Finally he bound her legs and arms with rope so that he could carry her corpse to the beach for burial.

The Yard team and the Antiguan authorities were also impressed because they summoned Dr West to Antigua twice: first to give evidence at the committal hearing of a local youth charged with the murder, and later to testify at the actual murder trial. He remembered: 'The committal was a very long-winded process. We were out there for about ten days. While we were there, Hurricane Hugo struck and we decided to move out of our beachside hotel, where the rooms would probably have been under water, to a place on higher ground in town. We stayed at the police headquarters for the evening and watched the hurricane go round. Once the peak winds had passed, you could more or less stand up outside. It was an interesting night.

'The next morning we went round the island to look at the damage, which was quite horrendous in parts. Fortunately there were very few deaths. I did notice that the first thing the government did was to get troops out to repair the hurricane damage to the Antiguan cricket ground. It was nice to know that they had got their priorities right!'

The murder had been committed by a former prisoner who had been befriended by Mrs Hector. She ran a prisoners' charity and had given him work in her house and garden. He had initially been arrested because he was known to be associated with her house and grounds, but detectives soon found that one of his shoes was a perfect match for a footprint in blood which had been left on the dead woman's bedroom floor.

When the case came to court, Dr West was disturbed to find that the prosecution was being conducted by one of the most senior and experienced barristers in the Caribbean, while it seemed that the government had chosen a very junior lawyer to defend the accused.

'It was a real eye-opener,' he said. 'I was expecting a fair amount of cross-examination, and there were only two or three relatively simple non-controversial questions asked. I was a little uneasy about seeing somebody who was potentially going to be hanged being defended by an inexperienced advocate. Defendants facing a capital charge should have access to experienced counsel who can fully assess the prosecution case and robustly explore any shortcomings.'

CHAPTER 12

GANGLAND KILLINGS

Many deaths of criminals are the result of contracts or revenge, but not all gangland killings are the same. Organised crime is big business these days and the brutal men who run it think nothing of eliminating anyone who stands in their way. Occasionally they are so cavalier about murder that they do little to cover their tracks, but their executions are sometimes so vicious that there is little left of the body for the police to investigate. In these situations the pathologist, who can sometimes decipher so much from a tiny fragment of bone or a sliver of brain tissue, is invaluable to the detectives.

John Fordham

The fifty undercover detectives who make up Scotland Yard's Criminal Intelligence Branch have always been known within the force as 'the watchers, not the takers'. The special skill of the dedicated band of hand-picked men and women is to know absolutely everything about a criminal – his lifestyle, habits, family, friends and activities –

without his ever knowing he is under scrutiny. They never make arrests, because to do so would mean that they would have to blow their cover by giving evidence in court. Instead, all the invaluable intelligence they glean is passed on for other officers to use. Known by the cipher C11 in the 1980s, the branch used the most sophisticated camera and sound equipment to take clandestine photographs and make secret recordings of their unsuspecting targets. One criminal gang's rendezvous was captured by a telephoto lens hidden in a car headlight.

Mostly in their thirties, the officers are chosen for their experience, skill and quickness of mind. They are all – men and a few women – totally at ease in any company, never looking out of place in a chic restaurant or a rough pub. But their particular talent is in disguise. Taxi-drivers, street-sweepers, tramps, milkmen, pensioners, joggers – a target criminal could find himself in a street crowded with the most unremarkable cross-section of the British public and not realise that all were detectives communicating with one another by hidden microphones in their wristwatches and listening on earpieces built into their hats or wigs.

In 1981 a small team of volunteers was put together from within C11 for top-secret surveillance work which would involve greater endurance than the unit's normal tasks. After training with the SAS and the Royal Ulster Constabulary in Northern Ireland, they began undercover operations against major underworld gangs. Their job, unarmed, was to dig in as close as possible to their target and stay there for days at a time relaying all movements to a mobile headquarters by radio. Trained to remain in the same position for hours on end, they carried yeast tablets and special sprays designed to deter inquisitive dogs. Their tactics included living in dugouts, concealing themselves in natural cover or hiding in a pile of tyres. Most of their time was devoted to watching suspected terrorist groups.

Detective Constable John Fordham was a key member of this élite unit. Described by one senior officer as 'Britain's most experienced and best-trained surveillance operator', he once stood up to his neck in water for forty-eight hours watching a target. He repeatedly turned down offers of promotion, preferring to stay 'at the sharp end'. Indeed, one of his bosses said in one report that he had run out of superlatives to describe Fordham's work. He had been a detective for eleven years with four commendations to his name when he accepted the assignment which would lead to his death.

In 1984 his unit had been tasked to track down the gold ingots stolen in the record-breaking £26million Brinks-Mat bullion robbery at Heathrow Airport the previous year. Working with Flying Squad detectives who were leading the bullion hunt, Fordham and his colleagues eventually traced a number of addresses where the gold was thought to have been hidden. One of the most likely hiding-places, the police thought, was the home of a millionaire builder called Kenneth Noye. Noye lived in a £1m mansion, Hollywood Cottage, set in twenty acres of land at West Kingsdown in Kent, a perfect place to conceal the ingots. The grounds were patrolled by Rottweilers and surrounded by high walls topped by barbed-wire fencing.

In the early weeks of 1985, just over a year after the robbery, Flying Squad chiefs decided the time was right to move in on the men and locations where they believed they might find the stolen gold. Thirty-six search-warrants were issued, covering suspect properties all over the country, and a major police operation was mounted to co-ordinate the raids simultaneously, so that none of the suspects could be tipped off in time to move the loot. The Kent mansion was to be the first target which would trigger off the rest of the operation.

It was a bitterly cold weekend with snow still on the ground outside Noye's house when the order was given to move in. Scotland Yard technical experts had hidden a video-camera, with an infra-red lens capable of recording at night, in a bird-box in a tree just outside the grounds. But it could cover only the main drive and was not able to see what was going on inside the house. Senior officers guessed that the sudden unannounced arrival of a team of detectives armed with search-warrants at the main gate might cause panic among the occupants of the house. It was vital, they judged, to see what they did and, more importantly, where they went in the first few moments before police could force their way in. That was to be the task of the C11 special force.

Just after 6.15 pm on Saturday evening 26 January 1985 Detective Constable John Fordham and his regular partner Detective Constable Neil Murphy clambered over the barbed wire into Kenneth Noye's property to start the operation. They had been watching comings and goings at the mansion for several hours from a hide in the grounds of a religious retreat opposite. Moments earlier they had reported the arrival in a Cavalier car of one of Noye's closest associates and a principal suspect in the bullion-handling case, the businessman Brian Reader.

Both the detectives were unarmed and dressed in camouflage clothing with dark balaclava helmets. Their only link with their mobile control van nearby was by personal radio. Now they were under orders to move in. They had to creep close enough to the house to be able to see through the main windows and cover the doors before calling in the group who would execute the search-warrants. Through the windows they were to watch the reactions of people inside when their colleagues burst through the main gates and, if anyone ran away, they were to track where the escapers went in the grounds.

Police dog-handlers had secretly watched Noye's three Rottweilers for several days before the operation and judged them to be relatively docile family pets. The animals scented the two undercover men within minutes, however, and bounded up, barking wildly and snarling viciously. Neil Murphy immediately did as his training instructed. Curtly reporting on his radio: 'Dogs hostile', he dropped back over the garden fencing and made a noise to distract the animals from his colleague. For some unknown reason – perhaps because he believed the dogs to be just noisy and not really dangerous – John Fordham stood his ground. It was to prove a tragic error of judgement.

At 6.27 pm Fordham made his last radio transmission. 'Someone out, half-way down drive, calling dogs', he whispered into his mouthpiece. It was Kenneth Noye himself responding to the barking of the dogs. Armed with a shotgun, a torch and a kitchen knife, he immediately attacked the unarmed officer while DC Murphy watched helplessly from the shadows. Within seconds the enraged builder had plunged the kitchen knife ten times into John Fordham's body. By the time a police rescue squad, called up by Murphy, had raced to the scene, Noye was standing over the stricken detective, holding the shotgun to his head while the frantic dogs circled the dying man, baying for his blood which stained the snow-covered grass.

'He's done me. He's stabbed me,' was all John Fordham had time to whisper to a colleague before he died where he lay.

In the confusion that followed, Murphy reported having seen two men and a woman standing over his fallen comrade, threatening to blow his head off with a shotgun. One of the men aimed a kick at the detective where he lay. As he was led away for questioning, Noye told police, 'He shouldn't have been on my property. I hope he dies.'

Although police teams were stunned by the death of John Fordham, they pressed ahead with the operation and several arrests were made. A thorough search of the mansion and the grounds led to the discovery of eleven gold bars – a discovery that later helped to put Kenneth Noye in jail for eleven years for his part in laundering the proceeds of the Brinks-Mat raid.

Both Kenneth and Brenda Noye, along with their friend Brian Reader, were charged with the murder of John Fordham. When he came to trial at the Old Bailey for the murder of Fordham, Noye claimed that he acted in self-defence. The officer had no identification, did not identify himself as a police officer and actually attacked the house-holder, Noye told the jury. He was petrified by the sight of a hooded man in camouflage gear standing in his garden in the dark. He was convinced he was facing an intruder, not a policeman. 'I stabbed and stabbed in blind panic,' he said.

The jury believed him, and after a fifteen-day trial he was acquitted of the murder – to the fury of the police service and the astonishment of the public. The jury also accepted Brian Reader's defence that there was no evidence to show he had taken part in the murder. The murder charge against Brenda Noye was later dropped.

The jury had been unable to examine fully all the forensic evidence, for two postmortems were carried out on the body of the dead policeman. The first was conducted the day after the killing by Dr Rufus Crompton on behalf of the police murder squad. The second took place two and a half weeks later at the request of Mrs Brenda Noye's defence lawyers, and was carried out by Iain West.

*

The two experienced pathologists agreed on everything about the wounds and the cause of death. But in searching for clues which might assist his client's defence, Dr West spotted a significant extra detail. His conclusions would have caused a sensation had they ever been brought before the jury or made public.

Dr Crompton is head of forensic medicine at St George's Hospital Medical School, a part of the University of London. At 10.30 on the morning of Sunday 27 January 1985 in the mortuary at Queen Mary's Hospital, Sidcup, he began his autopsy on DC Fordham. A gaggle of grim-faced senior policemen were there, including C11's boss Commander Phil Corbett. Also present was the surgeon who had operated on Fordham in a futile attempt to revive him. He was there to describe the original wounds that he had seen, and to differentiate for Dr Crompton between those and the incisions which he and his medical team had had to make during their emergency procedures.

First of all, John Fordham's clothing was examined and photographs were taken to show that the cuts in the garments corresponded exactly with the wounds on the body. 'The body was that of a well-nourished middle-aged man 5 feet 10 inches in height and weighing 76 kilograms,' Dr Crompton wrote. 'There were ten recent stab-wounds, all consistent with a single-edged blade about 1cm wide.'

The pathologist then described in detail each of these stab-wounds, working from the top of the body downwards and beginning on the front. His list starts: 'There was a nick to the margin of the right ear contiguous with a sliced scalp wound behind.' He went on to describe the four most severe stab-wounds, two of which punctured the left lung and two of which entered the heart. Having described a wound which entered the chest cavity but stopped just short of the lung, he reported:

Below this on the left was a 1.0cm long vertical stab wound 9.0cms to the left of the midline and 1m 34cm above the left heel. The track was downwards and backwards below the third rib for about 7cm to pierce the upper lobe of the left lung. The cutting edge was again downwards.

Below this was a 1.2cm long horizontal wound with the cutting edge medial. It was 1m 28cm above the left heel and 13cm to the left of the midline. The track was medial and back for about 6cm into the lower lobe of the lung.

Two cm below this and 12cm to the left of the midline was another horizontal wound with the cutting edge inwards. The track, about 7cm long, passed backwards and inwards, severing the bone of the fifth rib to enter the left ventricle of the heart.

Two cm below this was another horizontal wound, cutting edge inwards and 8cm to the left of the midline. The track was straight back for about 7cm through the sixth costal cartilege to transfix the lower margin of the right ventricle of the heart.

Dr Crompton then went on to make a highly significant observation.

The above two wounds had a small bruise adjacent to the inner margin, suggesting that the blade had been thrust in to its full length and the hilt had bruised the chest.

By the time Dr Crompton had completed his list of the pattern and nature of the stab-wounds, a picture of the fatal attack on DC Fordham was beginning to develop. Frenzied it certainly was. The angle of the knife had been altered several times and the direction of the cutting edge varied so much as almost to suggest a complete rotation, either of the knife in the hand or of the assailant's wrist. It was apparently a knife with a blade no more than 3 inches long and about ½ inch wide, being 2mm thick at the blunt edge. At least two of the blows were struck to Fordham's back, perhaps because his attacker moved behind him, he turned his back, or he was struck as he fell forward. Whatever the true case, these wounds cast serious doubt on the self-defence claims Noye later made.

Dr West's findings are by far the more interesting. The normal procedure during a postmortem examination is for the pathologist to give a running commentary of what he finds as he goes along. This is taken down in note form by an assistant, usually a police officer, who will also have a chart showing various elevations of the body on his or her clipboard. The pathologist will then annotate these drawings with the positions of any significant wounds or if, as in the case of Fordham, a chart is not available, will make his own drawing.

Dr West's drawings of Fordham's body, combined with his observation of the wounds, led to a remarkable conclusion. Having described the wounds in similar detail to Dr Crompton's and confirming the findings of his colleague, he wrote:

I found no evidence of defensive injury on the deceased's body and nothing to indicate that he had struck out at his assailant, or that he had attempted to ward off any of the knife-blows with his arm or arms. The presence of bruising around many of the skin wounds indicates that the weapon had probably been thrust into his body to the full extent of the blade on probably four occasions.

315

So John Fordham had not attempted to ward off the blows. He had not fought for his life, although a knife had been thrust into his body up to its hilt at least four times. What was he doing during this attack? Was he just standing there, bravely taking it all?

Iain West's report went on:

> The nature of the wounds suggested no significant movement of the deceased's body whilst stabbing had taken place. It is frequent to find distortion of the wound margins when stabbing occurs, indicating the victim's attempts to move away from the knife. This pattern is not apparent in this case, suggesting that the deceased may well have been unable to move away from the weapon during the course of the infliction of the wounds.

So, was Fordham knocked unconscious? Dr West wrote:

> The pattern of injury suggests that John Fordham may well have been mobile for at least part of the time during which he was being stabbed. There was no evidence of head injury to suggest that he had been rendered unconscious, but *the pattern of stabbing suggests that Fordham could have been physically restrained by one person while the stabbing was being conducted by another person.* If he was being held by his left arm, and the arm was pulled away from the deceased's body, this would account for the pattern of stabbing seen on the left side of the chest.

So was more than one assailant involved in the killing of John Fordham? Dr West said later, 'It was the relatively undistorted nature of some of the wounds and the line and pattern of stab wounds on the side of his chest which gave the real clues. These suggested quite clearly that they were done while he was immobile. You might see that pattern when somebody is lying on the ground, but you usually see it when somebody is being restrained by another individual. In this case, it is clear that the left arm is elevated at the time. The arm is lifted up so that the front and side of his chest is exposed and the stab-wounds have gone right round. It starts in front and goes right round. Alternatively, it could have started in the back and come round to the front, if he went forward. It is just that the arm is up. Normally when somebody is defending themselves they would parry, and it would be difficult if not impossible to get that number of stabbing blows in under the arm like that.'

That startling conclusion from Dr West was never put before the murder trial jury. In May 1985, during the committal proceedings, the murder charge against Brenda Noye was suddenly dropped. So, since that evidence had been produced solely for her defence, her husband's lawyers, and those defending Brian Reader, were not obliged to refer to it. In the event they relied totally and, as it turned out, successfully on the self-defence argument.

While Noye was in prison, Hollywood Cottage was sold and the proceeds frozen by the High Court. In 1995 Brinks successfully sued him and recovered £3m, including the value of the property, in compensation for his part in the crime.

The Surrey torso murder

There is nothing particularly exceptional about the St Helier tavern at Rosehill near Carshalton in Surrey. It is just a typical pub. Among the horse-brasses and beneath the mock oak beams, an assortment of regular customers and casual passers-by drink daily in the two bars.

Like most pubs, the St Helier has some questionable characters among its clientele and, like most pubs, it witnesses ferocious arguments from time to time and even the occasional fight. So when a group of burly men, slightly the worse for drink, began to raise their voices one day in May 1992, nobody took any notice. The row appeared to have ended when one of the participants swung a punch at another and was restrained by his friends.

Shortly afterwards the group left the pub, and if the other drinkers thought any more about it, they probably expected the combatants to settle their differences over a bout of fisticuffs in the car park. But, to their horror, a shot rang out within minutes and someone ran into the pub calling for an ambulance and the police. Almost before the landlord could lift the receiver to dial 999, however, there was a squeal of tyres and two cars roared out of the car park.

By the time the emergency services arrived on the scene a few minutes later, the only evidence that there had been a shooting was a pool of blood on the ground and the ashen faces of a couple of shocked eyewitnesses. No victim, no gunman, no bullet, no gun. After questioning staff and regulars at the pub, taking statements from eyewitnesses and trawling through underworld informants, detectives were soon sure that the incident was part of a gangland vendetta – it had been a punishment shooting.

The victim, it seemed, was a thirty-nine-year-old car dealer called Stephen Davison, a father-of-four from Swindon in Wiltshire, who was missing from all his usual haunts. The police made public appeals and checked on hospitals, but no one had seen Davison and no one had treated a man with bullet wounds. They became aware that they were dealing with a murder inquiry, but where was the body? The murder squad had a pretty good idea who their suspects were, but how could they make arrests without finding the victim?

The first breakthrough – although no one recognised it as such – came within a few days when, on 7 June 1992, several plastic bags were found floating on a lake in Priory Park, a local beauty spot at Reigate in Surrey more than ten miles away from the scene of the shooting. Inside one of the bags was a large grotesque lump of flesh.

'The police surgeon saw it and was not sure whether it was animal or human,' said Iain West. 'So I drove down from central London, wondering whether I was going to find that it was somebody's loin of pork which was judged to be past its best when brought out for Sunday lunch and had just been thrown away. But it was fairly obvious once we had unwrapped the various layers of plastic round the parcel that this was part of the left side of somebody's chest – with a section of the abdomen, ribs, a little of the spine and part of the breastbone.'

Working through the early hours of the morning in the local hospital mortuary, Dr West carried out a detailed postmortem on the grisly find. His report reveals how much information a skilled pathologist can glean from looking at such remains – a meaningless mass of bones and flesh to the layman. For the detectives anxiously peering over his shoulder, his task was simple. All he had to do was tell them who this man was and how he died.

After photographing the torso and having it X-rayed, Dr West quickly set to work. Oddly, the heart, lungs, diaphragm and liver were all missing, but there were plenty of clues to be going on with.

'Most pertinent was that there was a bullet wound on the left side of the chest and what appeared to be an exit wound on the right side of the abdomen,' he said. 'I was quite satisfied that it was a bullet wound. Although externally it was beginning to be altered by decomposition, there was a track that one could follow through the damage on the rib.

'Looking at the bones that remained, we had part of a pelvic crest in the abdominal section and the way in which the pelvis and part of the spine had been cut suggested a relatively strong high-speed electrical saw. I can't think of a chainsaw with quite as narrow a blade as that, but there was certainly circular scoring on the surface of the bone.'

In fact his postmortem report is much more specific:

Dismemberment appears to have been performed by a variety of implements. In the shoulder region a part of the skin margin was notched and showed a pattern suggestive of the use of a knife with at least five separate knife-cuts.

The left arm had been removed around the armpit region by cutting right through the humerus and leaving the head of the bone still embedded in the shoulder socket. The report goes on:

The anterior and lower border of the defect in the shoulder over a distance of 8½ inches showed an abraded margin, made not by a knife but by the blade of a coarser implement, possibly a power saw or some other power cutting-tool.

The margins of excision on the front of the chest and abdomen show again a mixed pattern of knife-cuts with notching of the skin and areas of abrasion on and near the margins, suggestive of the use of a power tool. On the margin of the central abdominal region there was a dentate pattern to the skin edge, the intervals between each skin peg being 3mm.

There was a slit 5mm wide in the bone of the left iliac crest, indicating the use of a broad-bladed power tool such as a circular stone- or metal-cutting blade. There was a cut from a similar implement on the body of the first sacral vertebra. On the back of the torso the excision appears to have been made with a knife with the skin margins being heavily notched.

Why such precise detail of the way in which the body had been cut up? Well, if and when the police arrested a suspect, they might be able to recover the power tools which had been used, and then Iain West's evidence would be vital to convince a court that those precise implements, owned no doubt by the suspect, could be matched to the torso.

But before that stage could be reached, there was much more to be done. How, for instance, had this unfortunate and as yet anonymous man died? That question was easy to answer. There was that bullet wound in the chest. Again his measurements were precise.

This included an eccentric abrasion rim measuring between 1 and 1.5mm on its rear and upper border and up to 0.5mm on the lower and front border. The central defect in the wound measured 7mm by 7mm. The wound was surrounded by a well-defined circular imprint . . . slightly blackened, and there was a definite arc of blackening at its lower margin.

Dissection of the underlying soft tissues revealed a firearm projectile tract passing through the chest wall in a downwards direction. The projectile had struck the 8th rib, bevelling the inner aspect of the upper margin of rib 8¼ inch to the left of the centre of the breastbone. A small dark particle was retrieved from the wound track. The projectile had entered the left chest through the pleura adjacent to the 8th rib.

The next task was to find the exit wound, and that too was fairly obvious.

On the right side of the abdomen 5 inches to the right of the midline and ¾ inch above the umbilicus was a roughly circular defect measuring ⅜ by ⅜ inch. There was no abrasion rim around the defect but there was a track communicating with the underlying abdominal muscles. There was considerable decomposition of the skin around this wound. The appearances are those of a firearm exit wound.

There was not much more to be learned from the torso, except to note that the ribs had been hacked at with a knife and some had been attacked with a saw. This first report ends with the sentence: 'There were two slightly raised pigmented moles on the front of the central upper abdominal wall'. Dr West had spotted a tiny detail which was to prove decisive in identifying the body.

When he returned a week later to separate the skeleton from the soft tissues and take away samples, he made much more precise measurements of the location of the moles and the distance between them.

Detectives were sure this had to be the body of Davison, but how could they prove it?

'We took lots of muscle from the remains of the chest and

all the hair that remained – it was very fine pale hair – and sent it for DNA testing,' said Dr West. 'But we were unable to get DNA groups out of it because of the state of decomposition. So then we were stuck. If we could not identify him from DNA, how were we going to identify him?'

Soon an ingenious solution to the problem was devised. The missing man's family supplied a colour picture of a grinning Stephen Davison wearing nothing but a tiny pair of swimming trunks and striking a mock body-builder's pose. The picture was enlarged and there, sure enough, were two well-defined moles on his chest. Now convinced that the torso was that of Davison, Iain West ordered that the photograph be made into a large print, and adjusted so that the chest area was exactly the same size as a large transparency he had of the torso.

'We had a photograph of the remains with the umbilicus and one nipple to orientate ourselves,' he said. Once this was done, he overlaid the transparency of the torso on it. The two pictures matched, and the two moles married up on the screen in precisely the same position, so there was little doubt. The torso found in Priory Park was that of Stephen Davison.

'That was a perfect example of another aspect of identification which we sometimes have to use,' said Dr West. 'Usually, though, it is superimposition of a face. Nowadays it can be done with video, whereas it used to be done with still photographs. That is how most of the victims of Fred West, the Gloucester builder, were identified, using video superimposition.'

Meanwhile, as the police inquiry took shape, Iain West had taken the remains back to his laboratory at Guy's Hospital, where with his staff he began the painstaking search for more clues. This included the cleaning and drying of the bones, including the ribs, one of which had evidence of an earlier fracture which had healed. Dr West wrote:

> The posterior ends of the ribs were splintered and had possibly been cut with a saw. The humerus had been cut with a saw. The spine and pelvis appeared to have been cut with a saw-like implement, probably a power saw or some other disc-shaped cutting implement. There is a groove typical of that made by a circular-bladed power tool in the remains of the left ilium.

Several weeks went by and then a team of detectives from the Flying Squad, whose job it is to deal with the most violent criminals, became impatient with the lack of progress in the inquiry. They began to lean on their informants, and by early September they had been given a detailed version of what had happened to Davison and who was responsible.

First, two men were arrested and charged with the bodyless murder. Then an early morning raid on a gipsy camp in Streatham, south London, was followed by a crucial discovery on a farm near Dorking in Surrey. A squad of Surrey detectives quickly summoned Iain West to the scene. He takes up the story in his official report.

> I was taken to a small stable in the north-east corner of the field. I was there shown an excavated hole in one corner of the stable block. At the base of the hole was an object concealed by blue plastic. I was present throughout the subsequent exposure and retrieval of the plastic bags and their contents, which proved to be the lower torso and thighs of a white adult male.

This section of body had been wrapped in three plastic bags, and Dr West returned to East Surrey Hospital in Redhill to examine them in detail in the mortuary. Once again there was clear evidence that the dismemberment had been carried out by a mixture of knives, saws and power tools. There were blue fibres embedded in the flesh along one of the cuts, and a black fragment, similar to the one recovered from inside the torso, was retrieved from the pelvis. There was a good anatomical match between the two pieces of body. Careful attention was now being paid to every detail that might help to prove that this was the body of Davison. In this new find the penis and scrotum were present, for instance. The dead man was uncircumcised, as had been Davison. Dr West was making calculations, based on the length of the right femur which had been recovered, to estimate the height of the dead man. It was 45.9cm, which gave him an overall height of 5 feet 7 inches, give or take an inch and a half. Police knew that Davison had been 5 feet 10 inches tall.

Now it was time to draw some conclusions and make a formal statement for the court:

Both of the specimens found on 7 June 1992 and on the 11 September 1992 have come from the same white male. I have seen a photograph of Stephen Keith Davison which shows two moles on the upper central abdomen. These moles correspond to the positions of moles seen on the torso which I examined.

There is a single firearm entry wound with a corresponding exit wound on the body. Assuming that there was a single firearm wound and that the entry and exit holes are related, then this wound would have been lethal. Even if the entry and exit were unrelated the presence of a firearm entry wound on that part of the left chest would indicate that the deceased must have suffered injury to his left lung which would have been fatal unless treated.

The parameters available for identification indicate that the remains are consistent with those of Stephen Keith Davison. The probable cause of death has been the effects of a low-velocity firearm wound to the chest. Low-velocity wounds usually are seen as the result of the discharge of a pistol or revolver.

With the body identified to the police's satisfaction as that of Davison, and two men charged with the killing, the legal process took over, but Iain West's involvement with the case was not ended. Now it was the turn of the defence to challenge his findings.

Almost a year after the shooting at the St Helier tavern, Davison's family had still not been able to hold his funeral because his remains had not been released by the coroner. The prosecution were keen to help, but the defence lawyers were delaying matters.

In a letter to the coroner, the defence solicitor Audrey Oxford suggested a solution to the impasse. She suggested that 'the two parts of the torso' be 'videoed separately and then placed together without any form of propping up' to be used for 'comparison and matching purposes if another portion of body arrives'. She continued:

I know not whether the parts of the torso have been filled out . . . our intention would be for them to be re-assembled prior to this videoing. If you are agreeable to do that on the basis that you were, at some future date, anxious to tie and match other parts to the two parts in hand by this suggested method or, indeed, if you can think of a better method to deal with it, then we would be obliged. However, whatever method is agreed and upon completion and inspection by us, then we will be quite happy for the body to be released for burial upon the basis that parts of the torso are not cosmetically enhanced.

The police asked Dr West to comment on this proposal, and he replied that the skeleton had been retained and reconstructed. 'The only materials remaining in the mortuary are the residual soft tissues which have been extensively dissected. It would be impossible to reconstruct the torso in the manner suggested. In particular it would be impossible to reassemble the skeleton within the soft tissues. I am not aware of any way in which video-taping the soft tissue remains will be of any assistance.' He said later, 'I had taken the bones out of the body to clean them up, to look at the machine marks and to examine the bullet wound. They wanted me to put them back into the soft tissue, which was obviously impossible.'

Still the defence fought on to discredit the suggestion that the torso was that of Stephen Davison. They focused on the discrepancy between Iain West's estimation of the height of the dead man and Davison's height. They produced X-rays to suggest that Davison had never suffered a broken rib. They suggested that the torso in the pond had been there too long for it to have been associated with the fight at the St Helier tavern.

Patiently Dr West answered each point in a supplementary statement.

Estimation of stature of a length of the single femur gives a rough guide to height. The error of any estimation based upon the femoral length, however, is such that it would not be possible to exclude the femur coming from a man 5 feet 10 inches in height.

I am unable to confirm either the presence or absence of a fractured rib on the copies of the miniature X-rays.

The part of the torso found in Priory Park showed a state of decomposition indicating that the disposal was likely to have occurred during the previous weekend. This takes into account the fact that a dismembered body would decompose more rapidly than an intact body, and it is likely that the gases produced during putrefaction would cause the remains to float within a day or two of being placed in the pond.

When the case came to trial, the Old Bailey heard first from a teenager who gave evidence from behind a screen. She said she had been eating an ice lolly and chatting with her friends outside the St Helier pub when she heard a loud bang. Moments later, a man was dragged by his heels through the fire exit and driven off in a horsebox.

The key prosecution witness was the man who had buried the portion of the body found on the farm at Dorking. Michael Bond took the police to the spot where the remains were hidden, and turned Queen's evidence against the two leaders of the gang along with another witness, Kevin Lewis. So desperate was the underworld to stop these two from giving evidence that the police had to give both men and their families round-the-clock protection. Bond was threatened with a shotgun, firebombed, and had his van daubed with curses and then stolen. He was moved by police to a secret address when his children received threats at school, but even then he was tracked down. Lewis told the court that a £20,000 contract had been taken out on his life.

Despite this intimidation, the true story slowly emerged.

The leader of the gang, a thirty-seven-year-old taxi-firm owner, Tony Crabb, had blasted his victim at close range then driven the body to a lonely caravan park, where the head and hands were cut off and burned and the torso was buried. Later that same night he and Gary Taylor, a nightclub bouncer, dug up the rest of body and cut it into pieces. Part of it was thrown into the pond at Priory Park, and when, some day later, Crabb spotted a lump floating on the surface, he swam out to it naked and pushed it back beneath the water.

When it came to giving a verdict, it was Dr West's evidence that finally satisfied the jury. The torso was that of Stephen Davison, they decided, and he had been the victim of a gangland killing. They found Gary Taylor and Tony Crabb guilty. Crabb was jailed for life for the murder and dismemberment. Taylor got nine years for helping to cut up the body. Bond got two years for his part in the crime.

'We never found any more of the body,' said Iain West. 'If the first piece had been disposed of in a different way, the whole case might have remained an unsolved mystery for ever.'

The story had an interesting postscript. Tyrone Evans, a violent and dangerous twenty-eight-year-old, was arrested and charged with obstructing police by dismembering the body of Davison and trying to conceal this crucial evidence by hiding it in plastic bags. As he was being driven from prison to Sutton magistrates court for a remand hearing one day, he overpowered his lone police guard and was whisked away by two men in a waiting Renault 5 Turbo car. The escape set off a nationwide hue and cry for Evans, but he was on the run for only four days before giving himself up. Three months later Evans himself was dead, having taken a drugs overdose in Belmarsh Prison before he could stand trial for his part in the murder.

Graeme Woodhatch

Graeme Woodhatch, a thirty-eight-year-old roofing contractor from Hampstead, north London, was admitted to the local Royal Free Hospital on Thursday 21 May 1992. That afternoon he underwent a routine operation for piles.

Three days later, on the Sunday morning, he was feeling much better and, dressed in a shirt and trousers, went to make a call from the public telephone outside McLaggan Ward on the fourth floor. It was 10.30 am and the hospital was quiet, when a bang was heard from the vicinity of the public telephone, followed by a scream and a crash. As staff rushed to the scene, they found Mr Woodhatch lying just outside the door of the ward. His head was in a pool of blood and the telephone receiver was dangling.

Hospital emergency procedures were quickly put into effect and Mr Woodhatch was given artificial respiration and blood transfusions as the staff fought to resuscitate him for forty-five minutes. Eventually it became clear that he was beyond help, and he was officially pronounced dead at 11.31 am. It looked as if he had collapsed through loss of blood resulting from a haemorrhage associated with his recent operation.

During the afternoon the dead man's distraught family began to arrive at the hospital and the talk was of one thing only – the death threats Graeme Woodhatch had apparently been receiving. This disquieting news caused one of the doctors to visit the morgue to take another look at the body. To his horror he spotted what he thought was a bullet wound in the head.

By this time it was almost 6 pm – some seven hours after the original incident – and the area CID team were alerted. Two detective constables arrived at the hospital and supervised the taking of X-rays of the body before it was moved to

St Pancras mortuary. Detective Superintendent Duncan MacRae took charge of the investigation, the local coroner was informed, and Iain West was contacted at home.

'By that stage they had discovered that the hole behind the left ear was a bullet wound,' he said. 'In answer to my questions, they said they had X-rays and the assumption was that we had one bullet in the head that had come out, though it didn't answer the question as to where the bullet was. I tried to insist that they X-ray the chest, as bullets sometimes travel down and get lost in that area, but the hospital was quite happy that the X-ray showed he had been shot just the once.'

The following morning Dr West carried out an autopsy and he immediately began to find evidence that Graeme Woodhatch had been murdered. He had been shot not once, but four times at close range.

'There was a dressing below the left collarbone,' recalled Iain West with a chuckle. 'I took the dressing off and said to the junior doctor from the hospital, "What's that?" She replied, "That's where we put a line in," and I said, "No, it's not – it's a bullet wound. Are there any more?" The reply was, "Oh no, there's no more," so I turned the body over and there was one in the back of the right shoulder.

'By this time I'd called in the mobile X-ray unit, and the X-rays showed the remains of two bullets in the head and two bullets in the trunk – one in the shoulder region and one in the chest. One of the fragments of bullet in the head had gone into an airspace within the facial bones. It was moving around, so it became a little difficult to follow. But neither of the shots to the head had killed him, as I recall. It was the one in the chest that killed him.'

Dr West's postmortem report tells the story of each bullet.

First, there was the triangular entry wound just below the dead man's left collarbone.

> The bullet track passed through the front of the left chest wall, penetrating towards the midline and piercing the first left rib just below the junction between the collarbone and breastbone. The bullet transfixed the upper lobe of the left lung, passing to the hilum of the lung. It then struck the body of the seventh thoracic vertebra and rebounded into the lower lobe of the left lung.
>
> I followed a bullet track into the posterior basal segment of the lower lobe of the left lung and retrieved a white metal bullet.

The second wound was behind the left ear.

> The firearm entry wound was surrounded by a zone of blackening and propellant tattooing which extended on to the rim of the ear. Within the area of blackening were a series of five superficial splits which ran in a line opposite the projectile entry hole.

Perhaps this was the first shot. One could imagine Mr Woodhatch standing with his back to the killer, the telephone receiver pressed to his right ear. Silently the gunman creeps up and puts the muzzle of the weapon behind his victim's left ear and squeezes the trigger. If that was the way it happened, this shot had a pretty devastating effect. Dr West reported:

> The wound track passed through the soft tissues overlying the left side of the jaw, striking the left ramus of the mandible and then entered the left maxilla,

transversed the left maxillary sinus and entered the nasal cavity.

With the clinical detachment which is the hallmark of his trade, he then simply wrote:

I recovered a distorted bullet from the nasal cavity.

If the shot behind Graeme Woodhatch's left ear was indeed the first, one might surmise that it caused him to spin round to face his killer, only to be shot again at point-blank range in the face.

The next bullet wound described by Dr West was just below the dead man's right eye on the right side of his nose. It, too, like the shot behind the ear, had been fired at close quarters, because all the tell-tale signs were there.

The wound was symmetrically surrounded by punctuate abrasions and superficial wounds in some of which were embedded black propellant particles. The bullet track passed through the nasal cavity just below the nasal bone, splintering the lower margin of the right nasal bone, and then pierced the left maxilla, traversed the left maxillary sinus and exited the outer cheekbone to strike the left zygomatic arch, causing the minor injuries on the skin of the outer left cheek. A distorted bullet was retrieved from the substance of the left massetter muscle below the zygomatic arch.

The fourth shot was through the left shoulder. Dr West reported:

I dissected the tissue all around the shoulder joint, looked at the humerus – the upper arm bone – but I couldn't see a hole. I could see that the bullet had gone through muscle to the surface of the bone, and then . . . nothing! It had to be in there, but there was no hole. In fact it had gone in at the junction between the cartilage covering the head and the neck of the bone. The cartilage would usually split with a bullet wound, but in this case it had flipped back down and was covering the hole. I found the bullet embedded in the head of the humerus.

It was one of these so-called hypervelocity stinger rounds – .22 rounds mainly designed for rifles.

There were also some grazes and abrasions, caused by bullet propellant, to the back of Mr Woodhatch's left hand and wrist. Perhaps these injuries were sustained as he instinctively tried to ward off the shots.

Dr West's report concluded:

Graeme Woodhatch was a man of medium build who has died as the result of firearm wounds to his head and chest. Natural disease has played no part in his death. The deceased has been shot four times by a small calibre low-velocity weapon, the two discharges to the face being at very close range. The bullets have penetrated the tissues of the face, causing bleeding into the airway, and have caused very serious injury to the left lung. There is no evidence to indicate that the deceased had been involved in any fight or struggle prior to being shot.

So, what was it all about?

There were red faces at the Royal Free Hospital and calls for an immediate overhaul of security within Britain's hospitals generally. Superintendent MacRae leapt to the defence of the medical staff, saying: 'The damage was inflicted by a small-calibre weapon. Although he was bleeding, it was believed initially that such injuries were sustained when he fell.'

But for him and his team there were more pressing matters and many more baffling questions to answer. Within days the murder squad began to uncover a lurid and unpleasant side to Graeme Woodhatch. He had, it seemed, a string of angry associates threatening to kill him over debts of almost £1 million. One gang had beaten him up after smashing their way into his village home at night and chasing him naked across a sportsfield. His ex-partner, Paul Tubbs, told newspapers: 'A contractor he welshed on beat him up badly only three weeks ago, and three months ago a man I can't name put a gun to his head. It was inevitable someone would murder him one day. He was a Maxwell without the brains. He just hoodwinked everybody.'

Police discovered that Woodhatch, a former Borstal boy, could hardly read or write but until weeks before his death had owned a £400,000 house, a £50,000 Porsche and a Mercedes. He had a string of girlfriends, took fabulous holidays abroad and boasted that he had superstar friends, including Rod Stewart and Martina Navratilova. His pride and joy was a Great Dane, and his hobbies were keeping fit, riding and collecting paintings. But those who worked with him claimed he had no friends at all and that he had beaten his wife Sue until their divorce three years earlier. His lavish lifestyle, they said, was paid for with gold credit cards and by cheating everyone he could.

His fifteen-year-old roofing company had gone bust because of his playboy lifestyle, and he was bankrupt, owing more than £400,000 in back tax.

Superintendent MacRae revealed that Woodhatch was out

on bail at the time of his death after being charged with making a death threat to a business colleague two weeks earlier. He was also facing a serious fraud charge at the time. 'We would dearly love to know whom he was speaking to on the phone. We would also like to talk to anyone who has business dealings with him,' he said.

The police interviewed Woodhatch's former wife, Sue, and his pregnant Israeli girlfriend, Etti Karrel. It was really the business connection that detectives were convinced would lead them to the killer, and gradually their interest began to focus on his two partners, Paul Tubbs and Deith Bridges. The pair had been impressed by Graeme Woodhatch's gift of the gab, and had taken him on a year earlier when his own business was heading for ruin. Soon they realised he was swindling them, and by the time of his death he owed the angry partners £50,000. Now the police had a motive, but they could not tie their suspects directly to the murder.

Then, almost eighteen months after the shooting, came an astonishing and totally unexpected breakthrough – from the other side of the world. A twenty-seven-year-old Maori woman, Te Rangimaria Ngarimu, known as 'Sparky', walked into a police station in New Zealand with a scarcely credible tale to tell. She had become a born-again Christian, she said, and wanted to confess to a killing in England to clear her conscience.

She had got to know Bridges, who was born in New Zealand, when they both worked in a north London pub five years earlier. They began to live together, and one night, when talk turned to Woodhatch, Bridges asked her to kill him for a fee. She agreed to do the job for £7,000 – an amount which would buy her the mobile home she had dreamed of. Tubbs supplied the money.

At the time of the killing there had been much speculation

that the .22 calibre bullets used to kill Woodhatch could have come from a pistol small enough to fit inside a woman's handbag. Could the murderer have been a woman – a jealous or spurned lover, perhaps? Nobody was prepared for the discovery that the murder was carried out by Britain's first female contract killer.

'Sparky' flew back to England to give evidence against her two co-conspirators, but after two days the trial had to be adjourned when Bridges, out on bail, was also shot in the chest and leg by a passenger in a passing car. When he was well enough to stand trial again some six months later, the Old Bailey heard the full story from the lips of the murderer herself.

She had never met Graeme Woodhatch and was given a photograph by Bridges to help identify her target. He also gave her the gun, which she loaded with hollow-tipped bullets to increase the damage. The day before the murder she travelled to the Royal Free Hospital, one of the busiest in Britain, but could not locate Woodhatch. The following day, dressed in a black baseball hat, black tracksuit, gloves and sunglasses, she took a taxi to the hospital, remembering Bridges' advice: 'Shoot him twice in the head and twice in the body to be sure of death.'

She found Woodhatch sitting down, using the telephone in the corridor, and recognised him immediately. 'I did not even have to look at the photograph,' she told the jury. 'I had my hand on the gun and took off the safety catch. I was pacing up and down, deciding whether to do it or not. I was quite nervous.' In the end it was 'Sparky's' desperate desire to own her own mobile home that decided Woodhatch's fate. 'Something just snapped, and I did it. Before I left, Deith told me just think about the house bus. I had always wanted one. It was going to be my home. I thought about it, and I shot him', said the young woman, who has degrees in maths and chemistry.

Everything happened so quickly that her recollections of the fateful moments were vague. Standing about three feet away, and holding the gun in both hands, she fired. 'There were four shots, but I remember pulling the trigger only once,' she told the court. 'That shot hit him in the face – he was facing towards me. I do not remember firing the other shots, although I heard four. I remember seeing him rolling around on the floor, screaming. He had his hands on his face.'

All her pacing up and down before the shooting had been designed to delay until a lift arrived to help her make a quick getaway. As the bell on the lift clanged above the stricken man's dying screams, the woman gave her victim one last look and coolly stepped inside.

Miss Ngarimu slipped away from the hospital in a taxi as pandemonium broke out on McLaggan ward. She went to Bridges' flat in Camden Town, where she wiped her fingerprints off the gun, stripped off her clothes, put them into a bag and left Bridges to dispose of them. Arriving at Gatwick airport for her 4.30 pm flight to New Zealand – over an hour before the hospital discovered they were dealing with a murder – she discovered she still had the photograph of Woodhatch in her pocket, and ripped it up in a blind panic.

That evening Paul Tubbs telephoned a friend and asked him to meet Deith Bridges to dispose of a holdall. When the friend received the holdall, he looked inside and found a gun, bullets, baseball cap and tracksuit. He threw it into a lake, from which police divers were later able to retrieve the gun to show it to Iain West.

'I examined the revolver together with the excised specimen taken from the left side of the deceased's face,' Dr West wrote in a statement given to the court. 'The pattern of the firearm wound behind the deceased's left ear is entirely consistent with the muzzle of that or a similar weapon being placed in loose or soft contact with the skin of the deceased when the cartridge was fired . . . in my opinion, a weapon identical to, or very similar to, this revolver was responsible for causing the firearm wound.'

'It was a Colt .22 Trooper target pistol,' he recalled later. 'There had been a muzzle imprint on the back of his left ear, and looking at the muzzle of the Trooper and looking at the imprint, they actually matched perfectly.'

Paul Tubbs and Deith Bridges were jailed for life. Te Rangimaria Ngarimu, too, was jailed for life. The judge told her that normally her crime would carry a recommendation of twenty years in jail, but because she gave evidence against the two men, he would recommend leniency to the Home Secretary. Her defence counsel told the court that she was now 'a sinner but not without hope of ultimate salvation. That is something with which she consoles herself'.

Iain West is still amused when he thinks of the Woodhatch case but his sympathy lies with the medical staff who failed to spot the bullet wounds. 'I've done it myself,' he said. 'I missed an air pellet in somebody's scalp once, mainly because I thought I had got out the pellet which related to another wound. In fact it was not that one, and when I went back and had a second look at the body, there was another wound in the back of the head. Graeme Woodhatch had been treated in hospital for a number of days, so it is not that surprising, I suppose.'

Murder at the 39 Club

Gang warfare exploded on the streets of London's Chinatown with terrifying ferocity early one summer morning in 1982.

Customers in the 39 Club, an illegal gambling den tucked away in a seedy basement were just preparing for the last mah-jong game of the night when two men burst in. It was 1.30 am on 18 July. Armed with broken bottles and staves, the intruders lined the eight occupants of the club up against the wall. Expertly they soaked each man in petrol, doused the stairway leading to the street, and torched the place as they fled. One of the eight gamblers sprinted up the stairs after them, and this action saved his life. Within seconds the Soho club was a blazing inferno, trapping the seven remaining men – six Chinese and a Vietnamese – and condemning them to a ghastly death.

The Chinese community is notoriously difficult to penetrate, and when Iain West began his postmortem the seven bodies before him were unidentified. They were simply and somewhat pathetically referred to as bodies 1 to 7. Despite the massive fireball that had engulfed the club, several of them were remarkably intact and free from fire damage.

Only one was naked, and that was body number one, a young slim man about 5 feet 4 inches tall, whom the emergency services had obviously stripped while trying to revive him. 'There were marks of treatment on the surface of the body in the form of injection marks in both groins and in the left forearm,' Dr West reported. He also noted that, like several of the other bodies, the effects of the fire had turned the skin a bright pink. This man's mouth was bruised, due to attempts to resuscitate him, and his throat, lungs and other air passages were all heavily congested with soot and mucus, a pattern that was to be repeated in all the bodies.

It is an important principle of crime investigation that, wherever possible, only one person should handle exhibits and items of evidential value. In the case of murder this principle is extended to the pathologist, whose investigations are best helped by an examination of the body *in situ* or, if that is not feasible, as in this case, at least in the state in which it was found.

Accordingly, each of the remaining six postmortem reports begins with a detailed description of the victim's clothing and personal effects as Iain West carefully worked from the outer layers of clothing to the body beneath. In several of the cases it was this description that eventually led to the successful identification of the dead men. Reading the reports, one gets a sad picture of the débris of human existence that we all gather to ourselves and which, in death, becomes so meaningless – seven pence in pocket change, four keys on a loop of string, a Crédit Suisse medallion, a 'Valentino' belt buckle, a packet of cigarettes and a green and gold lighter, a penknife, a ballpoint pen, a tube ticket, a payslip, a pair of glasses, a pocket calculator, a pair of green socks, a pair of St Michael's underpants.

Body number two of a middle-aged balding man wearing a charcoal pinstripe suit, showed signs of having been in a fight before the fire. Dr West wrote:

> There is bruising on the inside of the left side of the cheek and left corner of the mouth which has occurred during life. The injury is consistent with the effects of a punch to the mouth. There was bruising on the centre of the right chest adjacent to the breastbone, which could have been caused by a blow to the chest.

Body number three had a denture plate on his lower jaw and an enlarged heart. The pathologist could tell from this that he had suffered from high blood pressure for a long time, but there was no evidence of a recent heart attack.

These two bodies – numbers two and three – had been found huddled together in the toilet inside the small lobby at the foot of the stairs leading to Gerrard Street and safety. So near and yet so far. Dr West reported that the skin on their hands and feet was heavily wrinkled where the bodies had lain in pools of water after the fire brigade had pumped hundreds of gallons into the club to quell the flames.

The remaining four bodies had all been extensively charred. They had been found trapped in a tiny office and a small bedroom right at the back of the club, furthest from the exit. Body number one, the young man the ambulancemen had thought they might save, had been found between two of these bodies and probably shielded from the worst effects of the fire because of this.

Of body number four Dr West wrote:

There was extensive charring of the surface of the body with destruction of the majority of the skin on the back. A clout nail was sticking out of the front upper part of the left side of his chest. This was not associated with any bruising and appeared to be a postmortem injury. The scalp and skull were partially burnt through on the right side. The feet and lower parts of the legs were burnt off. The burnt remains of a foot were present with the body.

He went on to describe a 'large heat haematoma over the surface of the brain with extensive heat destruction'. The heart, too, 'showed extensive heat change'.

Body number five was also badly charred on the head, face, neck, arms and back, and frozen 'in the pugilistic attitude'. This man's right leg and right foot were also burnt away. The brain and heart were affected by heat damage.

Most of the skin had been burned away from bodies

numbers six and seven. All in all, a grim and sorry sight. For Dr West, deciding on the cause of death was easy. All seven had died as a result of asphyxia and the inhalation of fire fumes.

Who were these unfortunate people? The coroner needed to know for the inquest.

In order to help to determine their identity, Dr West called in Derek Clark, a leading forensic odontologist. Now a highly specialised form of forensic investigation would be brought into play. Mr Clark undertook a dental examination of each body. Carefully marking up a dental chart for each man as he worked meticulously through each mouth, he prepared the way for final positive identification. If the police were able to get some idea of who the dead man was, then Mr Clark's chart could be compared with the records held by the man's own dentist.

This examination threw up very few clues. Of body number three, for instance, Mr Clark wrote:

Partially carbonised head. Wide dental arches suggesting
a heavily-built male. All teeth present were grossly
carious and the mouth had been generally neglected.
There is unlikely to be a dental record of this body.
However, the worn-down appearance of the front teeth
plus the apparently missing upper left second incisor
might assist in identification.

Two of the men had dentures, but, by the time he had finished, all Mr Clark could say for certain was that three of the bodies had readily identifiable features. If he were shown photographs of two of the men alive, he thought he could say if they were the ones he had examined in death.

The police brought in Chinese-speaking officers to trawl

through the Oriental communities seeking information, looking for clues and trying to identify the victims. Gradually the information came in. The first three bodies were physically identified by relatives and friends, and the other four through items of property which Iain West had examined and so carefully listed in his report.

Body number one was twenty-five-year-old Kin Hong Tang, who lived just a few doors away from the club. He was also known as Hong Ji, Hon Jah and Hung. Number two was Ho Po Man, also known as Ballsuk, a forty-one-year-old from west London. Number three actually lived in the same building as the club itself. He was the oldest victim, aged sixty. His name was Fat Hou, sometimes called Kan Fat Hau. Numbers five and six both came from west London. Kin Choi Chau, with an alias of Ah Sey, was forty-two, and twenty-six-year-old Ba Tan Duong was the only Vietnamese among the dead, the others all being Hong Kong Chinese. Number seven, twenty-two-year-old Man Pong Shing from Letchworth in Hertfordshire, was ironically known by the nickname of Lucky Baby. And number four, Chun Hung Pang, was twenty-nine, came from Ilford and was known as Mah Bau Hung.

The tragic night when the 39 Club burned down almost claimed another victim because by 2.30, with police and firemen clearing débris outside, there was a huge explosion caused by a build-up of leaking gas. Shards of glass pierced the back of the police officer in charge of the clear-up operation, Chief Superintendent Cyril Gibbons, puncturing his lung. His life was saved by a doctor searching for survivors, who held the officer's damaged arteries together to stop blood pumping from the wound.

Eventually the full story of the vicious attack emerged. It was a savage revenge carried out by two Vietnamese boat refugees living in Britain. On the night of the murders, six Vietnamese had been in the club playing fan-tan. One member of their party won £70 and the men began to celebrate. The excitement developed into a row and they were asked to leave, but refused. Eventually the club doorman took one of the Vietnamese into the street, where a fight broke out. The group marched off down Gerrard Street, armed themselves with sticks and broken bottles and returned to the club, bent on revenge. But the police were called and they dispersed, only for two of the most determined of them to return later with murder in their hearts.

A year later two Vietnamese boat people, twenty-three-year-old Vu Linh Nguyen and twenty-one-year-old Van Tinh Phan, were jailed for life at the Old Bailey after being found guilty of the murders. They had been identified by the man who so narrowly escaped with his life.

'The problems of that case were not establishing why or how they had been killed but establishing who they were,' recalled Iain West. 'Fire causes major problems because one identifies using a number of parameters. Visual identification is obviously the first method to be used, but one has to be very careful about visual identification where there has been either decomposition or damage to the body. And I do know of several cases of misidentification by visual means.

'One has to rely on more objective evidence for identification, and obviously the best identification would be something like fingerprints or DNA if you have the individual's DNA on record. It is unlikely that you would have an individual's DNA on record, so fingerprints are probably the best, although we did use DNA to identify a chap who set himself on fire in his car as a protest outside no. 10 Downing Street in Whitehall some years ago. We checked his DNA back with his relatives to confirm his identity. If you haven't got somebody's fingerprints or footprints, and if they are not on file, you may go back to their house to look for objects that they handle regularly to make a match.

'In one case, I remember, the lower half of a young girl was found in a plastic bag shoved underneath a Rolls-Royce parked in the street in Mayfair. The body came in and was looked at by Keith Simpson initially, but he was going away on holiday so I was asked if I would take it over. It was clear that it was the body of a young female, not European, possibly Asian, possibly Middle Eastern. We knew that there had been a young Middle Eastern girl reported missing. We X-rayed the limbs and pelvis; she had been simply dismembered at waist level. No trace was ever found of the upper half of the body. We were left with a pelvis, two legs and two feet. She was starting to decompose, but I was able to confirm her age. We went to the flat of the missing girl, but couldn't find any traces which connected with the body. Two detectives and a fingerprint officer then went out to the missing girl's home in Saudi Arabia.

'They had taken footprints from the body and began to search the home for a likely place where they might find footprints from the missing girl. They went into the girl's bedroom and saw a desk. They reasoned that a young girl might sit barefoot at her desk, rocking back in her chair with her feet propped against the front edge. When they tested their theory, sure enough there were footprints on the front edge of the desk. When they brought them back to England they matched the prints from the body, and she was identified on that basis. I had a lot of admiration for the team involved in the investigation and in the novel way in which she was identified. We still do not know who killed her, however.'

Dr West went on to outline the particular problems of

identification in the case of fire when fingerprints and foot-prints are destroyed. 'It is fairly common to find the skin destroyed or damaged seriously by fire,' he said. 'You have then to look at the next best means of identification, which is probably dentistry. If there has been considerable dental restoration, the chartings may allow a very accurate assessment of identity. That assessment can be even more powerfully corroborated if there are dental X-rays because they will show you not only where fillings are but the precise shape of the fillings. If you X-ray the dentition in an unidentified body and compare the shape of the fillings, and their arrangement, with the records of a missing person, you may get an accurate identification. I remember the case of a woman whose body had been badly injured during the Brighton bomb, where I looked at the shape of a root filling in a fragment of the jaw and found it corresponded precisely to the shape of a root filling on an X-ray that her dentist sent in.

'Dental evidence may be as good as fingerprint evidence in respect of identification – the possibility of there being two radiologically identical root fillings with this identical pattern being so remote as to be unimaginable. It is better evidence than DNA when the only source of DNA is from relatives of the deceased.

'One of the problems we find nowadays is that young people have very good teeth and there isn't much to find on their dental records. We might be looking for abnormalities of the teeth or abnormalities of the arrangement of their teeth that might have been noticed by their dentist; many of them have few fillings. In looking for other good indicators of identity one may find someone who has undergone neurosurgery. If you look at the shape of any skull defects seen on the X-ray of the body and compare them with an X-ray of a missing person, you may be able to match them up. One of my colleagues had a case where the shape of a metal plate found in the X-ray of a patient's skull matched up perfectly with the shape of the plate found in the deceased; again, identity was confirmed that way

'Metal plates are not very common. I've done many post-mortems on cases where people are thought to have had a 'silver' plate put in their skull during the war because of an injury to the head. I've never yet seen one. My colleague's seen two. I have, however, seen people who've suffered severe fractures where pieces of metal have been used to bridge fracture lines.

'On occasion, also, you X-ray the skull specifically for the shape of the frontal air sinuses. The shape of the frontal sinus is thought to be relatively unique to the individual. So, if you have a missing person who has had skull X-rays, you may be able to compare the shape of the sinuses with those on the deceased. If they match up, all the evidence suggests that you've got a good identification.'

But Dr West pointed out that examining skulls is not always a satisfactory way of identifying a body. 'One of the bodies found in the King's Cross fire was a man with a bone flap and a metal clip in his skull. Despite that, he has still not been identified. Unfortunately there is no way of knowing whether your missing individual would have had skull X-rays or scans. There is no way of searching within the records of the Health Service to see who has had a particular procedure done.

'If you haven't got these indicators of high probability of identification, you then have to look at other aspects. It may be jewellery, clothing, that kind of order of identification. We know that you have to be careful in that area, because people do swap jewellery or even share clothing. There have been documented cases where people have been initially identified on the basis of objects in their pockets which apparently related to them but turned out to belong to other individuals. It may have been stolen, or it may be that something was put in their pocket by the rescue services. I can think of one air crash in that respect.

'We had problems at the Clapham train crash because the bodies were strip-searched and the belongings put in plastic bags and left in the body-bags. Some of the body-bags contained items from more than one body, and it was difficult to match them up to the remains, particularly where you had bags containing parts from more than one body. In one case, there was a jacket in a bag containing one body, but the jacket belonged to another individual. In the case of a young female, there was a handbag with all the documentation placed in the bag with her body, but it was apparent that it wasn't her handbag. There was a photograph of the owner, and you could see from the features of the deceased that it couldn't have been the same.'

Dr West then went on to deal with an aspect of the identification process which became controversial in the aftermath of the Marchioness pleasure-boat disaster on the River Thames on 20 August 1989. On that occasion the hands of several of the deceased were removed and taken away from the mortuary so that sophisticated fingerprint techniques could be used on the damaged skin for identification purposes. 'As far as the removal of hands is concerned, it is done as a matter of last resort. If the fingerprint people say that they can't get prints by any other means, you have to go along with them. The usual situation is where you have a murder case where the victim is decomposed, and you've got to exclude his or her fingerprints or footprints from the scene. If the prints can't be taken from the dead body, as they can in most cases, you have to remove the hands and then replace them after the postmortem. Unpleasant, but essential in certain cases. When a drowned body cannot be identified by other means, the hands may have to be removed

'Where we are left with no clothing and no jewellery, and in cases where the body is so badly damaged that you can't see scars or any other abnormalities, you have to assess any disease processes, any internal evidence of surgery or internal evidence of congenital abnormality. You would also take X-rays to see if there is evidence that may assist. Samples are now regularly taken for DNA.

'You are left with a small group of individuals at the end of the day where decomposition or incineration is so severe that there is virtually nothing there to go on. There was a fire in a hotel in London where there were sixteen victims, and it took days to remove the last victim because the fire kept smouldering on. All I was left with was part of the spine, a few bits of the pelvis, a very small section of the base of the skull and some charred ribs. That body really had to be identified on the basis of exclusion. We knew that this particular man had been in the building and had never been seen. His wife was in the room with him when the fire started, therefore his body had to be the remains which were found.

'Very few bodies are not identified,' concluded Dr West. 'I can think of perhaps six or seven in twenty-five years. Oddly enough, the first postmortem I ever did at St Thomas's when I started in forensic medicine in London was that of a woman who had obviously been living rough who died of a pulmonary embolism, and we never identified her. I've only ever had one unidentified murder victim – a woman strangled in a hotel in central London.'

The firebombing of the 39 Club was a case which was memorable to Iain West for another reason. The detective in charge of the case was Detective Chief Superintendent George Churchill-Coleman, who at that time was head of CID in London's West End and later found fame as the longest-serving Commander of Scotland Yard's Anti-terrorist Squad. 'We were using a temporary mortuary at the time,' Dr West recalled, 'and I vividly remember that at some point during the autopsies George Churchill-Coleman went out of the postmortem room. He came back later with two pieces of metal in his hand, asking if anyone had an exhibits bag for them. "We've got two dead soldiers outside; an army ambulance has just brought them in," he said. They were the first victims of the Hyde Park bomb (see Chapter 2) and the first indication I had of what was to be an extremely long and busy day. I had been carrying out the Chinese postmortems when the bomb went off but I didn't hear it.'

CHAPTER 13

DEATHS 'IN CUSTODY'

Among the most controversial cases of sudden death are those where the victims are alleged to have died at the hands of the police or other representatives of authority. The unexplained death of somebody under arrest, in prison or in secure mental accommodation always brings calls for an official inquiry. And if a member of the armed forces is implicated in the death, voices are inevitably raised in parliament. Technically all such incidents are termed 'Deaths in Custody' and Dr West has been involved in helping to unravel some of the most noteworthy of these cases over the past two decades.

Lee Clegg

Throughout the spring and summer of 1995 a major campaign captured the imagination of the British public. Involving generals, MPs, ministers, lawyers, newspapers and large numbers of ordinary citizens who signed petitions, it was an orchestrated attempt to win freedom for a young soldier serving life for the murder of a joy-rider in Belfast.

To his supporters, the case of Private Lee Clegg was a simple one of a soldier penalised for doing his duty. The twenty-two-year-old paratrooper had been a member of a four-man army patrol which flagged down a car in the back streets of West Belfast one Sunday night in September 1990. Having slowed down, apparently to comply with a check-point, the car, a dark blue Vauxhall Astra, suddenly picked up speed and roared off, driving straight at one of the soldiers who stood in its path. Suspecting that the car contained IRA terrorists and fearing for the life of their colleague, all four members of the patrol, including their officer, opened fire. Between them they fired nineteen rounds.

The trouble was that the car did not contain terrorists, just local teenagers out for the evening enjoying a prank or two. The seventeen-year-old driver, Martin Peake, was hit in the head and died instantly. His passenger Markievicz Gorman was wounded, and in the back seat eighteen-year-old Karen Reilly was hit and died a short time afterwards.

For the troopers, the action they had taken had to be justi-fied under their rules of engagement, which allow every soldier to open fire in self-defence whether or not he has been fired on first. The entire case was to turn on this point. The whole patrol insisted that Private Barry Aindow, the sol-dier at whom the car had been driven, was in mortal danger. He had been the first to open fire in self-defence, he claimed. To reinforce this point, he faked an injury by allowing one of his colleagues to jump on his leg so that he could say the speeding car had actually hit him.

When the case came to trial, Private Clegg told the court that he fired three aimed shots at the windscreen as the car approached and one as it passed. The Crown's case was that he fired all four shots at the back of the car after it had passed. The judge, sitting without a jury, decided that the round recovered from Karen Reilly's body had been fired by Private Clegg's weapon, and that the bullet had entered the vehicle through the rear of the car, passing through the back seat. There was no scientific evidence to prove that Clegg had fired his first three shots at the front of the car, since no bullets had hit the windscreen. The bullet that 'contributed significantly' to the death of Miss Reilly was fired from almost directly behind the car, about 50 feet back, and it entered a few inches above the rear bumper. Clegg denied firing this round, which had the appearance of being an aimed shot. The judge ruled, however, that Lee Clegg had fired the final shot when all possible danger to his patrol had passed and the car was going down the road. He sentenced the trooper to life for the murder of Karen Reilly and to four years for attempting to wound Martin Peake.

Private Aindow was given seven years for the attempted murder of Peake, and was convicted of attempting to pervert the course of justice. His sentence was cut to four years, and by 1995 he was free. Lance-Corporal Stephen Boustead was cleared of attempted murder and attempted wounding, and Lieutenant Andrew Oliver was acquitted of perverting the course of justice.

The campaign to free Clegg began to take off in January 1995, when he lost his appeal to the House of Lords against conviction. The Court of Appeal had already turned him down.

Eventually lawyers for the freedom campaign turned to Iain West, knowing that he was not only Britain's leading Home Office pathologist but also a noted ballistics expert. Armed with the trial transcripts, the original postmortem report, the medical records and a pile of scenes of crime photographs, Dr West set about reading himself thoroughly in to the case.

He noted particularly the size, shape and direction of entry of the fatal bullet wounds on Karen Reilly's body, and formed an opinion on how she had been hit and the way in which her body had reacted in the split second after the bullet's impact. He also paid careful attention to the bloodstaining in the back of the Astra car and the direction in which the splashes of blood had fallen. He soon determined that a series of practical tests – a reconstruction of the fatal shooting – would be the only satisfactory way to get at the truth.

Accordingly, an Astra car of precisely the same vintage and construction as the death vehicle was obtained. And on 4 June 1995 at an army rifle range at Lydd in Kent the tests took place, with a series of shots being fired from the same type of weapon and from a similar distance at the car. The ammunition was identical to that used by Clegg on the fatal night, and the experiments were supervised by another eminent forensic expert, Dr Graham Renshaw.

'The forensic science evidence in Northern Ireland was that the last bullet Clegg fired must have gone through the back of the car, and that this bullet, which was recovered from Karen Reilly's body, could only have gone into the car by that route,' said Dr West. 'There were two particular bullet holes in the near side of the car. The original experts thought that one of them would have been caused by a round which fragmented completely; the other, they said, could not have caused the deformity which was found on Clegg's bullet inside Karen's body.

'The two bullet rounds that she had in her chest were very close together. One went right through her chest and her arm – no one has any idea who fired that shot. They are, however, extremely close together as though it had been two shots fired almost simultaneously, one rapidly after the other – possibly two shots from the same weapon.

'The other Irish scientist had excluded the possibility of

both of the shots which struck her occurring from the same angle. I took the view that if they occurred from different angles, then her body would have had to go through very major changes in position between the first and second shots. I thought that was unlikely, given the pattern and distribution of bloodstains that one could see on the photographs of the back seat of the vehicle. The easiest way to investigate the problem was to see how bullets, fired from the same type of weapon into an Astra car, would behave.'

Revealing the key findings of the test firings, he continued, 'If you fire bullets through the back of the car, in the same manner as the bullet which allegedly killed the girl, you would expect them to go through the tailgate, through the back of the seat and through the upholstery. The bullets we fired never came, though; they fragmented within the seat and did not come through intact. What had apparently been very convincing in the courts in Northern Ireland was the shape of a hole in the back of the rear seat – a roughly banana-shaped defect – which corresponded to the shape of the bullet found in her body. In our test firings we produced an almost identical banana-shaped hole in the back of the seat, and yet that bullet had fragmented.

'On the other hand, one of the shots we fired through the side of the car during the experiment, when it was retrieved from the mass of cotton wool inside the vehicle, had bent at the same place and deformed in a very similar manner to the bullet found in Karen's body.'

At the end of the experiment Dr West and Dr Renshaw issued a joint statement with Clegg's lawyer, in which they said:

The prosecution in the Clegg case laid great emphasis on the shape of the entry hole in the rear of the vehicle and the wound to the girl. It was the prosecution's case that this round did not fragment. We have shown that it is likely that it did. Conversely, we have been able to demonstrate that Karen Reilly was struck not once but twice from the side of the car, meaning that there is no scientific evidence, based on our tests, that Private Lee Clegg fired after the vehicle had passed him.

The injury to Karen Reilly's head and the pattern of bloodstaining on the car seat is consistent with Karen Reilly having been hit by two missiles as described.

So, after these exhaustive scientific and ballistics tests, what was West saying about the prosecution case?

He was saying that it was flawed in three vital areas. The identical round fired at the rear of the car had broken up and failed to pierce the back seat. Bullets fired from the side might not have fragmented, as the judge in the 1993 trial had accepted. And Miss Reilly was hit twice by bullets fired from the side of the car. Clegg could, therefore, have 'legally' fired the fatal bullet, although his advisers were to continue tests to see if the bullet which killed Karen Reilly actually came from his rifle.

With the crucial evidence now available and the clamour for action growing louder by the day, the Cabinet met to consider the case. The IRA ceasefire had been in place for almost a year and the peace negotiations were at a delicate stage. Everyone realised that Clegg's freedom would have to be handled extremely skilfully.

In the event, the Northern Ireland Secretary, Sir Patrick Mayhew, referred the matter to the Life Sentence Review Board. The panel of twelve civil servants judged that Private Clegg had been sufficiently punished and was unlikely to re-offend. They freed him, with riots following in the streets of

Belfast and Londonderry, and calls for the immediate release of paramilitary terrorists. Just one month had elapsed since the experiments had been conducted.

Private Clegg and his supporters continued to fight for his conviction to be quashed and began to build a case upon the new evidence for the matter to be put back before the Northern Ireland Appeal Court. Meanwhile, the Army Board decided that Lee Clegg could resume his military career without a stain on his character.

Joy Gardner

Joy Gardner, aged forty and an illegal immigrant from Jamaica, died in hospital on 1 August 1993, four days after a struggle at her home in Crouch End, north London, with three officers from Scotland Yard's deportation squad. They had arrived with two uniformed local police and an immigration officer to execute a deportation order which had been issued eighteen months earlier, and their job was to escort the reluctant deportee to the aircraft which would take her back to her homeland.

But Mrs Gardner was not prepared to go quietly. She became angry, hysterical and very violent. In front of her six-year-old son Graham she ripped off her nightclothes, smashed two china ornaments to use as makeshift weapons and launched a ferocious attack on the officers – two men and a woman. As they sought to restrain her, she bit two of them, drawing blood. Eventually they managed to overpower her and bound her with a leather belt with handcuffs threaded through a loop at the front. A gag made of surgical tape and twisted to the thickness of a pencil was put in her mouth and taped round her head. But still she struggled until she collapsed across a table and fell on the floor where she lay still.

The officers turned away to collect her clothes; then one of them noticed she was not breathing. A paramedic crew tried resuscitation for about forty-five minutes and then took her to the Whittington Hospital, north London. She never regained consciousness.

The tragic case led to an immediate outcry from the voluble black community, and the Metropolitan Police Commissioner, Sir Paul Condon, moved swiftly to placate the anger of local people. Amid accusations of a knee-jerk reaction designed simply to avoid a riot on the streets, he immediately suspended the three officers from duty and disbanded their squad. Days later, the independent Police Complaints Authority appointed the Essex force to investigate the incident.

The investigation took many months, and eventually, to the consternation of the government and the astonishment of the police, the three police officers were charged with manslaughter. This was not before an astonishing battle had been fought out by opposing pathologists over the actual cause of death. It was a case which would turn entirely on medical opinion, and that opinion was bitterly divided.

The first postmortem on Mrs Gardner's body was performed jointly by Dr Paula Lannas of the London Medico-Legal Centre and Iain West's deputy, Dr Richard Shepherd, acting for the Police Complaints Authority. Dr Lannas said Mrs Garner had died of a blow to the head. This view was backed by one neuropathologist who specialised in studies of brain tissue. But Dr Shepherd insisted that she died of asphyxia caused by the gag. He sought backing for his view from Dr Helen Whitwell, a Birmingham Home Office pathologist and neuropathologist. His report pointed to the presence of petechial haemorrhages around the dead woman's eyes. Petechiae are a classic sign of suffocation which occur during or shortly after the person asphyxiates. But Dr Royden Davies, a heart specialist at the Whittington Hospital who treated Mrs Gardner, said the signs were not there when she was admitted. They had not shown up until days afterwards.

Iain West was called in as a private consultant to make a further postmortem examination on behalf of Joy Gardner's family.

By this time, the medical argument between brain damage and asphyxia was well developed and eminent specialists were joining in the debate weekly, like rugby forwards joining a scrum.

But Dr West, who had been away on another assignment, was largely unaware of the dispute and had not read Dr Lannas's findings at that stage. He and Dr Ian Hill, a member of his staff who was representing the Police Federation, undertook the second postmortem in the presence of Dr Lannas and Dr Shepherd.

'We found no bruise on the back of the scalp whatsoever,' he said, 'but we did find an additional injury. They had discovered one bruise on one temple and we found an additional bruise on the other side of the head. Neither was deep. Neither had extended down to the surface of the skull, so there obviously had not been a heavy impact to the head. A bruise does not simply disappear. You have either to excise it or it disappears through decomposition – and there was no sign of decomposition. There was a collection of bloodstained fluid at the back of the head; this might have looked initially like a bruise, but that is not uncommon when someone has been lying on their back being ventilated in an intensive care unit for days. I've seen it occur in other cases where blood and fluid collect in a layer between different areas of the scalp.'

By now Dr West was leaning towards the Shepherd view that asphyxia was the cause of death. Dr Whitwell came to London and performed a third postmortem, assisted by Dr West, and she, too, came to the same view. During that third autopsy, the two pathologists dissected the body very thoroughly in order to investigate allegations from Mrs Gardner's family that she had been severely beaten up. They found no injuries to suggest that she had been in any way attacked, simply bruises consistent with her having been involved in a struggle.

'My view at that time, and what will remain my view, was that she had died as the result of the effects of gagging,' said Dr West, as he set out to discuss the argument against brain damage caused by head injury. 'The police officers said that the only time head injury could have occurred was when there was a tussle and she ended up on the floor with one of their men on top of her. This occurred before she was cuffed; she was still fighting, still able to bite, so the fall obviously wasn't sufficient to knock her out.

'At the trial, Paula Lannas had suggested that she may have repeatedly banged her head on the floor, but there is no evidence from any of the witnesses to support that. And there is no medical evidence that you could actually do potentially fatal damage to your head by striking your head against the floor while lying on the floor. We have seen people in prison who had repeatedly banged their heads against walls, but they are not lying down while doing it.

'Frankly, if someone is going to die from a head injury with that rapidity, you have a severe head injury, or other factors have intervened. Certainly, you can get concussional head injury associated with that degree of contusion, but if you are concussed you don't normally need to be restrained. We know people can behave irrationally when concussed, but they would not try to bite and they would not die unless something else occurs. And that can be obstruction of the airway. They may be in a position where they can't keep the airway clear; the tongue might fall back or they might vomit and inhale.

'There were indications at postmortem – from the pattern of pneumonia in her lungs – that Joy Gardner had aspirated vomit into her lungs. I'm not sure at what stage. It could have been at the time of gagging or it could have been during the resuscitation procedures that followed.'

Dr West went on to explain the perils of using gags. 'Gagging is a dangerous pursuit. Gagging may kill for a number of reasons. Firstly, it may provoke vomit, often through panic. The vomit can escape and enter the airway. There are even dangers with the use of an incomplete gag. In this case, the officers appear to have made the assumption that if you leave a space at the top of the gag then the person will still be able to breathe. But they clearly didn't realise that a gag may press against the tongue. For a time the person may keep the tongue pushed forward in order to assist with breathing, but that does not last for long before exhaustion occurs. That assumes that they are not fighting. If they are fighting and struggling, the oxygen requirements of the heart are enormous – several hundred per cent above the basal level. A gag will also tend to accumulate secretions around the throat, which may also cut down on the air supply. In those circumstances you will have a very restricted airway, and I think that's what happened in this case. I think she went into sudden dysrhythmia. The heart's action suddenly altered into a lethal rhythm and she had a cardiac arrest.

'As I said at the trial, gagging is an all-or-nothing event.

Most people who are gagged survive without any harm. Occasionally people will end up with problems caused by reduction of oxygen supply to the brain. Relatively few people die, usually from asphyxia or from inhaling vomit.

'Joy Gardner did not asphyxiate in the classic sense. She died in a situation where she had a high oxygen demand when she had a partial obstruction of the airway; she developed a lethal dysrhythmia when her heart was already working overtime in response to the situation to produce the high levels of adrenalin that must have been present in her body.'

And, with classic understatement, he added, 'A recipe for trouble.'

His postmortem report put it another way:

In my opinion, Joy Gardner died as the result of irreversible anoxic cerebral infarction and bronchopneumonia resulting from suffocation induced by the use of a gag.

In June 1995, at the end of a four-week landmark Old Bailey trial, all three police officers charged with Joy Gardner's manslaughter, Sergeant Linda Evans, and Police Constables Colin Whitby and John Burrell were acquitted. They were quickly reinstated and the Police Complaints Authority announced that they would not be disciplined.

Kevin Gately

15 June 1974 was a beautiful summer day in central London. But the warm weather and the peaceful holiday atmosphere was to be marred by an ugly street battle between police and protestors.

It was a period when violent clashes between right-wing and left-wing groups – mostly idealistic students – were commonplace in the British capital. Scarcely a week went by without a march, a meeting or a picket in which hundreds, sometimes thousands, of chanting, banner-waving protestors would take to the streets proclaiming some cause or other, usually involving a country and people on the other side of the world.

The most troublesome of all the demonstrations were those which focused on domestic politics, and at that time the left and right were polarised in a much more overt way than we have seen before or since. The police had become skilled over the years at keeping the two factions apart, but had not yet adopted the now familiar tactic of announcing different starting times and routes for the opposing groups – a tactic which grew directly from the events of that day.

On this occasion the right-wing National Front had booked the Conway Hall in Red Lion Square, Holborn, for a rally. The left-wing Liberation Group were demanding the right to mount a counter-demonstration against the meeting and were being allowed to march through the square. The infamous 'Battle of Red Lion Square' was about to begin.

Everything went according to plan initially. The National Front were held back at the Theobalds Road entrance to the square while the Liberation march entered and made its way to the agreed area on the north side of the square, where they were being allowed to hold an open-air meeting. But suddenly a small group of demonstrators launched a ferocious attack on the police cordon protecting the front of Conway Hall, using lengthy staves to which their banners had been attached in the manner of lances.

In the midst of this mêlée was a twenty-year-old maths student from Warwick University taking part in his first demonstration. Standing at 6 feet 9 inches tall, Kevin Gately must have been difficult to miss in the crowd. What exactly happened to him is still a mystery, but everyone who knew him insisted that he was not a violent person. Kevin was, by all accounts, a genuine gentle giant.

When the leaders of the counter-demonstration shouted the order to turn and charge at the police cordon, Kevin was apparently in the third or fourth rank. The police were given the order to draw truncheons, and both foot and mounted officers began to fight back. Another student later reported that, without warning, Gately suddenly slumped unconscious against him, his head held on the other man's shoulder because of the crush. As the crowd parted momentarily, the stricken man fell to the ground with several other demonstrators toppling on top of him. Witnesses next saw Kevin's body, easily identifiable by his red checked shirt, 'coming out of the feet of the police as a rugby ball coming out of a scrum'.

A rapid rescue sortie was mounted by the police and Kevin was rushed to University College Hospital, where he died of a massive brain haemorrhage soon afterwards. The death of Kevin Gately quickly became a cause célèbre, and the government ordered a public inquiry under Judge Scarman into the Battle of Red Lion Square.

But the nearest anyone ever came to learning what really happened to the unfortunate student resulted from the inquest, and Iain West's evidence in particular.

For a forensic pathologist, every postmortem examination is likely to form the basis of future court action of one form or another, so postmortem reports are treated, from the outset, as though they are formal statements. Each pathologist has his own style, but there is a universally accepted form of words and a precise structure which helps all the participants and those later reading the report to fully understand what is being said.

In the Gately case, Dr West's report begins in the familiar way with the statement:

At 9.25 am on Sunday 16 June 1974, at St Pancras Mortuary, Camley Street, London NWI, Detective Chief Superintendent Lewis identified to me the body of Kevin Gately, aged 20 years.

Having listed the names of the police officers and medical personnel present, he went on to describe his external examination of the body – the body of a very big man.

He was a well-nourished young man, 6 feet 9 inches in height with a trimmed beard and long scalp hair. His span was 6 feet 5 inches, and the length of his digits in both hands and feet were within normal limits for his height.

The report then went on to list seven marks of injury which Dr West spotted on the body:

There was a small roughly oval bruise on the left side of the scalp about 1¼ inches behind and slightly below the middle of the back of the left ear, ¾ inch in diameter. The bruising extended through all the layers of the scalp.

There was a small linear abrasion with surrounding bruising 1 inch in length over the left side of the forehead about 2½ inches above the left eyebrow.

There was a very faint superficial discoloration of the upper left cheek and temple.

Superficial abrasion about ½ inch in diameter to the right of the point on the chin, with slight bruising following the line of the right side of the jaw for a distance of about 1½ inches.

Small abrasion on the front of the left knee about ½ inch in length.

Recent bruising on inner aspect of the left upper arm about 1½ inches in length and about 3 inches below axilla.

Small bruise over the right ankle.

But it was when the report turned to the internal examination, particularly of the skull and brain, that the significant findings were recorded. Of the skull, Dr West wrote:

No fracture. The thickness of the skull was normal at the occipital and frontal regions but was slightly thinner than normal in both temporal regions, measuring about ¹⁄₁₀ inch in places. It was also thinner than normal in two areas at the vertex.

Turning to the brain itself, he noted:

The dura was firmly adherent to the skull and there was no evidence of extradural haemorrhage. There was a bilateral subdural haemorrhage, consisting of a mixture of blood clot and free blood, overlying both frontal parietal regions and around the base of the brain. The haemorrhage was considerably larger on the right side and had produced some flattening of both cerebral hemispheres. There appeared to be separation of some connecting veins draining into the superior sagittal sinus. There were traces of blood in the subarachnoid space over the cerebral hemisphere, but the arachnoid membrane appeared intact and blood appeared to extend into the membranes surrounding some of the cranial nerves.

The brain showed superficial contusions along the medial aspects of the frontal and parietal hemispheres. A cut section of brain revealed clear CSF [cerebro-spinal fluid] filling the ventricles and no evidence of intracerebral haemorrhage.

The cerebral arteries were unremarkable and there was no evidence of aneurysmal formation or haemorrhage from them.

So what did all that mean in layman's terms? In his conclusions, Dr West went to some lengths to explain.

Death has resulted from compression of the brain by a large subdural haemorrhage resulting from a head injury. This type of haemorrhage characteristically is caused by a blow to the moving head causing the brain to move inside the skull, thus tearing small communicating veins running between the brain and the membrane beneath the skull (the dura).

It is not uncommon for there to be no fracture of the skull and also relatively slight injuries to the scalp. Superficial contusion of the brain is sometimes seen in association with subdural haemorrhage.

He went on to deal with the bruises on Kevin Gately's head.

The bruise behind the left ear could have been caused by a blow by or against a hard object, resulting in the formation of the subdural haemorrhage. The injury to the chin is less likely to have caused the subdural haemorrhage, although injuries in this site are known to give rise to loss of consciousness, as is commonly seen in boxing.

It is a case which lives in the memory for Iain West because it was his first experience of high-profile pathology in the political cauldron of London. 'I'd been doing full-time forensic medicine only for a matter of months, and my boss Hugh Johnson was away on holiday. He was not due back until the Sunday, and I took a call at home on the Saturday night to be told that a very tall young man had gone down at the demonstration and died a short time later, amid allegations that he'd been hit by a police truncheon.

'I did a postmortem the next morning, wishing my boss was back because obviously this was a political hot potato. I found this injury behind his ear, obviously an impact by or against something. It didn't look particularly like a truncheon injury – it looked more like an object with a rougher surface. That appeared to be the only significant injury on his body. He'd died of an acute subdural haemorrhage which had developed very rapidly, rather more rapidly than normal and it seemed most likely to me that he'd been knocked over and struck his head on the kerb or been hit by a piece of sawn timber – and there was plenty of that around at the time. But there was nothing that was characteristic of a truncheon injury, and I've seen plenty of truncheon injuries subsequently to confirm that view.

'Anyway, I was playing it rather carefully at that time, so I didn't give a cause of death until Hugh Johnson had come back, as I wanted him to have another look. He had another look to see if I'd missed anything, and to my relief he confirmed my findings. Asking him to have a look meant we would both have to give evidence at the inquest. My level of experience at that stage was limited, and it was a case that I did not want to deal with on my own.'

Indeed, Dr Hugh Johnson, then Reader in Forensic Medicine at St Thomas's Hospital Medical School, not only agreed entirely with Iain West's findings but went further in offering an opinion as to how the young man received his fatal injury. He reported:

> The impact of the head injury appears to have been at the site of the bruised region behind the left ear. The small size of this bruise and the absence of a fracture of the underlying bone suggest that this blow was of only moderate force. Such a blow could have been caused by a blow from an implement or from a missile or from a kick or from a fall on to a hard object. It is impossible to state from examination of the injury itself how it was caused.
>
> Dr West had carried out a full, careful and thorough examination, and I agree with his findings in their entirety.

So had a policeman clubbed Kevin Gately to death with a truncheon, or had he died as a result of being hit by a missile thrown by a demonstrator, or a knock on the head when he stumbled and fell in the crowd?

When it came to the inquest before the St Pancras coroner, Douglas Chambers, a month later, Dr West was not able to give a conclusive answer to those questions. Under questioning by counsel for the Gately family, he agreed that the blow to Kevin's head might have been made by a blunt instrument such as a police truncheon. 'But that is only one of many possibilities,' he said in giving evidence. 'What caused the blow is a mystery. I found no indication from my examination of the injuries to help me decide.' The injuries were also consistent with someone having fallen and perhaps hit their head on the pavement, because it was a blow of only moderate force, he said. The death was due to a massive brain haemorrhage.

'Well over half a pint of blood inside the skull is an awful lot of blood,' said Dr Johnson, adding, 'I don't think that any medical man can give an opinion definitely.'

The two doctors who had treated Gately when he first arrived at UCH had apparently not been fully aware that Gately had been taking part in a violent demonstration. They were clearly at something of a loss to explain his condition. Professor O.M. Wrong said the student had been 'so deeply unconscious that we would not have expected him to survive'. Dr Terry Feest told the jury that he had not been able to find any cuts or bruises on Gately's head. But Dr West intervened to explain that it was not unusual for a bruise to take some time to appear.

It was just as well that Iain West had called for a second opinion because of the controversial nature of the young student's death and the insistence of the demonstrators that he had been killed by the police. At the end of the inquest, the jury returned a verdict of death by misadventure but made three recommendations that were accepted by the coroner. They were:

- Demonstrations of diametrically opposed factions should not be allowed to take place in the same vicinity at the same time.
- More attention should be paid to objects carried by demonstrators – a reference to the staves which had been disguised as poles to support flimsy banners.
- That when casualties were taken from demonstrations to hospitals it should be made clear to hospital staffs that they had been in a demonstration.

Almost a year later, at the public inquiry into the Red Lion Square riot, counsel for the tribunal told the chairman, Lord Scarman, that there was no evidence that Kevin Gately had been struck by a police truncheon. He pointed out that the young man stood 'literally head and shoulders above the crowd yet no one testified that he had received a blow from a truncheon – or anything else'.

When Lord Scarman made his final report, he recorded no definite finding on Kevin Gately's death but gave the opinion that it was almost certainly not due to police action. The student was a victim of the general riot situation, and those who began the fighting carried a heavy measure of moral responsibility, he declared.

Colin Roach

On Wednesday 12 January 1983 at 11.30 pm, twenty-one-year-old Colin Roach walked into the foyer of Stoke Newington police station in north London, put the single sawn-off barrel of a shotgun into his mouth and pulled the trigger. That is the police version of how a sad, troubled and depressed black man took his own life.

But his death – tragic yet seemingly straightforward – sparked off a remarkable series of protests and accusations against the local police which persisted for years. Within hours, groups of angry local people began to gather outside the bizarre location of his death, and within days forty-seven people had been arrested after three violent demonstrations. Soon there were vigorous calls for a full inquiry, not only into the death but into the general policing of Stoke Newington.

Quite simply, the black community of Stoke Newington

were so distrustful of their local police force that they not only believed officers were capable of murdering Colin Roach, but actually convinced themselves that he had been killed in the police station and the death made to look like suicide.

So, was it suicide, or is it possible that someone else pulled the trigger? And, if so, was the murderer really a policeman or could a mystery killer have quietly slipped into the entrance hall of the police station behind Colin Roach and calmly slipped out again when the deadly deed was done?

If Colin had decided to take his own life, why should he choose the foyer of a police station? asked his friends. He was a happy, placid young man with no history of mental disturbance, they claimed. A tailor's cutter, he had a wide circle of friends both black and white, his share of girlfriends, and an enthusiasm for sport. He had dabbled in boxing and was thinking of taking up martial arts. The day after his death he was due to go to France on holiday with a friend and two girls.

Apart from one minor brush with the law two years earlier, he had not been in trouble until six weeks before his death, when he had pleaded guilty to theft of a wallet. He was given a three month sentence, reduced on appeal to three weeks, and spent Christmas in Pentonville Prison. Friends said the sentence seemed to have shocked him, and that something sinister had happened to frighten him while he was in jail.

After his death, many of his closest family and friends spoke of something troubling Colin that caused him to behave in a totally uncharacteristic way. On the afternoon of his death, he visited his sister in hospital where she had just had a baby. He left home again at about 9.30, taking nothing with him. Where he went is a mystery, but he was later seen walking nearby carrying a shoulder bag and a towel.

The last person to see Colin Roach alive was his friend Keith

Scully, who took him for a ride in his car. 'He asked me to take him home,' said Mr Scully. 'Then he said he didn't want to go home, just drive about. He said someone was after him. Someone was going to get him and kill him. I said: "Who, and why?" He said, "I can't tell you. They will get you as well."' According to Scully, Roach was petrified at this point. 'He was sweating, holding his head in his hands, and he kept looking behind him all the time. He kept saying, "Drive faster", and that he didn't want to go anywhere where people knew him.'

Roach asked Scully to take him to Bethnal Green police station, saying, 'Someone's going to get me and I want to get in there to be safe.' But he suddenly changed his mind and agreed to be dropped off near Stoke Newington police station. 'He said: "It's all right, I will be safe here," and walked into the police station,' said Scully. 'I could see him standing there. He hadn't gone through the glass doors, he was just standing there facing the glass doors and looking. No one was near him, although I did see someone walking up the street in my mirror before I drove off.'

Where Scully says he saw Roach standing would have been obscured from the view of the front desk of the police station. At about 11.30 pm, officers on the station desk heard a bang. They ran out to find Colin Roach lying, still outside the inner glass doors, with a sawn-off shotgun, a shoulder bag and a towel beside him.

It was the way the police handled the death in next few hours that fuelled suspicion that there was more to it than met the eye. Keith Scully had been sufficiently worried to fetch Roach's father, who reached the police station at 12.15. He was questioned from then until 2.45 am before he was told his son was dead. When he was finally told, officers refused to accept his protestations that his son did not have a gun, and would not let him see the body. His wife was also told nothing, despite repeated telephone calls to the police station. Meanwhile, however, the Press Bureau at Scotland Yard was giving details of the death to the media and implying to reporters that Colin Roach was mentally disturbed. Earlier than usual, and even before the family had been told, the police announced that suicide was the cause of death.

All this haste was a reflection of the way relations between the police and the local community had broken down. Pressure groups had been calling for a full inquiry into policing in the area for some time amid allegations of police brutality and harassment of blacks. There had even been suggestions that other deaths could not be properly explained by the police. In one case, a black family were awarded £50,000 compensation after police illegally entered their home and beat them up.

The case remained high-profile in the press until the inquest before the St Pancras coroner, Dr Douglas Chambers, at Clerkenwell County Court some five months later. The jury, five men and five women, including six blacks, were told that Colin Roach had believed he was hearing frightening voices when he came out of prison and had been given drugs by his doctor to help control the condition. Amid uproar in court, they returned a suicide verdict.

It was not a verdict which satisfied the Roach Family Support Group, and after repeated unsuccessful calls for an inquiry they set up their own, made up of people without political interests in the Hackney area. When they published a report five years later, they declared that there was insufficient proof of suicide.

Colin's family could not identify the holdall found with him, and the report claimed that the shotgun was too big to have been concealed in the holdall anyway, and must have found its way into the police station some other way. The gun itself was never scientifically linked to Roach. There were no fingerprints, although he was not wearing gloves, and no fibres from either the holdall or the towel he was carrying. Police made no attempts to trace the gun in the London area. Two pathologists were unable to explain the position of the body or the changes in the position of the towel he carried. That was the official position of the Roach family and their supporters – a suspicious and slightly sinister mystery. Or was it?

The services of Dr West in this most unusual case were sought by solicitors acting for the Roach family. In a two-page commissioning letter to him, they outlined the sensitivities of the situation – in particular the issues that were causing such suspicion of the police among local people.

Gareth Peirce of B.M. Birnberg & Co. wrote:

We were informed by the police that death had been caused by the firing of a single cartridge of a small shotgun placed inside the mouth, and that there were no external injuries to the head.

When asked by members of the community why there would not have been very extensive damage to the head, the police informed the family that a low-velocity cartridge would not necessarily cause any external damage.

We would be obliged if you would ask for and inspect on our behalf any photographs taken of Colin Roach *in situ*. One of Mr Roach's complaints was that he asked to see Colin's body but was told that he could not, and the explanation given was that there was such a mess. As the police have subsequently said there were no external injuries, the family would like to know whether there was in fact a great deal of visible mess or not.

Her letter went on to ask Dr West to examine the levels of drugs in Colin's body, to check for fingerprints on the gun and to examine the gun itself. A full report from Colin's doctor and a list of twenty specific and searching questions was enclosed.

Iain West began his investigations with a postmortem examination at Hackney mortuary on 11 February 1983, a month after Colin Roach died.

His report makes fascinating reading, not simply because it is an example of forensic investigation at its most precise, but for the insight it gives into this tragically common form of death – usually suicide but occasionally murder. Most people imagine that putting a gun inside your mouth and pulling the trigger must be a particularly gruesome and messy business. But, in this case, Dr West describes in a clinically dispassionate way exactly what happened to Colin Roach. After explaining that he had found no bruising or grazing on the body and no evidence of defensive injuries to the hands or forearms, he began with the scalp:

> The scalp was not lacerated and showed no surface injury. There was bruising on the undersurface of the scalp owing to the marked disruption of the bones of the skull. There were no scalp bruises which could not be accounted for by the fractures in the skull.

Moving on to deal with the skull and the mouth the report declares:

> There had been a single discharge of a shotgun into the deceased's mouth. The muzzle of the gun appears to have been situated just inside the teeth at the moment of discharge. The contents of the cartridge had travelled backwards and slightly upwards, causing a groove to be

cut in the upper surface of the tongue. The shot had struck the upper part of the cervical spine and the base of the skull, causing fractures in the rear section of the base of the skull (the occipital bone) and fractures in the first cervical vertebra.

There had been disruption of the upper and lower jaws, the centre part of the lower jaw being separated from the rest of the jawbone. The upper jaw had been fractured near the left second upper premolar tooth and between the right upper lateral incisor and canine teeth. Fractures of the lower incisor and inner premolar teeth. Separate fractures of the sides of the lower jaw. Fragmentation of the facial and nasal bones and of the front part of the rear section and the whole of the middle section of the base of the skull. The disruption of the jawbones is partly the result of movement of the gun barrel during recoil and partly the result of gases produced during the discharge of a shotgun cartridge disrupting the facial bones.

The release of gases had clearly caused the most devastation. Dr West's report points this out:

There were multiple fractures in the vault of the skull and these, together with the fractures in the base of the skull, had been caused by the release of a large quantity of gas, under pressure, into the mouth following the shotgun discharge.

Remarkably, however, there were apparently few injuries to the soft tissues of the mouth.

There were lacerations in the lining of the mouth and

lacerations on the lips and gums. All were entirely
consistent with injuries produced by shotgun discharge. I
found no injuries in the mouth to suggest that the
deceased had been punched or kicked in the mouth.

He went on to say that the brain had been extensively lacerated and to report that he had removed pieces of shot from
the remnants of the brain, skull and scalp.

Iain West has considerable experience in firearm injuries.
So there is a sense of intense interest about the next section of
his report, which deals with his visit to the ballistics section of
Scotland Yard's Forensic Science Laboratory to examine the
single-barrelled sawn-off shotgun.

The gun was a 12-bore shotgun, 20½ inches long,
excluding the shortened wooden grip which had
separated from the gun. The barrel was 15⅜ inches long.
There were no obvious teeth-marks on the barrel near to
the muzzle. I would not normally expect to see teeth
marks in this situation.

When it came to his conclusions, Dr West was quite clear that
it was a case of suicide.

The fatal injury has been caused by the muzzle of the
sawn-off shotgun being inserted into the mouth just
beyond the teeth, with the teeth gripping the barrel. The
position of the muzzle, the angle of the shot and the lack
of any signs of violence, other than those associated with
shotgun discharge, indicates that this was a self-inflicted
injury. The mouth is a common site for suicidal shooting.

Dealing with the murder theory, he went on:

Homicidal gunshot wounds to the mouth are much less common than suicidal wounds. Homicidal wounds are usually associated with the gun being forced into the mouth with the muzzle being pressed into the throat. Other injuries might also be expected; these would include damage to the lips caused by forcing the gun into the mouth, marks of restraint on the arms and probably other marks of violence caused when the victim is being subdued, e.g. bruises to the head as the result of blows, and injuries to the hands and arms caused by the victim trying to defend himself. I found nothing on the deceased's body to suggest that he had been involved in a fight or struggle, or that any attempt had been made to restrain him.

Attempting to answer some of the doubts raised by the family, and dealing with the issue of Colin's mental state and the medication he had been taking in the weeks leading up to his death, Dr West then offered an explanation.

The fact that only traces of chlorpromazine were found in the deceased's blood indicates that he had not taken the drug for some considerable time prior to his death. If Colin had been psychotically disturbed in the period leading up to his death, then failure to take the prescribed medication would cause the symptoms to become worse. The general practitioner's statement indicates that Colin was quite disturbed when seen, and chlorpromazine would appear to be an appropriate treatment for his state. I have seen nothing to suggest that he would be unable to acquire and handle a gun.

Dealing with the tricky issue of whether or not the police

should have allowed Mr Roach to view his son at an early stage, Dr West first explained the appearance of the body and the devastating effects of the gas discharge inside the skull.

'Release of the gas into an enclosed space such as the mouth will cause widespread destruction of solid matter such as bone. This would explain the quite marked distortion of the skull and face of the deceased. It is quite common for the fragments of skull to be blown through the scalp under these circumstances, although, in the case of Colin, serious scalp injury did not occur.

'It may be that the police felt that his features were so distorted that he should not be viewed until reconstruction had been performed after the postmortem. It is, of course, important when examining a scene for trace evidence to try and exclude as many people as possible in order to prevent contamination. It is my experience that relatives are excluded from the scene of death partly to spare them some distress and partly to prevent contamination of any trace evidence which might be present.'

Discussing the case later, he said, 'It was a classic contact wound with the back of the mouth and palate causing massive disruption to the head. All the indicators at postmortem were those of self-inflicted injury. It was suggested that you could put a gun muzzle in somebody's mouth while they were yawning, but that would be extremely difficult. Certainly you could force a muzzle into somebody's mouth, but if you force a sawn-off shotgun into somebody's mouth when they are not compliant, damage to the lips and teeth would be expected. There was none.

'The next question is, where would the gun go to when it had been fired? When we did the experiments in the laboratory with the family solicitor present, the gun was recoiling seventeen or eighteen feet.

'I have little doubt that Colin Roach shot himself. It would be very difficult to engineer it in any other way.'

John Mikkleson

John Mikkleson cut a distinctive figure wherever he went. He was not only a Hell's Angel, he was a black Hell's Angel – a genuinely rare combination in the 1980s.

To the thirty-four-year-old biker, the fact that he was both black and a Hell's Angel made him doubly a target for police harassment. There has never been any love lost between the rebel motorcycle gangs and the forces of law and order. In the North Kensington area of London where John Mikkleson lived in a largely black community, there was strong suspicion among the local people that the police picked on them for racially motivated reasons, so there was a certain inevitability about the fact that Mikkleson met his death as a result of a clash with the police.

It happened one balmy summer evening in late July 1985. John Mikkleson, who was a member of the Windsor Chapter of the Hell's Angels, went out on a drinking spree with two other members of the Chapter, Martin Griffin and Alan Krafft. For once, they left the bikes behind and went by car.

All went well in the early part of the evening, but as the trio got more and more drunk, their driving became more and more erratic. As they moved from pub to pub, drinking and taking drugs, it was only a matter of time before they came to the notice of the police. Eventually the attention of a mobile patrol in a police van was drawn to the unusual sight of three drunk Hell's Angels in a car. The police began to follow the vehicle and were led all the way to Krafft's parents' home in

Feltham, west London. When the officers asked who owned the car, a violent fight broke out and the policemen drew their truncheons.

What happened next was all too predictable, and sounded perfectly reasonable at the later inquest into Mikkleson's death. PC Richard Peacock told the court that he urged Mikkleson to 'calm down' but it had no effect, and the biker put an arm round another officer's neck and 'began to strangle him'.

'I felt if I didn't do anything, my colleague might die, so I drew my truncheon and hit him across the head,' said PC Peacock. 'It had an immediate effect. He released my colleague and I pushed him sideways.' The officer added that he thought Mikkleson was lying flat out because he was 'an exhausted drunk'.

What happened next was to lead to serious problems for seven police officers. An unconscious John Mikkleson was arrested, and his limp body was loaded into the back of a police van to be driven to Hounslow police station. There he was dumped on the charge-room floor, with his hands cuffed behind his back, for more than an hour while as many as twenty police officers stepped over him or walked round him. Eventually a worried policewoman, who could not get a response from him and could not see any vital signs, telephoned for an ambulance. Frantic attempts to revive him at the hospital proved futile, and he died.

Because of the circumstances and manner of his death, it was going to be vitally important to establish precisely how John Mikkleson had died and what had caused it. Two post-mortems followed in quick succession, both attended by a host of police top brass, and representatives of the coroner's office and the Police Complaints Investigation Bureau. The matter was sensitive in the extreme. Both autopsies tended to suggest that Mikkleson had died from inhaling his own vomit.

Tests revealed that he had three times the legal blood-alcohol limit for driving, and had been taking drugs.

When lawyers for the dead man's family asked Iain West to conduct a third postmortem three days later, the coroner himself came to observe along with the doctors who had conducted the first two examinations.

Dr West had studied the statements of all the police officers before he began, and one particular aspect caught his eye. 'He was arrested, tossed semi-conscious into the back of a police van face down with his hands cuffed behind his back, and arrived at the police-station in a sort of moribund state,' he said. 'My view was that there was pressure on the back which restricted his breathing.' The findings of his postmortem soon confirmed that view.

> There were bruises on the deceased's back consistent with somebody applying their bodyweight across his back and perhaps, at one point, kneeling on his back.
> There were bruises and grazes on the front of the chest, which could have been caused by the deceased lying face-downwards on a flat surface and weight being applied to his back. The grazing could have been caused by being forced to the ground in this manner. The bruising was not extensive. The forehead bruising and grazing could have occurred during this process – particularly if the head was grabbed from behind and forced on to the ground. The rim of minute bruises around the back of the head would be consistent with a grip applied to the back of the head, forcing it forwards – though I could not say at which stage this occurred.

The time of death was also a key issue, and again Iain West's report addresses the problem.

I feel that death probably occurred some considerable time before Mikkleson arrived in hospital. I found nothing to indicate that he was likely to have remained in coma for a prolonged period. The process of dying may have taken some considerable number of minutes, but I feel from the circumstances that it is likely to have occurred much earlier.

The report dismisses the suggestion that a constable took Mikkleson's pulse on the way to hospital because he would have been in deep shock some time before death, and a pulse would not be detectable at the wrist. Referring to the officer who took the pulse, Dr West wrote: 'It is not uncommon for anxiety to cause transmission of a pulse from one's own digital vessels and to give an impression of a pulse on someone who is already dead. Therefore I never rely on the detection of a wrist pulse in this type of situation.'

When it came to the witness statement he made for the coroner's court, the picture which emerged was clear.

There were multiple injuries on the deceased's body consistent with a fairly violent struggle. There was a bruise over the scalp behind the left ear consistent with a blow from a truncheon.

The deceased was moderately intoxicated at the time of his death, but in my opinion the level of blood alcohol was not sufficient to account for death on its own.

John Mikkleson died as the result of inhaling vomit caused by a number of factors:
- A concussive head injury leading to temporary loss of consciousness.
- A moderate degree of alcoholic intoxication, although not severe drunkenness.

- Pressure on the back, leading to compression of the stomach region against the ground.
- Some degree of compression of the neck, albeit of short duration.

I find nothing to suggest that Mikkleson had been subjected to the use of excessive force. The blow to the scalp behind the left ear which could have rendered him unconscious was not delivered with the use of great force. The skull was thinner than average at this point, and if a hard blow had been delivered, it would undoubtedly have fractured his skull. I found no evidence to suggest that any other deliberate blow had been struck on the deceased.

There is no postmortem evidence to suggest that the deceased had inhaled a large quantity of gastric contents. It is likely that the quantity inhaled was small, and if treated at an early stage, he could well have recovered from the aspiration of vomit.

Then, no doubt in an attempt to be fair to the police officers who had not attended quickly enough to the dying Mikkleson, Dr West added: 'The signs of drunkenness and the signs of a head injury may appear to be identical even to a medically trained observer. It is impossible for a lay person to distinguish between unconsciousness due to severe drunkenness and unconsciousness due to a concussive head injury, particularly where, in the latter instance, the individual has been drinking.'

The inquest jury ruled that John Mikkleson had been unlawfully killed. They told the Hammersmith coroner, Dr John Burton, that they felt his death was manslaughter because of the police's lack of care.

His funeral procession through the streets of west London was a colourful affair with hundreds of Hell's Angels from all over Britain and Europe paying their respects with all the pomp and primitive ceremony of their proud yet sinister organisation.

The Mikkleson case was one, Iain West feels, which threw up a number of important points for the police to note. 'I accept the need to restrain individuals, but one of the problems with restraint is that, in certain instances, it may be dangerous – particularly in people who may be taking certain types of drugs.

'It is well known, for instance, that a person who takes crack cocaine and gets into a fight may suddenly die – mainly because of the effect that cocaine has on the heart and on a chemical which circulates in the body known as adrenalin.

'People who are drunk obviously have a problem too, because they may vomit and inhale vomit. People who are obese, if you place them face down, may find it difficult to breathe because you are pushing the abdominal organs upwards towards the chest cavity, effectively splinting the diaphragm.

'If hands are cuffed behind the back and the abdomen forced face downwards, you may actually splint the accessory muscles of respiration around the shoulders, making it very difficult for the individual to breathe. We occasionally see deaths occurring in that way.'

Kenny Baker

The quiet Surrey village of Woodhatch, near Reigate, had never seen anything like it. It was as though the action of a Wild West movie were being filmed in the leafy lanes of their dreamy hamlet.

The time was 10 am on 27 November 1990, and a Securicor van had just pulled up in the local garage forecourt. Two of the three-man crew got out to buy coffee. Suddenly there was a blood-curdling yell, and two burly men sprinted towards the van. They wore children's party masks and were brandishing guns. They had just made it into the back of the security vehicle before the next part of the action began.

With a cry of 'Stop! Armed police! Put down your weapons', a team of policemen wearing flak jackets and baseball caps moved into position carrying automatic weapons. They fired into the sides of the van, and the two men surrendered. But as police blocked the getaway of the gang's open-backed truck, two other robbers spun round to face their ambushers. Pointing their weapons at the police, they made as if to open fire. The response from the police marksmen was immediate. A fusillade of shots rang out. One man fell, wounded in the shoulder. The other, wearing a Ronald Reagan mask, was hit in the stomach and the head. His name was Kenny Baker, and he was dead.

The consequences of the incident for the police were immediate. No matter what the circumstances, any police officer who shoots and kills a civilian will face a rigorous investigation which could end in prosecution and imprisonment. Within hours of the shooting, Detective Superintendent Pat Crossan of Surrey police was appointed by the independent Police Complaints Authority to investigate.

For Iain West, who conducted the postmortem on the dead robber, the matter was no less serious. It was a routine examination on a dead body and would be treated with his usual thoroughness and impartiality. But because of his close working relationship with police officers, he dared not run the risk of being suspected of showing favour to one side or the other.

If the policemen had been trigger-happy, he would say so. If not, he would say that, too. 'One is dealing with these cases completely independently and objectively,' he insisted, 'irrespective of whoever has asked you to deal with it. I give my findings and my conclusions based on those findings. It may not always suit them, but those are my conclusions and those are my findings.'

Baker, a big man, had been hit twice and, from the nature of the wounds, Dr West could tell a great deal about both shots. One of the bullets had hit him in the face just below the nose at the junction of the right nostril, the upper lip and the cheek. The postmortem report devotes a whole page to a minute description to the track of the bullet and the destruction it caused. The most significant passage reads:

> The projectile entry track ran downwards, backwards, and inwards to the left, towards the left angle of the jaw. It was roughly 45 degrees backwards and 45 degrees to the horizontal and to the vertical planes.

So, in the case of this bullet, Baker was shot from above and to his right by an officer firing down at him. The damage in the mouth and cheek area was considerable, with the jaw being broken, and Dr West recovered a number of broken teeth, bone fragments and parts of the core and jacket of the bullet itself.

But it was the other bullet which did the lethal damage:

> The bullet track entered the left flank of the abdominal wall piercing through the underlying muscles producing a torn track up to 5cm in diameter.

He went on to describe the bullet's passage through the kidney and other vital organs, leading to the critical statement:

The projectile severed the aorta below the left renal artery and the adjacent inferior vena cava.

There were teeth in the stomach and circular bruises on the wrists indicating that the mortally wounded man had been handcuffed, but otherwise there was nothing remarkable about the findings.

Dr West's conclusions were concise and unequivocal. He wrote:

He has been struck by two projectiles. The abdominal wound appears to be a low velocity injury produced by a bullet which had fragmented and expanded. This has been primarily responsible for death and was associated with the considerable haemorrhage. The second wound was to the face and showed the features of a high-velocity injury. *This appears to have been caused after the bullet wound to the left side of the abdomen and during the process of dying, as there was relatively little bleeding associated with this injury.*

So was Baker 'finished off' by a police marksman standing over him as he lay dying on the ground? Apparently not, for Dr West added: 'Both of the injuries are consistent with remote range discharges.' He said later, 'The shot in the face was from a high velocity rifle, but that did not produce the lethal injury. It was the shot across the abdomen from a low-velocity round – 9mm from a pistol or an MP5 – that produced the lethal injury.'

A year after the shooting, the remaining members of the robbery gang stood trial at the Old Bailey. Dennis Arif, who had held the security guards at gunpoint, was jailed for twenty-two years. His brother Mehmet, who had been shot in the shoulder, and their brother-in-law Anthony Downer were both jailed for eighteen years.

The gang had been following the Securicor van, which contained £800,000, and intended to drive it away. But they were suspected of a series of armed robberies and had been watched for months by police surveillance teams who tracked them all the way to Woodhatch. When they were arrested they were carrying a small arsenal of weapons, and a further frightening stockpile was uncovered at a safe house in south London.

The jailing of the Arifs brought to an end the infamous reign of one of the most successful criminal family dynasties in Britain. Inside prison, the three men were to join their brother Dogan Arif, jailed in 1989 for an £8.5m drug-smuggling racket. The money the brothers lost when the deal to import three tons of cannabis from Australia was uncovered by customs officers sent the family back to its roots – armed robbery. A large Turkish Cypriot family, the Arifs were raised in south London, where the brothers built a lucrative power base around property, pubs and clubs, all sustained by brutal shootings, stabbings, robbery and drug dealing in the streets of Southwark, Rotherhithe and Walworth.

Some eighteen months after the shooting, an inquest jury returned a verdict of lawful killing on 'Crazy' Kenny Baker. He was aged fifty-two when he died, almost twenty years older than Dennis Arif, the man who had led him into the ill-fated criminal enterprise.

And what of Iain West's view on such crimes? The man who sees the end product, quite literally, of violent wrong-doing tries to remain totally detached from all the bloodshed. But sometimes even he is shocked. 'I sometimes find it quite dreadful that an individual will kill during the course of a robbery that can only be expected to net a few pounds,' he said.

Orville Blackwood

In the ill-starred annals of criminal history, Orville Blackwood would never find a place as a successful robber.

He was jailed in 1983 for four years for holding up a betting shop armed with a toy gun, but the judge told him, 'You made it inevitable you would be found out.' On the way to the shop, Blackwood had called at a police station to ask directions. At the shop, he scribbled 'Blackwood was 'ere' on a poster and told the manager he needed money for his bus fare home. He grabbed a handful of cash.

That pathetic venture into crime led to tragic consequences for the young Jamaican. From prison he was transferred to a mental hospital, where he was diagnosed as having symptoms of paranoid delusion, and then he was moved to Broadmoor, Britain's foremost hospital for the criminally insane. And there, nearly five years later, he died in controversial circumstances.

By then, Orville Blackwood was thirty-one. He had completed his sentence, but was being further detained under the Mental Health Act. He had twice unsuccessfully applied to a tribunal for a transfer from Broadmoor and was due to resume a third application. His lawyer claimed he was non-violent and lucid, discussing family business in letters he wrote from the hospital.

But Blackwood was a diabetic, concerned about his health, and anxious about the weight he was gaining from the anti-psychotic tablets the hospital had prescribed for him. On the day he died, an argument developed over taking the pills. Orville, a big man of over 20 stone, hit out at his doctor, and it took nine staff members to restrain him. He was injected with two tranquillising drugs. Within a minute he was dead. He was the third young black man to die in similar circumstances at Broadmoor in the space of a few years, and his death sparked off furious calls for an inquiry, which was quickly granted. In the meantime the dead man's family called in Dr West to conduct an independent second postmortem on the body. The first autopsy had been inconclusive.

Before he began, Iain West studied the file on the case and paid particular attention to the toxicology report by his colleague Patrick Toseland of the clinical chemistry department at Guy's Hospital.

Dr Toseland had found evidence of two drugs in Blackwood's body – promazine and fluphenazine. He reported:

> The toxicological evidence shows quite clearly that *no more than the designated amounts of promazine and fluphenazine were given to the deceased*, and that death occurred very shortly after the injection of the fluphenazine compound.

He went on to discuss a number of cases of sudden death caused by the use of these drugs, adding:

> It is accepted generally in clinical practice that the prescribing of two separate phenothiazine drugs is not a desirable course, although it is common in psychiatry.

And then Dr Toseland appeared to contradict his earlier statement by declaring:

> *Although the dose of fluphenazine is in excess of that recommended in the National Formulary*, there are many examples of patients receiving more than the

recommended dose, as in these cases of constant therapy some degree of tolerance will occur, necessitating increased dosage.

In the conclusions to his postmortem report, Dr West postulated a number of possible causes for Orville Blackwood's death and indicated how thoroughly he had explored every possible avenue. He found bruising on the left arm which might have resulted from attempts at restraint, but could find no evidence of pressure on the chest or neck which might have inhibited the dead man's breathing.

Nor did I find any evidence that any attempt had been made to control him by the use of a 'sleeper'. The usual form of 'sleeper' hold is an arm hooked around the neck from behind causing constriction of the carotid arteries and thereby depriving the brain of its blood supply. When this occurs, it is usual to find minor marking on the surface of the skin and sometimes bruising around the carotid arteries.

The presence of occasional petechial haemorrhages (burst blood vessels) in the deceased's left eye is of little significance. They are, of course, seen in instances where there has been some obstruction of the airway. In that situation they are usually seen in both eyes and in the lining of the mouth. When an active adult suffers some obstruction to the airway, such as during suffocation or strangulation, providing they are conscious, they will tend to resist, and the process of struggling will usually cause florid petechial haemorrhages to be seen in the eyes and mouth, as well as on the surfaces of a number of internal organs. Where the individual concerned is large or powerful, there would be evidence of petechial haemorrhages in the areas that I have described and signs of the struggle on his trunk and limbs.

There is nothing to indicate that the deceased would have been deliberately rendered unconscious at any stage by infliction of head injury, by the use of a choke or stranglehold, or by the use of drugs.

He goes on to discuss signs in the liver of a disease called sarcoidosis and examines the possibility that the drugs given to Blackwood might have produced a condition known as Neuroleptic Malignant Syndrome, which results in high temperatures and seizure.

But one by one the pathologist rejects all the possible causes, and concludes:

It is my view that this tragic sudden death has resulted from an acute reaction to the phenothiazine drugs that he was given. It is likely that the reaction was in the form of lethal disturbances in his heart rhythm.

Commenting later, Dr West said, 'These drugs can have effects on the cardiovascular system – the blood pressure, the heart and the way the heart beats. Over the years I have found that individuals from the Afro-Caribbean community have a greater propensity to have an adverse reaction to such drugs. I remember another case where a young black man suffering from a mental disorder became violent towards his mother, and she called the police. They managed to pacify and control him without leaving a mark on him. The doctor was called and gave him a tranquilliser intravenously – he died almost immediately it was given. Another one of these idiosyncratic reactions to this group of drugs. I have seen it in all races, but it certainly seems to be more common in Afro-Caribbeans.'

Two years after Orville Blackwood's death a second inquest was held. It had been ordered by a High Court judge after Blackwood's mother, Clara Buckley, campaigned for a judicial review. But the second inquest, like the first, returned a verdict of accidental death.

When the report of the official inquiry into the incident was published in September 1993, it concluded that Broadmoor had problems of racism, low nursing skills and an overwillingness to use physical restraint. But it did not lay the blame for Orville's death on any individual, and was rejected by Mrs Buckley as a cover-up.

CHAPTER 14

CHILD ABUSE

The year 1984 was a tragic one for cases of child abuse, but two cases in particular shocked the nation and brought the plight of cruelly treated children to the forefront of public attention. The deaths of two little girls led to a full-scale inquiry and radical changes in the way social services departments and social workers handled problem families under their care.

Jasmine Beckford

When little Jasmine Beckford finally died, she weighed just 23 lb. She was 3 feet 5 inches tall, but skeletal. She was four years old. At the end, she had no fewer than forty injuries to her head and face and was covered from head to toe in bruises. Her deformed left thigh was ulcerated and there were burns on her hands. In Iain West's expert opinion, she died from brain injuries after three or four heavy blows to the head.

Her father, a twenty-five-year-old scaffolder, Maurice

Beckford, was jailed for ten years for manslaughter. Her mother, Beverley Lorrington, twenty-four, was sentenced to eighteen months' imprisonment for cruelty.

During the last ten months of her life, Jasmine was subjected to the most horrific attacks. Every part of her body was injured. Her left pelvic and pubic bones were broken and her injuries were due to repeated episodes of physical violence and chronic neglect. Yet, somehow, her parents were always able to convince visiting social workers that the child was away staying with her grandparents, so no one was able to come to the aid of the wretched tot.

When Iain West came to conduct the postmortem on tiny Jasmine one Friday in July 1984, even he could not have been prepared for the pathetic sight which met his eyes.

'You detach yourself, but it is difficult to detach yourself completely from some cases,' he said. 'With Jasmine, it was a pretty instantaneous reaction, almost disbelief. It was: How can a child get into this state, in this day and age, in this country? But you must put those thoughts to one side.'

The child's body was first photographed, clothed and unclothed, and then X-rayed. In the precise language of an official postmortem report, Dr West began by describing the external appearances. He wrote: 'She was a thin little girl 3 feet 5 inches in height and weighing 1 stone 9 lb.' After a description of the child's clothing and bandaging, the report noted the marks of previous injury. It is not a report for the squeamish, and as you read it you wonder at the cruelty meted out to this poor defenceless girl. There was a deformity of the left thigh

with extensive scarring of the anterior aspect of the thigh and front and sides of the knee. There were punctuate and linear scars on the back of the left thigh and lower left buttock and oval linear scars behind the left knee.

Ten areas of previous injury were described, including ulcers on the pelvis, the legs and the ankles, and scars all over the little girl's head and virtually every other part of her body.

In describing the recent marks of injury, Dr West needed four pages of closely typed detail to enumerate the marks he found, meticulously listing every bruise and graze as he worked though each area of the body. He wrote:

There were eleven injuries on the left cheek and jaw outside the level of the mouth.

He went on to list twenty-two groups of such injuries on the head and neck alone. A typical notation was:

A group of irregular punctuate and linear abrasions consistent with fingernails, on the right cheek covering an area 2 inches by 1 inch and extending in a line down the cheek.

She had a split lip and bruises in and around the mouth, indicating punches. Jasmine's trunk, legs and arms were a mass of bruises, some of them he described as 'consistent with knuckle marks' or 'grip-type bruises'. The child had been thoroughly and regularly battered.

When it came to the internal examination, Dr West described two recent fractures of the ribs and fractures of the pelvis and the pubic bones on both sides. The undersurface of the scalp was badly bruised.

But it was the brain which was to give clues as to how the child died.

The left cerebral hemisphere was covered by a thin layer of fresh non-adherent blood clot with a smaller quantity overlying the right cerebral hemisphere.

There was contusion of the right lobe of the cerebellum. The brain was swollen with flattening of the gyral pattern, displacement of the left uncinate gyrus. There was splitting of the corpus callosum between the two cerebral hemispheres with visible contusion on the frontal poles, both subfrontal regions and traces of subarachnoid bleeding in the left temporal region.

Even to the untutored layman's eye, the message is clear: serious brain damage. Dr West's conclusions confirm that. He wrote:

[Jasmine] was a very thin little girl who has died as the result of severe head injuries. There were multiple old scars on the deceased's body consistent with repeated episodes of physical abuse.

There were numerous fresh injuries consistent with the effects of severe physical beating conducted within the period of a day or so leading up to her death. There were marks which included injuries such as might be left by slaps and punches, and some of the injuries to the face were consistent with the effects of hard punches.

The fatal brain injury had been caused by blows to the child's head.

Then, in a damning final paragraph, he wrote:

The overall appearances are suggestive of the child being subjected to repeated episodes of severe physical violence and to chronic and severe neglect.

It was undoubtedly one of the worst cases of long abuse I have ever seen,' he said later. 'She was the victim of severe mental abuse as well as severe physical abuse, no doubt. She was wasted and her last eighteen months must have been miserable.

'I remember her leg, which was thick and covered in ulcers. When you felt the leg, there was no muscle there, just hard calcified tissue because the fracture in the area had not been treated properly. The bone was just calcifying and ossification was occurring in the muscle as a result of trauma.

'I understand that that was due to the fact that the accused had heard from one of his weight-lifting friends that one of the ways to treat fractures was to use weights, so he left weights lying against her leg.

'She had almost complete separation of her lip from her upper gum but very little bruising there, indicating that the beatings had continued after she was dead.

'She had severe head injury – a subdural – and multiple fractures, particularly around the lower limbs and pelvis. There were certainly over twenty fractures of both lower limbs.'

Tyra Henry

Baby Tyra Henry never regained consciousness after being dropped in a fight between her parents. The twenty-one-month-old infant was in the arms of her mother, Claudette, when her father began punching the defenceless young woman. Some of the blows fell on the baby, and when the enraged father offered to take the baby out of harm's way, her mother readily held the child out to him.

But nineteen-year-old Andrew Neil changed his mind and

withdrew his arms, leaving the baby to fall like a doll, hitting her head on the floor where she lay moaning and twitching. Panic-stricken, Neil scooped up Tyra and took her to the bedroom to wipe blood from her lips and then, unbelievably egged on by Claudette, he bit the child in a crazed attempt to bring her round. By this time, Neil was hysterical and blaming Claudette for the incident. Then he simply left the flat in Brixton, south London, which he shared with the baby's twenty-year-old mother and did not return until the following night.

That is the version of events Claudette gave to the jury when Andrew Neil appeared on a charge of murdering his daughter a year later in August 1985.

Meanwhile, Claudette bathed the unconscious tot and put her to bed, sitting watching her for an hour to make sure she was still breathing. The child had not opened her eyes and there was a bruise beginning to form on her cheek. The next morning, Claudette went out to look at a new flat, leaving the unconscious Tyra all alone. It was while she was out that the baby's aunt, Paula Neil, found the tragic infant and rushed her to hospital.

In the evening, Andrew Neil held an uproarious party at the flat to celebrate his twentieth birthday.

Two days later, Tyra died.

Under a care order, she was supposed to be living with her grandmother, Beatrice Henry, whom she called 'Mummy', and seeing Claudette only during the day. But when Mrs Henry's electricity was cut off, the baby moved in with her real mother without the knowledge of the local social services.

When it came to the trial, Roger Robinson, professor of paediatrics at Guy's Hospital, who had attended Tyra, said he had never seen such severe brain injuries associated with ordinary falls in the home. On hearing the 'dropping' story, he

said: 'In no way could that produce the injuries in this child –
this is not the way brain damage happens.'

It was only two months after examining the body of Jasmine
Beckford that Dr West stepped into the mortuary to perform
a postmortem on Tyra Henry. He might have been forgiven
for a sense of depression in the face of this appalling inhu-
manity to tiny children.

Like Jasmine's, Tyra's small body was a mass of bruises,
scratches and abrasions. But this time there were also bites.
She had been bitten in many areas, on her face, back, chest,
buttocks, arms and legs, and some of the bite-marks were
particularly inflamed.

> Bite-mark on the back of left chest with well-defined
> tooth impressions, some giving the impression of the
> teeth being dragged across the skin.

This is one typical notation in the postmortem report. Many
of the other bite-marks were described as 'suction bites', and
many 'showed the imprint of the teeth of both jaws'.

When it came to his conclusions, Iain West's report had a
depressingly familiar ring to it.

> Tyra Nichola Beatrice Henry was a well-nourished little
> girl who has died as the result of complications of severe
> head injury. Pre-existent natural disease has played no
> part in her death.
>
> There is postmortem evidence of two heavy impacts on
> the back of the head, one resulting in a fracture of the
> skull. The head injuries are consistent with the child's
> head being struck against a hard surface and could have
> been caused by throwing the child across a room with the

403

head striking a hard surface.

There were numerous bite marks on the child's body, all but two consistent with marks made by an adult mouth. The two bite-marks on the back of the left wrist and hand could have been caused by the child's own mouth, and are consistent with the injury produced by forcing the wrist and hand into her mouth.

Some of the bite-marks made by an adult have been inflicted with considerable force.

Virtually all of the injuries appear to have been caused within a day or so prior to her admission to hospital.

So that was it: a comprehensive picture of cruelty on a horrific scale.

When Iain West entered the witness box at the Old Bailey, his testimony against Neil was devastating. His evidence simply showed that the baby's injuries included fifty-seven human bite-marks, brain damage caused by a fractured skull, and bruises all over her body. The massive brain injuries were consistent with the baby being thrown across a room and hitting her head on a wall, he told the stunned jury.

When passing sentence on Neil, Judge Robert Lymbery referred to the 'very large number of non-fatal injuries caused by biting and scratching, and the totality of this presents a horrifying picture of the body of that small child. I have no doubt whatever that you inflicted those injuries. Shorn of any emotion, one can only say this is an appalling case of cruelty.'

It was not the first time that Andrew Neil had faced a court over cruelty. Almost eighteen months before Tyra's death, he had been sentenced to a detention centre for battering Tyra's brother Tyrone when the boy was three months old, causing him to be blinded and brain-damaged. That conviction was quashed on appeal.

This time, however, the brutal baby-batterer was not so lucky. Judge Lymbery sentenced him to life imprisonment on 25 July 1985.

'There was brain damage in this case, but the most striking thing about Tyra was the number of bite-marks on the body,' said Dr West. 'She was simply covered in human bite-marks and numerous tooth-marks. Again, it was one of those cases which one looks at in disbelief that someone could do this. There was no doubt that Tyra had been picked up by the mouth and shaken, like a terrier might pick up a rat.'

So how does a pathologist, who is also a human being and a father, react when faced with such appalling scenes? 'Once you start working, anything subjective is controlled,' said Dr West. 'It is the same as doing anything unpleasant. You must retain complete objectivity, despite the nature of the case. If you become emotionally distraught every time you see an abused child, you have lost the necessary objectivity to deal with the case.' The set formula that modern pathologists use to carry out postmortem examinations helps to overcome any fleeting emotional responses in cases of child abuse.

'A homicide postmortem involves a very much more extensive examination,' said Dr West, 'and includes areas that you would not normally examine in a non-homicide case. You may be looking for evidence of injury which is not apparent on the skin or not apparent on X-ray, for instance.

'Examinations may take hours, followed up by a microscopic examination of the body tissues and organs some days later; other tests may be necessary. Examination of the brain by a neuropathologist or examination of other organs by a specialist pathologist is commonplace.

'Everyone assumes, when you deal with a child abuse case, that you would feel anger against whoever has done it, but that is not necessarily the instance. I have seen cases where a child has been injured by somebody obviously at the end of their tether, and it may be that the system has failed them as much as it did the child. Perhaps in other instances the system is not necessarily at fault, it may just be a situation where no one has recognised the stresses that a young mother is being subjected to – what they are undergoing. But in the majority of instances, these people are not a danger to society.'

Then he went on sadly, 'The examinations of both Jasmine and Tyra have left images that I will always have in my mind – the state of their little bodies the first time I saw them.

'I will never forget them.'